# Distant Voices Still Heard

*For our students*

# DISTANT VOICES STILL HEARD

### Contemporary Readings
of French Renaissance Literature

*edited by*
John O'Brien and Malcolm Quainton

LIVERPOOL UNIVERSITY PRESS

First published 2000 by
LIVERPOOL UNIVERSITY PRESS
4 Cambridge Street
Liverpool
L69 7ZU

**British Library Cataloguing-in-Publication Data**
A British Library CIP record is available.
ISBN 0 85323 785 9 *cased*
ISBN 0 85323 795 6 *paper*

Typeset by Northern Phototypesetting Co Ltd, Bolton, Lancs.
Printed and bound in the European Union by Redwood Books Ltd,
Trowbridge, Wilts.

# Contents

# Editors' Foreword

This book arose from a perceived pedagogical need. It seemed to us that a book was needed which would be of assistance to students as they intensified their study of French Renaissance literature – a book that would attempt to bridge the transitional moment between the specific study of a very limited number of Renaissance texts and the larger demands that are made by more advanced study in Great Britain and abroad. This period of transition will often be the final year of the undergraduate degree and the first year of graduate study. It is moreover at these periods that students frequently encounter in a serious, professional way the theoretical readings that have informed the study of the French Renaissance during the last thirty years or so.

The aim of this present publication is therefore multiple. First and foremost, it seeks to introduce maturing readers to representative interpretations of early-modern French literary culture using the perspectives of contemporary literary theory. The volume proceeds by way of paired worked examples from five Renaissance authors who, we believe, represent a broad chronological span and, we hope, achieve a reasonable balance between prose and poetry. Readings include structuralism, psychoanalysis, and feminism, and they focus on issues such as the problem of interpretation, the role of the reader, the nature of the text and the question of gender. The Introduction supports this enterprise by tracing the development of contemporary critical methodologies of Renaissance literature as a means of situating the readings undertaken in the body of the book. It also addresses broader issues in the interpretation of sixteenth-century literature, such as questions of historical distance and difference.

In a volume of these dimensions, which needs to keep to manageable size, it is not possible to include every strand of literary theoretical thinking about the sixteenth century that has engaged the attention of critics over the past thirty years. We are aware that some readers might wish to see greater space devoted to deconstructive interpretations, to New Historicism, or to recent enquiry into post colonialism. To some extent, this is offset by the Introduction which attempts to give an overview of the field and directs readers to further exploration of critical approaches that interest them. Moroever, the contributions themselves are by no means univocal in their use of theory. Readers will quickly see that there is a certain pervasive eclecticism which allows contributors to engage their chosen text from a variety of angles. This book is thus not intended to be an exhaustive contribution to its subject area, but to introduce some of the major literary theoretical methodologies and to show how these affect, practically, the ways we read French Renaissance literature.

We wish to express our thanks to the staff at Liverpool University Press, especially to our editor, Robin Bloxsidge, who has supported our project with patience and good humour, and to Frances Hackeson. We also wish to thank Ann Fincher-O'Brien for help with bibliographies and preparation of the manuscript.

*John O'Brien*
*Malcolm Quainton*

Introduction

# The Time of Theory

*John O'Brien*

Have we anything still to learn from literary theory? The question could be phrased in another way and in another tense: was there anything ever to be learned from literary theory? The switch in tense and its modifying adverb contains a history as well as an outlook. For supporters of the second question, the moment of literary theory has a specific history, and one that is now past; it is linked to a constellation of names – Barthes, Lacan, Foucault, Derrida, to name only the most obvious – and to a period of time in the third to last quarter of the twentieth century that appears *passé* as we enter the twenty-first century. On this view, the moment of theory was just that – a moment describable in the past tense and seen as a fragment of a longer perspective, a longer view which is synonymous with the sweep of literary history. Theory thus represents a detour on the pathway of history, a moment when time was temporarily out of joint.

The question of time and tense is at the heart of the issue which theory carries along with it, and no less so when we come to speak about theory and French sixteenth-century literature. For in Renaissance studies, it is tied to the problem of anachronism and periodicity. If one wanted to chose a symptomatic moment when this cluster of points surfaced directly in the study of the sixteenth century, it might be the rejoinder made by the French Renaissance scholar, Jean-Claude Margolin, to the opening chapter of Foucault's *Les mots et les choses*. In that chapter, Foucault had claimed that the key to the Renaissance outlook is interpretation; knowledge of the world depends upon the ability to recognise, read and organise signs. Things are linked to each other through the theory of resemblances, such resemblances being recognisable and decipherable because they bear within them 'signatures'. Hence what can often seem to us a vast rag-bag containing everything from alchemy and magic to rational knowledge and the classical legacy was in fact a systematic relation of knowledge interpretable through divination and erudition working respectively on the natural sign and the written sign.[1] It is this system that Foucault terms the Renaissance 'episteme', that is to say 'a configuration of relations which functions as the conditions of existence of particular forms of knowledges and sciences'.[2] Margolin's retort concentrated on the idea of man and humanism that emerged from Foucault's work.[3] It was a controversial topic, for the Renaissance is commonly credited with introducing the notion of humanism and placing man centre stage in the world order. Margolin took issue with the fact that although Foucault claimed to represent the human sciences, this crucial humanist notion of man was absent from his thinking. Rather than directly attacking Foucault's arguments about the French Renaissance as such, Margolin queried his underlying paradigm. Margolin's challenge – not a debate, since Foucault did not respond – had none of the heated controversy which surrounded the Barthes-Picard affair of a few years' earlier, partly because it was not regarded as emblematic of the struggle between *la nouvelle critique* and its opponents. Yet a fundamental disagreement, an essential disparity of outlook, remained. Theory and history seemed polar opposites, with the privilege given by Margolin to a metaphysical concept of Man underpinning the further notion of 'histoire événementielle', in other words history as fact, 'out there', indisputably ascertainable and verifiable by heavy recourse to archival evidence; history was a vast storehouse of 'pièces justificatives' ('documentary evidence'), of which indeed literature was one.

Such an outlook itself had a well-defined history. It could be illustrated by the numerous literary histories that were, and to an extent still are, current in Renaissance studies. But it has been common in theoretical circles to start from another, yet complementary angle and invoke E. M. W. Tillyard's book *The Elizabethan World Picture* (1943) as characteristic of the mind-set that predominated in scholarly circles before the advent of theory. In truth, Tillyard's work was expressly indebted to an earlier study, Arthur Lovejoy's *The Great Chain of Being* of 1936, and spawned later analyses such as C. S. Lewis' *The Discarded Image* of 1964.[4] In all these studies, examples from Renaissance literature, primarily English Renaissance literature, were collected to restore and compose a picture of the metaphysical system underlying sixteenth-century writing. This metaphysical system could be found in its entirety in none of the writers instanced (except perhaps encyclopedic writers such as Du Bartas in France), but, it was argued, underpinned them all. Literature was essentially used in these books to illustrate the history of ideas, and a hierarchical system based on the ultimate orderliness of the universe. In the same way that literature could become the handmaid of history by supplying evidence for a largely political view of Renaissance culture, so too it could be integrated into more 'serious' disciplines such as philosophy or intellectual history. Literature became subservient to the Idea. The condition of such an existence was that Renaissance literature was dismembered wholesale and anthologised, almost in an ironic inversion of the Humanist precept of imitation, and then distributed in the form of quotations and centos in support of more 'rigorous' fields of study. Not that useful work was not done along the way: Tillyard realised the Medieval roots of much that was thought of as typically Renaissance, a point likewise repeatedly underscored by Lewis who rejected the term 'Renaissance' as misleading, a product of the propaganda of the sixteenth-century Humanists. In fact, the term 'Renaissance' as a description of a particular period in early modern Europe had been only systematically applied by Michelet and Burckhardt in the nineteenth century.[5] Lewis certainly overemphasised the persistence of the medieval, but his essential point about period labels is a salutory reminder that 'Renaissance' can give quite the wrong impression about the true extent of continuity and change between the late medieval period and the early modern.

It might be expected that such a view of history – interpreted either as an activity confined to days and dates, or as an abstraction towards a transcendent Idea – would have attracted the critical attention of Marxist criticism. In fact, while Marxism had much to say about the realist novel, it had, at that time, little to report about the Renaissance. One slight exception to this rule was the Marxist critic, Henri Weber, whose monumental 1956 work, *La création poétique au XVIe siècle en France*, opened with a section on the social, economic and political background to the poets' work. But the Marxism was pushed no further and, in truth, it was hardly a noticeable feature of this work which is still remarkable for the sensitivity of its analyses in a style not entirely dissimilar to American New Criticism. Weber's analyses have, in fact, little in common with (for example) Lukacs, and little also with the cultural criticism evolved by Bakhtin (supposing that the latter was a Marxist, which cannot be taken for granted). Bakhtin's day had not yet come.

## THE CODE AND THE TEXT

When the text was not a more or less transparent document, designed to support the paradigms of literary history, then it fell back into the realms of subjectivism: history was thus used as a mechanism of control by which to establish the worth of literary data; the documentary value of literature vied for precedence with the 'text-in-itself'. As François Rigolot points out in his contribution to this volume, the attraction of Structuralism, at least in its Jakobsonian manifestation was that it 'was able to explain the functioning of the "literary object" beyond *history* and *the subject*, cleansed of any interpretative leanings' (Rigolot's italics). The literary text was no longer dependent either on its documentary force or on its hermeneutic possibilities. On the contrary, what Structuralism now promised its adherents was, in Rigolot's words, 'the unshakeable guarantee of scientific rigour'. Rigolot characterises his early work as having been influenced by this approach and he admits its limitations, particularly its schematism. It is significant in this respect that Rigolot returns to his subject – *Pantagruel*, chapters 10–13 – after an interval of twenty-five years: those years have seen some of the most significant developments in the application of theory to literature. But Rigolot argues convincingly, apropos of his topic, that Jakobsonian linguistics should not be relegated to the past of literary analysis, but still have an active role to play. The six factors which Jakobson identified in any act of linguistic communication can be shown still to illuminate this episode from Rabelais in ways which add to its significance and our understanding. Since Rigolot is especially clear about Jakobson's premises in the two essays 'Linguistics and Poetics' and 'Two Aspects of Language and Two Types of Aphasic Disturbances', there is little need to rehearse them here. Yet in re-emphasising the enduring value of the Jakobsonian linguistic approach, Rigolot re-alerts his readers to the importance of metaphor and metonymy, which were later to assume such importance in Lacanian psychoanalysis, and shows how Baisecul and Humevesne are able to manipulate to extraordinary effect the processes of selection (related to metaphor) and combination (related to metonymy). Although seemingly incomprehensible to us, the speeches of Rabelais' two litigants are susceptible to analysis with the tools Jakobson supplies. However – and it is a crucial qualification – Rigolot is quick to point out the limitations of his method. For one thing, Jakobson's system accounts for the function, but not the content of the litigants' speeches: however intelligible the communicative functions become in the light of semiotic analysis, the content of the speeches of the two litigants remains stubbornly impenetrable to us. We understand the signs, but cannot understand the meaning. Thus it follows that interpretative methodologies will inevitably leave a 'remainder', segments or levels of texts that cannot be encompassed in any one critical approach and which thereby display the relativity or contingency of that approach, at the same time that they propel the reader and the critic to new interpretations; not in expectation of reaching, one day, the definitive reading which brings an end to all interpretation (and thus to the very act of reading itself), but in the hope of understanding the modalities of communication that allow the discourse of these two Renaissance litigants to re-echo 'across the vagaries of time' and restores to them 'their urge to signify'.

Rigolot's conclusion to his essay in this present volume complements the view he adopted in a 1995 article entitled 'Interpréter Rabelais aujourd'hui: Anachronies et catachronies'.[6] The sub-title of the article provides its starting point, since it focuses on the issue of anachronism and asks whether reconstruction of the intentionality of an early modern text must be left to philologists and historians or whether certain concepts of our postmodern consciousness might help illuminate aspects of Rabelais. To this end, he distinguishes between 'anachronie' and 'catachronie'. The former is 'la projection aberrante du présent sur le passé' (p. 270) ('the aberrant projection of the present onto the past'), whereas the latter is 'l'illusion, tout aussi aberrante, de pouvoir saisir le passé indépendamment du présent qui conditionne la saisie (on croit pouvoir faire abstraction de sa situation existentielle pour reconstituer un passé hypothétique...)' (p. 270) ('the no less aberrant illusion that one can grasp hold of the past independently of the present that conditions the very attempt to do so (one imagines one can step outside one's own place and time in order to reconstruct a hypothetical past...)')). Rigolot can thus rightly underscore that solid and wide-ranging historical erudition about the sixteenth century is an absolute pre-requisite to any critical interpretation of French Renaissance literature, while introducing a relativist note (derived from Hayden White and New Historicism – see later) about our involvement in any past that we study and the precariousness of any framework we evolve.[7] When critics speak of Rabelais' polysemousness or linguistic ambiguity, Rigolot argues, these are not anachronisms imported into the Renaissance work, but at the very heart of the humanist culture with which Rabelais was imbued. To regard our modern sensibility as being necessarily in conflict with Renaissance outlooks is consequently a false dichotomy; and Rigolot phrases in this way the only temptation to be avoided: 'Encore faut-il résister au plaisir de les [= les grands textes de la Renaissance] moderniser, pour mieux les actualiser' ('Nevertheless one must resist the pleasure of modernising them [= the great Renaissance texts], so as to grasp their topicality all the better'). The verb 'actualiser' (literally: 'to update') links Rigolot's *Poétique* article with his essay in this present volume, where he uses precisely the same verb. The critic's aim is not to indulge in either 'anachronie' or 'catachronie', but to remain open to the topicality they contain, their relevance to our intellectual situation.

Rigolot had already made an important contribution in a further area also, the status of the Text. Barthes' influential 1971 essay, 'De l'oeuvre au texte' ('From Work to Text'), makes a seven-point case for distinguishing between the work (static, monumental; connected with meaning, closed back upon the signified; guaranteed by an authorial presence and the process of filiation) and the text (mobile; giving predominance to the signifier over the signified; 'plural', decentred, without closure; possessing no authorial stamp or guarantee).[8] The Text (so capitalised in Barthes) seemed to constitute a new, semi-personified entity offering the literary scholar two main advantages: first, as Barthes himself pointed out, it was not entirely synonymous with the term 'literature', but could be used to move into adjacent and perhaps complementary areas such as film or advertising or indeed any domain susceptible to semiosis (Ann Jones, in this volume, takes advantage of this). Text is, says Barthes, a productivity, a work, a field of investigation, not a thing to be found on library shelves. Secondly, Text encapsulated in its very principle the disjunctive mobilities, the ludic qualities, that contemporary criticism came to identify as characteristic of the Renaissance as of other periods of French literature. Jean Paris' *Rabelais au futur* and Michel Beaujour's *Le jeu de Rabelais* give rein to precisely that 'play of the signifier', stressing the comedy at the expense of a purely serious view of their author.[9] In *Le texte de la Renaissance*, Rigolot enlarges upon and systematises the underlying conception of text on which these critics implicitly depend. He asks whether it is possible to reconcile 'text' and 'Renaissance', in other words semiology and literary history. Endorsing a palpably Barthesian notion of text ('Un texte se définit non par sa monumentalité, mais par sa «mouvance», son instabilité fondamentale') ('A text is defined not by its monumentality, but by its "slipperyness", its fundamental instability')[10], he defends his choice of this term by claiming that (i) 'text' supplies a lexical deficiency; it is a reality which has no name in the Renaissance; (ii) it allows us to dissociate semantic representation from its manifestation (i.e. the book as a concrete object); (iii) modern semiotics is in some respects close to Humanist philology in its rejection of linear discourse and its acceptance of 'productivity'.[11] The first and third of these arguments are defences of the value of modern theory to analyse Renaissance literature, and will recur in a variety of forms among other contributors to this volume.[12] The second argument is really a way of distinguishing 'text' from 'work'. Rigolot's work thus provides an instance of careful textual practice combined with the systematic application of theoretical terminology and pespectives, largely drawn from structuralist narratology in the case of *Le texte de la Renaissance*. Thus for Rigolot it is not unreasonable to speak of the Renaissance text, since sixteenth-century works reveal consistent practices that enable us to posit such a phenomenon.

It is worth noting that the semiological theory which Rigolot employs is part of a larger movement commonly called 'the linguistic turn', in other words the way in which language has come to the forefront of our awareness of what is important about texts.[13] This movement has its ultimate origins in the work of Ferdinand de Saussure, the Swiss linguist whose lectures were collected after his death and published by his pupils in 1916 under the title *Cours de linguistique générale*.[14] Saussure's advance was to consider language as a series of signs. Each sign was composed of a signifier ('signifiant'; the acoustic or written representation) and a signified ('signifié'; the concept to which it pointed). The signifier and the signified bonded together to form the sign. The operations of language, moreover, work by a system of differences. Each signifier was accorded meaning because of its difference from the neighbouring signifiers; 'pat' is understood for what it is by its difference from 'pet' or 'pit', for example; indeed, Saussure would claim, 'pat' only is what it is because it is not 'pet' or 'pit'. Each signifier thus has no endemic properties, but signifies negatively, in other words because it is not something else; to use Saussure's own formula, language is a system of differences without positive terms. Saussure also maintained that the link between the signifier and the signified was arbitrary. There is no inherent reason why 'pat', 'pet' and 'pit' signify what they do; they signify by a convention of the English language. If the language one is speaking changes – from English to French, for instance – a new range of signifiers will have to be learned, a new range of conventional acoustic and graphic traces used to represent the same meanings. Even this brief sketch of Saussure's central tenets cannot properly give a true flavour of the impetus he was to impart to theory in the hands of Barthes, Derrida and Lacan. It is not too much to state that without Saussure, twentieth-century literary theory would not have made the advances it has. Without Saussure, it is difficult to imagine, for instance, the type of shift from work to text that Barthes describes, nor his subsequent development of the notion of *écriture* ('writing'), notably in *S/Z* (1970).

## THE FATE OF READING

One effect of the structuralist approach symbolised by Rigolot's analysis of Rabelais was to radicalise the theory and practice of reading. Floyd Gray, who, like François Rigolot, had received early training with Alfred Glauser, has dealt with precisely these problems over a broad range of critical works.[15] Like Glauser, Gray takes the process of reading and writing as complementary activities; they are, he states in his article here, 'correlative phenomena, the one participating in the fulfilment and determinacy of the other'. This view has arisen, Gray notes, from the twentieth-century shift from the author as source and the work as object, to the idea of writing as a speech act and reading as a subjective experience. Gray is alluding, among other things, to the articles by Barthes and Foucault on the question of the author, as well as to work on reader reception theory associated with the names of Iser and Jauss.[16] Collectively, these critics propose that the meaning of the work of literature resides less in the author – whose intentions may be inscrutable, historically irrecoverable or unknown – than in the reader and his/her experience of the text; that readings are historically and socially situated, are provisional, and will vary over time; and that writing and reading are two facets of a related activity, since writing implies reading as a preliminary (French Renaissance literature is an excellent illustration of this last point).

Gray begins by showing how Marguerite de Navarre is effectively absent from her own work by the fact that the work was originally published anonymously, and secondly – and perhaps more importantly – by the delegation of the roles of narrator and commentator. Once the question of the author has been thus bracketed, the workings of the text can be analysed as the imminent source of readerly satisfaction and signification. In line with Barthes' 'Introduction à l'analyse structurale des récits',[17] Gray underscores the role of structure in the pleasures and frustrations of reading a piece such as *Nouvelle* 10 of the *Heptaméron*. The parallels, the crises and reversals, the twists and turns of the plot, the strained relations between the characters, the delay and postponement which do not cancel meaning but intensify it, all these contribute to the narrative complication with which the reader must contend in order to reach the outcome (which in this case coincides with the climax). In this reading, the sheer materiality of the reading process is paramount, emphasising concomitantly the reader's ability to negotiate the various peripeteias which are the mainstay of the *nouvelle* under consideration.

These narrative characteristics presuppose a reader who is unusually skilled in handling narratological devices and in relating these to a larger interpretative framework or frameworks. That the interpretative framework is itself so contradictory requires special exertion from the reader. Indeed, Gray is of the view that one should read *Nouvelle* 10 not so much for the story of Floride and Amadour as for the spectacle of *écriture* itself, with all its pleasures and frustrations; the cult of intersubjectivity, of relations between characters and their outcome, is ultimately less important, because more predictable, than the means by which these are communicated. This is a bold, almost Aristotelian view (character is subordinate to plot), but Gray is convinced that this is the only way forward. He boldly labels as wrong any attempt to side with one or the other of the interpretations offered by the *devisants*, and right, the effort to follow the line of the text, however blurred and embroiled this may be. One might readily argue that to give the reader such a responsibility is itself a significant Renaissance phenomenon. Rigolot had demonstrated that the reader of Rabelais' work has entrusted with 'la responsabilité du sens' ('the responsibility for meaning'), 'la charge de la bonne interprétation' ('the onus of the right interpretation'), 'invité seulement à prendre ce qu'il lit "en bonne part", c'est-à-dire dans une bonne intention' ('invited only to take what s/he reads "in good part", in other words in the right spirit') (Rigolot (1995), p. 281). Gray too highlights this same fact: 'while the *devisants* deconstruct the text, we are expected to reconstruct it, returning to the story itself to re-evaluate the significance of its foldings and unfoldings'. Such foldings and unfoldings, one might remark, are not only images of the text's complexity; they are also images of the reader's activity. As Cave points out,[18] folding and unfolding recall the etymology of the French words 'im-pli-cation' and 'ex-pli-cation', and so the task of untying the knots and interpreting what lies hidden within the text – although, as Cave warns, what is unfolded in one place can become re-folded in another. Thus if at one level the reader is simply another interpreter, like the *devisants* themselves, at another level s/he has the possibility and indeed even the responsibility of unravelling the tangled skeins of the text. In other words, the reader is required to exercise judgement in the Montaignean sense of the term – to evaluate and weigh the data, without presupposing the absolute truth value of what is being assessed and without relying on the authority or *parti pris* of others. Reading is nothing other than the formation of judgement.

Although Gray does not mention this, his conception of the reader's task fits in well with Cave's analysis of reading as a form of enactment.[19] In this paradigm, the reader is literally on the same level as the fictional characters, obliged like them to confront the obstacles to understanding, the pressure that the text exerts on the reader's competence. This notion of literary competence – the strategies by which the reader makes sense of texts[20] – occurs again, this time in punning form, in Ann Moss's contribution on 'De l'amitié'. Her reference to 'insuffisants lecteurs', echoing Montaigne's phrases 'un suffisant lecteur' and 'l'indiligent lecteur',[21] forms part of her argument about the historical distance she divines separating both Montaigne's time and our own, and Montaigne's era and the past of classical antiquity. This initial point recalls the hypothesis put forward by Thomas Greene in his powerful and finely spun study, *The Light in Troy*.[22] For Greene, the historical gap which the Renaissance perceived between its present and a revered classical past gives particular edge to the sixteenth-century practice of literary imitation (*imitatio*); the quotations and allusions which populate Renaissance literature are both evidence of the classical heritage and the Renaissance's inability to rival the master texts on which it depends, or ultimately to re-connect with the past it promotes so strongly.[23] What Moss likewise undertakes is a linguistic archaeology, unearthing the half-obliterated signs of a style of reading now fallen into disuse, in this case the Renaissance use of commonplace books as a necessary preliminary to independent writing of one's own. Moss demonstrates that Montaigne is making reference to this method of composition, which embodies a whole set of cultural assumptions and values not immediately familiar to our own habits of mind. Similarly, one of Malcolm Quainton's emphases is what he specifically terms 'palimpsests'[24] in Ronsard's *Sonnets pour Hélène* II. 30: the material in this sonnet is re-written, supplying two further poems on a parallel theme within the Hélène cycle and within other collections contemporary with the *Sonnets pour Hélène*. Quainton's striking demonstration implicitly contests the idea of the source: all three Ronsard poems exist within and between each other, expanding and mutating in a gyration of shifting poetic forms and variations, giving rise to new texts as they proceed.

Two issues emerge from this account, both related to the question of intertextuality which is at the root of the analyses by Moss and (in part) by Quainton. The first has to do with the nature of intertextual practice in the Renaissance. As a central feature of Renaissance writing, this has understandably been the object of much critical scrutiny. Greene's book and its premises have already been mentioned. Important studies by Gisèle Mathieu-Castellani, André Tournon, Antoine Compagnon and Terence Cave also deal with this crucial issue in ways which open it up for further investigation.[25] Mathieu-Castellani notes that three characteristics seem to describe the Renaissance use of intertext: 'la filiation' ('lineal descent'), 'l'engendrement' ('procreation') and 'la rivalité mimétique' ('mimetic rivalry'). These three types of relationship correspond to three uses of the intertext: as a guarantee, as an origin, and as a model. Yet, against these optimistic and well-behaved images of the intertext, Mathieu-Castellani then comments:

> Mais ... si ... on observe l'écriture dans sa pratique, dans son travail, dans son corps à corps avec l'écrit étranger qu'elle absorbe et digère, apparaissent alors des effets pervers: voici que la caution garantit une alliance contre nature du même et de l'autre, radicalement autre, voici que l'origine se révèle fictive, masquant d'autres ancrages textuels, et que le modèle devient antimodèle, contre lequel s'écrit le texte.[26]

> But ... if ... one observes writing in practice, in the work it performs, as it wrestles with the foreign body of writing that it absorbs and digests, then weird and wonderful effects can be observed: all of a sudden the guarantee sponsors an unnatural alliance of the same and the other, the radically other, all of a sudden the origin turns out to be fictitious, concealing other link-ups

in the text, and the model becomes an antimodel, against which the text is written.

The connection between classical text and Renaissance re-writing is far from being the straightforward process of inheritance that the paternal images of genealogy and transmission imply; the Renaissance's own image of *transmissio studii*, 'the handing on of learning', purposely conceals the distortions and difficulties which the process embodies. As Mathieu-Castellani shows, it is a problem not only of how to integrate fragments of previous texts, but also of what tonality these fragments impart when imported into their host text. Intertextuality accordingly implies a problematic re-writing of previous (inherited) materials, not a simple accommodation of the past with the present.

Like Mathieu-Castellani, Tournon brings out the resistances, the discontinuities, and sudden shifts that the Renaissance technique of literary imitation implies. Drawing on examples as diverse as Ronsard's *Amours de Cassandre*, Béroalde de Verville's *Le moyen de parvenir*, the 'Eloge des dettes' in Rabelais' *Tiers Livre* and chapter 17 in the *Quart Livre*, he seeks to show how such examples exhibit their own inconsistencies, sometimes – as in the case of Rabelais or Béroalde – quite blatantly advertising their incongruities as a source of pleasure or humour for the reader. The problem thus becomes, for Tournon, not how to discover the secret unity of such texts, but how to respect and account for their disparate, heteroclite nature. As soon as the reader attempts to grasp the meaning of a sequence of allusions or quotations, the anomalies set up centrifugal tensions that make the Renaissance text impossible to weld into a satisfactory, unified whole. Tournon summarises his approach in this way:

> Toute méthode qui uniformise son objet, en escamotant les anomalies et ruptures provoquées par l'hétérogénéité, tend à laisser à l'écart des traits spécifiques lourds de sens; on ne peut y trouver qu'un procédé d'exploration partielle, apte à identifier les matériaux, mais inefficace dès qu'il s'agit de leur agencement.[27]

> Any method which regularises its object, sweeping aside the anomalies and sudden breaks caused by heterogeneity, tends to leave out specific features laden with meaning; such an approach can only be a tool of partial exploration, suitable for identifying materials, but unsatisfactory as soon as it comes to seeing how they fit together.

Tournon fully recognises the reader's temptation to extract comfortingly uniform aspects from a literary text, whether in the guise of thematic constants, overarching ideas and self-enclosed episodes; like Rigolot in a not dissimilar context, Tournon acknowledges that the reader may fall prey to the delusion that the literary work can be interpreted without any 'remainder' or 'leftover' or that any such remainder can be safely dismissed as incidental or exegetically unimportant. As with Mathieu-Castellani, the thrust of Tournon's argument is to contest vigorously such tidy schemes and to require of readers of Renaissance works an alertness and an intelligence that make of them, in the tradition of Barthes, co-producers of textual meanings, not passive consumers.

This project brings its own problems, however; and this leads us to the second aspect of Renaissance intertextuality mentioned earlier. The fine discriminations of texts seem to call for a reader who would be a polymath, able to spot any allusion or quotation and see its relevance to the passage at hand. In turn, this turns reading into an elitist activity, the prerogative of the few armed with the requisite knowledge.[28] This is a perennial problem in reading sixteenth-century texts (but not only these). Different solutions (though perhaps only partial solutions at best) can be offered for this difficulty. Moss conceives of the scholar's task as restoring to our active repertoire something forgotten in the cultural archive. Here the difference between the sixteenth century and our own is not the subject of lament, but the stimulus to the establishment of versatile strategies for overcoming, or at least mitigating, cultural differences. Quainton offers another outlook. Acknowledging that reading involves a constant tug and pull between the subjective experience of the reader and the expectations of the text, he views reading not as a once-and-for-all activity where the reader drains the text of its potential, but as an evolving process which sees changes in cultural perspectives as part of the experience of reading, alongside difficulties of language and form. A third model is offered by Mathieu-Castellani and Tournon. Mathieu-Castellani's use of the term 'anomalies intratextuelles' ('intratextual anomalies'),[29] and Tournon's expression 'marques' ('marks') or 'indices de lecture' ('reading cues'),[30] are indebted to Riffaterre's work on 'agrammaticalités' ('agrammaticalities'), in other words disturbances in the fabric of the text which orientate the reader towards the discovery of 'some originating pre-existent word group (the *hypogram*) of which each segment in the poem is a variant'.[31] In this form, Riffaterre's theory is open to charges of elitism or of establishing a normative reading. Specifically within Renaissance criticism, Francis Goyet accuses

Riffaterre of failing to distinguish between *imitatio* – which he regards as being backed by a theory – and intertextuality, which Goyet regards as a practice of some texts.[32] Modifying his view, Riffaterre then held that the reader need not be able to locate any particular intertext, but must nevertheless work with the presupposition of intertextuality.[33] Riffaterre further distinguished between intertext, a form of source criticism, and intertextuality, a feature of literary texts as such.[34] He has also dealt with the question of readerly competence and attempted to answer Goyet's query about 'le cas du lecteur inculte' ('the case of the ignorant reader')[35] by arguing that the loss of readerly recognition of the intertext in modern culture can always be counterbalanced by the fact that the text itself offers pointers to its own interpretation – that the text is its own most reliable decoder.[36] It remains true, nevertheless, that Riffaterre seems 'essentially concerned with the effect on the reader of a textual presupposition which gives structural and semantic unity rather than fracturing the text under consideration'.[37] The point made by Mathieu-Castellani and Tournon is precisely the opposite of this, and it is clear that theories about Renaissance intertextuality are caught in a powerful and yet unresolved dialectic between reading as integration and reading as fragmentation, and between the text as making specific demands of readerly knowledge and competence and the text as offering the reader clues to its own interpretation.

## THE TEXT AS DANAID

At the beginning of his chapter on Montaigne in *The Cornucopian Text*, Terence Cave cites Montaigne's essay 1.26, 'De l'institution des enfants' ('Of the Education of Children'), with its initial striking image of the Danaids ceaselessly yet fruitlessly drawing water from their pitchers:

> Je n'ay dressé commerce avec aucun livre solide, sinon Plutarque et Seneque, où je puyse comme les Danaïdes, remplissant et versant sans cesse. J'en attache quelque chose à ce papier; à moy, si peu que rien.

> I have not had regular dealings with any solid book, except Plutarch and Seneca, from whom I draw like the Danaïds, incessantly filling up and pouring out. Some of this sticks to this paper; to myself, little or nothing.[38]

For Montaigne, this is specifically a reflexive moment, a moment when he comments on his relations with his predecessors and his own work. Cave offers the following commentary:

> The paper on which the text of the *Essais* appears is ... a place of difference: it allows the rewriting and naturalization of foreign texts; it thereby permits the search for the identity of a *moi* in contra-distinction from what is 'other'; but at the same time it defers any final access to the goal of the search, since the self is expressly an entity dissociated from the activity of writing.[39]

Although Cave repudiates any affiliation to particular critical models or schools of thought, prudently asserting that to do so 'would have been to reduce sixteenth-century texts to the status of local illustrations of a modern theory',[40] his commentary nonetheless deploys to powerfully impressive effect methodologies and vocabularies which are broadly theoretical in inspiration and are associated with the work of Derrida, Barthes and, to a lesser extent, Lacan. The extract from *The Cornucopian Text* quoted above owes its impact to Cave's ability to map out in careful detail the teasing convolutions, paradoxes and intimate contradictions of the Renaissance text. Thus, in Cave's hands, the passage from 'De l'institution des enfants' is both an attempt to enact the appropriation of foreign materials that might help define a new Montaignean self and yet the deferral of that appropriation through the division separating the *moi* from the writing which is supposed to be the expression or fulfilment of it. That fundamental ambivalence is also played out in the rest of the quotation from Montaigne, as Cave goes on to show: the admiration which the essayist displays for Plutarch and Seneca is in complex tension with the vacuity and inanity signalled by 'aucun livre solide' ('no solid book'); Plutarch and Seneca are the exceptions, made almost parenthetically, to a generalised argument about books and their status. Equally, the central image of the Danaids is, Cave writes, 'not a wholly reassuring figure of plenitude' (*The Cornucopian Text*, p. 271); the myth, after all, emphasises the futility and vanity of the Danaids' task, which they are obliged to undertake as eternal punishment for murder. Even allowing for any irony in Montaigne's appropriation of the myth, his ambiguous relationship to the medium of writing or his activity as a writer shows through.

Cave's later assessment of 'De l'experience' – and the closing lines of his chapter on Montaigne – might stand as a summary of his approach:

Full experience is always absent; presence is unattainable. All that the *Essais* can do, with their ineradicable self-consciousness, is to posit paradigms of wholeness as features of a discourse which, as it pours itself out, celebrates its own inanity. [...]. Whatever plenitude seems to have been proper to the past, whatever festivity is assigned to these terminal moments, Montaigne's writing is both the only place in which they [= figures of abundance] can be designated, and a place from which they remain inexhaustibly absent.[41]

Cave gives potent expression to the empty graphological gestures which, in his view, the *Essais* mime, of which they are aware, but which they are condemned to repeat in the absence of full experience that would authenticate Montaigne's text as its accurate record and natural counterpart.

The importance, radicality and originality of Cave's book cannot be underestimated, even now, over twenty years after it was published. It embodies most forcefully and exactingly Rigolot's astute dictum that we need, not to modernise Renaissance texts, but to be attentive to their topicality. Particular developments in theoretical thinking had enabled Cave to undertake his project with its special force. Most prominent among these was the work of Derrida, whose valorisation of writing and patient questioning of the metaphysics of presence have left a lasting impression on the study of literature. Derrida's critique arose from the observation that the Western philosophical tradition, since Plato and before, gave the priority to the Logos, understood variously as reason, the rational principle, the Word of God, mind. The characteristic of this term was that it assumed what Derrida called, in *De la grammatologie* and elsewhere, self-presence ('présence à soi'): it was readily described as possessing fullness, completeness, naturalness, immediacy. Logocentrism, as Derrida termed it, was held to constitute a guarantee of a self-validating absolute, a truth or a foundation for metaphysics, ontology and epistemology. In each case, a presence, directly available to our awareness and understanding, suffices to centre (to anchor or organise) the structure of a transcendent system in such a way as to fix the bounds, coherence and determinate meanings within that system. This same description, Derrida claimed, could be extended to an entire range of abstract concepts on which Western philosophical thinking had relied. Moreover, in the case of each concept, a positive term is set against an explicit or implicit negative term with which it is contrasted and from which, in principle, it is distinct. Derrida calls such pairs 'binary oppositions'. Noting that one term is always given precedence over the other, he proceeds to demonstrate that far from being separate poles of a stark antithesis, the two elements are imbricated in each other; the hierarchy and the neat distinction they appear to compose collapse when subjected to scrutiny. Thus our understanding of (for example) presence depends upon our knowing that it is the converse of absence. The 'properties' of presence arise out of their difference from absence rather than from inherent characteristics. In order to understand what presence is, we have first and foremost to understand what it is not.

This mobilisation of difference for a larger philosophical purpose is a bold extension of Saussurian linguistics and takes place within a framework in which Derrida examines the nature of such binary oppositions, and notably the speech/writing binarism. If speech is endowed with the qualities of presence – naturalness, spontaneity, immediacy – writing, in the Western tradition, has just the opposite characteristics: it is a mediate form, based not on the presence of the objects it discusses but on their absence, since writing stands in for things, as their symbolic representation. For Derrida, as for Saussure, signifiers owe their seeming identity, not to their own inherent features, but rather to their differences from other signifiers. Cave draws one conclusion from this in respect of the central issue of mimesis:

> Users of language are duped by deeply ingrained linguistic habits into supposing that discourse mirrors, represents, or mimes reality, and tend to underestimate its congenital inclination to deviate from the 'things' it purports to represent.[42]

Thus writing does not deliver full meaning, but defers it in a play of differences; linguistic signifiers seem to point to a transcendental signified that might anchor it in a secure referentiality, but are split from such transcendent referentiality; signifer is no longer bonded to signified, as in a Saussurian scheme. Writing promises, but does not deliver, the meaning towards which it gestures persistently; to believe that writing enacts what it promises is to take rhetoric and symbolic signs for reality. This deferral of (the full presence of) meaning through the play of graphological differences is caught by Derrida's neologism 'différance' – both 'difference' and 'deferral'. 'Différance' is the condition whereby a text provides the 'effect' of having a significance that is the product of its difference. However, since this difference can never come to rest in an actual presence or centre, its determinate signification is deferred from one interpretation to another in a 'play' of signifiers. At the same time, by close investigation of Rousseau's attitude to writing (and sex), Derrida shows in De la grammatologie that

writing, seemingly an addition to speech – speech's inferior, figurative, deviant representation – ends up by supplanting it: this is the
burden of Derrida's findings, a conclusion which he captures in the
suitably ambiguous French verb 'suppléer' and its associated noun
'supplément' (meaning both 'to fill up by addition' and 'to supplant').

It is this tight and powerful nexus of considerations which under-
pin Cave's analysis of Montaigne in *The Cornucopian Text*. The essay
'De l'experience' appears to be some record of experience – and Montaigne frequently exalts the claims of experience and life over book-
ish learning – yet it is Cave's contention that, in Montaigne, 'full
experience is always absent; presence is unattainable'. The synonyms
for presence – experience, wholeness, plenitude, abundance, not to
mention Nature – proliferate, but always (and only) through the
detours of writing. Yet since writing is 'a place of difference', it 'defers
access to the goal of the search': writing can designate such presence,
can sketch out 'paradigms of wholeness', but never give them, simply
and directly, to the reader; it perpetually *signifies*, but never just
*means*. What we encounter in the pages of the *Essais* is a rhetoric of
vivid (re)presentation, the rhetoric of *enargeia*, which highlights its
own workings in terms of vanity, futility and emptiness, at the same
time that, through rhetorical sleight-of-hand, it wishes the sign to be
taken for the thing, language for its object, signifier for signified.
Hence the correlation between modern theory and Renaissance texts.
Cave claims that 'perhaps the most significant development in recent
Continental theory is the attempt to devise a discourse which will per-
form the functions of rational argument while at the same time
unmasking and exploiting its hidden devices of rhetoric'.[43] For Cave,
the *interférence* between the referentiality of language and the orator-
ical strategies of the text (copiousness, abundance, sexuality, inebria-
tion) is a drama which is equally well played out, in a variety of forms,
throughout sixteenth-century literature, from Erasmus to Rabelais,
Ronsard to Montaigne.

It is worth considering at this point two objections to this position.
The first comes from Gérard Defaux, whose book *Marot, Rabelais,
Montaigne: L'écriture comme présence* is, as the title indicates, in no
small part designed as a refutation of Derridean logocentrism, in
other words, as Defaux explains quoting *De la grammatologie*, 'la
proximité absolue de la voix et de l'être, de la voix et du sens de l'être,
de la voix et de l'idéalité du sens' ('the absolute proximity of voice and
being, of voice and the meaning of being, of voice and the ideality of

meaning').[44] Using Erasmus' notion of 'oratio speculum animi' ('speech is the mirror of the mind') and Quintilian's 'pectus est quod disertos facit' ('it is the heart which makes one eloquent'), Defaux argues strongly that, while acknowledging the potential slippage between signs and meaning, words and things, the Renaissance continued to believe resolutely in the 'présence de la chose dans le mot, de l'esprit dans la lettre, de l'auteur dans son texte' ('presence of the thing in the word, the spirit in the letter, the author in his/her text').[45] Defaux openly champions therefore what he takes to be the Cratylism of the Renaissance, that is to say, the belief, expounded in Plato's dialogue *Cratylus*, that the relationship between names and their referent is motivated, not conventional.[46] This is the very opposite of the Saussurian position, and Defaux proceeds to emphasise the extension of this view:

> L'effacement de la matérialité du signifiant ayant nécessairement pour corollaire la valorisation et la promotion du signifié, la parole est alors essentiellement structurée et portée par une volonté quasi obsessionnelle de représentation, elle est l'instrument entre tous privilégié de la *mimesis*. Faite avant tout pour montrer, pour rendre la chose présente, elle est image, peinture ou tableau.[47]

> The necessary corollary of the effacing of the materiality of the signifier is the valorisation and promotion of the signified. Words are thus essentially structured and borne along by an almost obsessive urge for representation; they are the uniquely privileged instrument of *mimesis*. Designed above all to display things and make them present, words are an image, a portrait or a picture.

For Defaux, the logocentric optimism of an Erasmus or a Rabelais is entirely at one with the assumptions of their age.

Defaux's method is nowhere better illustrated than in his chapter on Rabelais, which expressly targets Derridean *différance* and readings deriving from this approach, above all Cave's reading of the prologue to the *Gargantua* as a case of plurality, in other words the notion that a text cannot be confined to one particular meaning, 'not because it is obscure, not because it has several levels of meaning, but because it is set up in such a way as to block interpretative procedures'.[48] Siding with Screech and especially Duval,[49] Defaux counters that the much-vaunted contradiction between the first and second 'halves' of the prologue to *Gargantua* – the text asserts a difference between surface and depth and then renounces it – is more apparent than real and derives from a misreading of the letter of the Prologue. Rabelais aims for a benevolent reader who takes the text 'in good part' (Defaux's analysis here rejoins Rigolot's); to see in Rabelais a hero of Derridean *différance* is to reduce Rabelais to our modernity, to make him say what we want to read rather than reading what he wants to say, to modernise him without actualising him, in Rigolot's phrase.[50] Cave might reply that he does not deny the ideology of perfect reciprocity between word and thing that the Renaissance seeks to foster and sustain, but that he is attentive to the disturbances within the text which are not readily accommodatable to that belief. Indeed, Cave has recently reiterated in more cautious terms that Renaissance texts are able to see closure and beyond closure; they can understand their own horizons and what lies beyond them.[51] He might accordingly agree with Barbara Johnson that 'the de-construction [*sic*] of a text does not proceed by random doubt or arbitrary subversion, but by the careful teasing out of warring forces of signification within the text itself.'[52] Certainly, he has subsequently been at pains to emphasise that 'one is not speaking here of an aesthetic or a rhetoric that makes interpretation arbitrary'.[53] For Defaux, in contrast, a pervasive intentionality[54] is inescapable in both the writing and the evaluation of such Renaissance works: 'dès qu'il y a langage, dès qu'il y a texte, il y a sens' ('as soon as there is language, as soon as there is a text, there is meaning') and attempts to suggest that a text is always in excess of its glosses are misplaced, while the search for plurality is 'le fruit d'une mauvaise lecture ou d'une approche critique impertinente dans son anachronisme' ('the product of a misreading or of a critical approach that is impertinent in its anachronism').[55]

Thomas Greene pays tribute to the influence of Cave's work in *The Vulnerable Text*, and in 'Dangerous Parleys', one of the essays collected in that volume, he refers in passing to Cave's commentary on the Danaids' passage while taking issue with Cave's view of the Renaissance text.[56] In 'Dangerous Parleys' and more particularly in another essay, 'Vulnerabilities of the Humanist Text', Greene examines the question of whether Renaissance texts can be said to possess a centre, a view which he sees Cave as undermining. He maintains that they can, and that such a centre, although wobbly, will act as an organising principle.[57] What is organised is however nothing solid and definitive. It is rather an aetiology, in other words 'a retrospective explanation of a textual coming-into-being, a process of accumulated significations through time (which does not of course exclude a concurrent loss of signification)'.[58] Thus each Renaissance text (or in the case of Erasmus, each adage) enacts that aetiology, which is the story of its own emergence, in Greene's version of reflexivity. But Greene rapidly adds that the aetiology of which he speaks 'provides at best a simulacrum of order, a flexible, shaky order that remains in the realm of becoming'.[59] In short, it is 'in a sense, a fiction'[60] and yet, through that semi-fictional aetiology, 'the Humanist text ... assumes deliberately its own concrete historicity, the perspectives, the prejudices, the semiotic vocabulary, of its age ...'.[61] These descriptions give some sense of what Greene understands by his coinage 'vulnerability': it is the condition by which the Renaissance text knows its own limitations, its own inadequacies, its own circumscribed particularity, which are all the effects of its historical place. For 'to embrace history is to embrace contingency, incompleteness, the vulnerability of the contingent'.[62] Hence Greene's Renaissance text is no less self-conscious and self-reflexive than Cave's, but is aware of its condition as one in which a utopian desire for plenitude is renounced in favour of acceptance of its own contingency. Indeed, the Renaissance text 'will never achieve absolute closure, freedom from deferral, perfect finality, those unreal dreams of the twentieth-century mind'.[63]

The 'Vulnerabilities' article ends with an Erasmian adage, to the effect that whoever cannot follow the straight road should follow the winding river.[64] Greene's article in this present volume employs the same image of meandering to describe Ronsard's 'Epistre à Villeroy', and it is possible to look at Greene's essay in the light of the criteria he established in his earlier article. With Ronsard as with Erasmus, the centre is decidedly wobbly and uncertain. Indeed, it may be preferable to speak of centres, in the plural, since the focus shifts from part to part, changing its classical model (first Horace, then Virgil) and illustrating the 'divine inconstance' ('divine inconstancy') which Ronsard admired in the Greek lyric poet Pindar and which Quainton, in an analogous Ronsardian context, explores in the steps of the dance, now fast, now slow, composing a pattern not obvious to the casual observer. In that respect, the poem's journey and the reader's itinerary are one, both launched on an uncertain future which reflects the status of poetry at that present time. Yet there is more than a structural principle at stake in Greene's reading of the 'Epistre'. He poses large questions about the relationship of the poetic artefact to the external force of history. Ronsard's poem comments on its own situation in the midst of civil strife, the French Wars of Religion; the poem is conscious of its own precariousness and no doubt the uncertainty of poetic productivity generally in a time of changing fortunes. In this light, the multiple foci of the 'Epistre' become more understandable:

the poet-narrator surveys the turmoil of past and present and seeks a point of reference that will give the poem and history some purchase, some stability. The name 'Villeroy' is that point of reference. As Secretary of State, Villeroy confronts every day the realities of political conflict, but nonetheless affords Ronsard the shelter of his estate at Conflans; he embodies that meeting place between the surging forces of history and the winding flow of poetry.

The final images of the 'Epistre' as an orange growing in Villeroy's orange garden at Conflans and of the collection it prefaces as a book in Villeroy's library may, in that regard, seem nothing more than an elegantly devised conceit. But Greene rightly insists upon the fact that the promise these images encapsulate is fragile: 'One is allowed to hope that both the books and the trees will survive the darkening storm, though we have no reason to think it will abate. The power of the estate's resistance has not yet been fully tested'. The poem has 'custody of beleaguered values ... on the eve of their probable disappearance'. Greene's analysis here is at one with his disquisition on anachronism in the essay 'History and Anachronism'. With typical finesse, Greene distinguishes between five types of anachronism in Renaissance literature. His own book *The Light in Troy* deals principally with the fourth of these anachronisms, creative anachronism, which 'confronts and uses the conflict of period styles self-consciously and creatively to dramatize the itinerary, the diachronic passage out of the remote past into the emergent present'.[65] However, it is the fifth, and last, type of anachronism which is of most interest to us in dealing with Ronsard's 'Epistre'. This last type Greene terms 'pathetic' or 'tragic' anachronism and he defines it as deriving from 'the destiny of all enduring human products, including texts, since all products come into being bearing the marks of their historical moment and then, if they last, are regarded as alien during a later moment because of those marks'.[66] These observations fit beautifully Ronsard's 'Epistre'. The constant incursion of contemporary history into the poetic text is not an incidental, but central to its genesis and the situation it has to face and wishes to discuss. Even the oranges at the close – at other times a transcendent, time-defying image in Ronsard – are a symbol of pathetic anachronism in just the sense Greene describes elsewhere. Ronsard could have used an image of iron resilience or proud monumentality. He chooses instead an emblem which bears the marks of its historical moment in the uncertainty of its survival, and the insecurity of its reception not only perhaps by the poem's dedicatee, but also and more importantly by us, the future readers of this 'Epistre'. The poem takes on the risk of its own anachronism by offering these marks, exposing its vulnerability, to our evaluation, in the knowledge that what we find alien or hard to assimilate (Greene mentions Ronsard's flattery of Villeroy as an instance) is proof that the passage of time cannot be entirely breached by the poem. On Greene's account, anachronism is thus not a feature external to the Renaissance text. It is a feature actively discussed and positively employed by those self-same texts, unalterably written into their constitution. It is part of their heritage and part of their destiny.

## 'NOUS NE SOMMES JAMAIS CHEZ NOUS' ('WE ARE NEVER AT HOME') (MONTAIGNE, *ESSAIS*, 1.3)

'Ici, dans le champ du rêve, tu es chez toi' (Lacan) ('Here, in the sphere of dreams, you are at home').[67] It is not difficult to understand the attractions of psychoanalytical criticism for the literary theorist. The easy relationship between psychoanalysis and literature – a marked feature of the practice of Freud and Lacan – helps reduce any feeling that theory is simply being imposed on an artwork: the organic connection between the two domains is strongly maintained. This connection is moreover not one of subordination; art is not reduced to the role of illustrating psychoanalytical principles. On the contrary, psychoanalysis can just as often start with the work of literature; literature is the site of psychoanalysis. In that respect, Lawrence Kritzman and Nancy Frelick are following in a well-established tradition, and one to which they have already made significant and distinguished contributions.[68] Yet this close relationship between art and psychoanalysis is at the same time a facilitating mechanism, allowing the foregrounding of substantial aspects of psychoanalysis, centred on the problematics of the human subject. The target of psychoanalytical criticism can be said to be Descartes' dictum in his *Meditations on First Philosophy*, 'Je pense, donc je suis' ('I think, therefore I am'),[69] with its underlying assumptions of the supremacy of the conscious rational self as the organising and controlling principle of the human personality, the commanding feature to which other faculties are subordinate. By contrast, the Oedipal processes mapped out by Freud over the course of his career describe a self irremediably split at every stage of its development. A quintessential self, displaying the unity of utterance, intention or purpose supposed by the Cartesian system, is, psychoanalysis would claim, an inadequate representation of the forces contending for supremacy within the Freudian or Lacanian ego. At best, such a quintessential self is a construct of narcissism bolstered by the Conscious ('le conscient'), which expressly suppresses drives and desires emanating from the Unconscious ('l'inconscient'). Subject to the censorship mechanism of the Conscious, the Unconscious nevertheless evades such controls to return in dreams, slips of the tongue, jokes, all of which reveal that a very different drama is being staged and played out on the Other Scene of the Unconscious, as Freud termed it. This conflict between conscious and unconscious, repression and display, likewise has repercussions for the concept of the author and the text. The challenge psychoanalysis offers to the unitary self and the consistent meaning attached to it has parallels in the status of the author. Once a focus of the text's meaning, the source of definitive utterance, the author is now shown to be riven by contradictions and incompatible urges: psychoanalysis, particularly in its Lacanian form, adds to the lesson imparted by Barthes and Foucault. Lawrence Kritzman encapsulates this point when he says in his article here that Lacanian theory rejects the notion of a self-contained subject and proposes instead 'one that forever exceeds itself': in other words, a self which is decentred, ex-centric, and composed of elements outside conscious or rational control. And the text which emerges from this bundle of warring impulses and desires is no less significant in the psychoanalytical scheme of things. Indeed, the text gives dramatic expression to this divided ego, revealing those disturbances in the psychological fabric. The text is, in Lacan's terms, the place where the Other – the Unconscious – speaks, since 'l'inconscient est structuré comme un langage' ('the Unconscious is structured like a language') and 'l'inconscient, c'est le discours de l'Autre' ('the Unconscious is the discourse of the Other').[70] The text, in short, analyses its author – and its reader.

Lawrence Kritzman's article in this volume pursues these points with particular vigour. Although he disclaims allegiance to specific psychoanalytical models, his indebtedness to that tradition offers him powerful analytical tools which he uses to great effect. He expressly states that Montaigne's essay 3.4 'anticipates the preoccupations of psychoanalytic theory'. In particular, 'the various categories of diversion anticipate the Lacanian revision of psychoanalytic theory by rejecting the concept of a self-contained subject'. The crucial term in both these statements is 'anticipates'. It symbolises both the relevance of Renaissance literature today and the relevance of contemporary theory to Renaissance literature: a theory – here psychoanalysis – allows us to draw out the implications of Montaigne's words, to see how they embody a psychic configuration of which the essayist himself may not have been fully aware, but which is featured in the very signifiers composing the text.[71] For Kritzman, Montaigne's essay 'De la diversion' implicitly acknowledges the presence of the Unconscious with one of its initial statements: 'Nous pensons toujours ailleurs' ('Our thoughts are always elsewhere'). The Unconscious weaves its way through the utterances of the essay, revealing the essayist's wish to postpone engagement with death. While such postponement is the condition of Montaigne's narrative dynamics – the essay *is* (about) digression[72] – it is also emblematic of other concerns. For 'De la diversion' not only traces, but more importantly enacts those tensions and evasions by which the human subject attempts to live through grief and bereavement, in short to survive. Part of that strategy of avoidance and survival will involve the diversions of rhetoric, using 'the magic of language' in order to effect a semblance of mastery over the chaos of death. Accepting the disparity between words and things comes at a price, however. Exiled from the plenitude of being, the human subject accepts the condition of loss in return for verbal control; an existential state is exchanged for a symbolic form. Kritzman phrases the consequences of this action in this way: 'The discourse on diversion is born from the fictions that supplement the ontological nothingness of the writing subject by compensating the absence through endless repetition'. Each new attempt at mastery is accordingly just repetition, delaying rather than confirming actual control, and demonstrating the vanity of words as well as the ontological vacuity of a creature who writes himself into existence through them. Yet the compulsion to repeat is unavoidable if the human subject is to survive, if writing is to continue, if reading is to advance.

This vocabulary of loss, vacuity and emptiness also explains Kritzman's careful avoidance of the term 'author' and his strategic choice of the expressions 'writing subject' or 'subject of writing' to characterise the essayist in 'De la diversion'. (Kritzman's use of the name 'Montaigne' likewise needs to be seen as a metonymy for the work and not as reference to a living person.) A fundamental tenet of Lacanian psychoanalysis is that the self is subject to the signifier: it is not only composed out of the letters and written into existence through the very letters on the page, but also subject to the ebb and flow of language, the twists and turns of communication always susceptible to sabotage by the unpredictable irruption of the Unconscious. As Lacan puts it in a suitably ambiguous phrase, the self is 'le sujet de la représentation', alternately in command of and yet submissive to the linguistic scenes in which it participates.[73] The expressions 'writing subject' and 'subject of writing' work in a similar way. They overturn the notion of an author, an authority who is the source of the literary work, by making the author a function of his/her work. The author is now a topic ('subject' in that sense) of the writing within which s/he appears. S/he is also subjected to writing, having no independent existence outside of the words on the page. A further blow is struck against the idea that the literary work is the free expression of an autonomous individual.

Another way of conceptualising this range of issues is through the Lacanian notion of the mirror stage ('le stade du miroir').[74] For Lacan, this putative event – a necessary myth in the formation of the individual – takes place when the child is between six and eighteen months old. At its heart is the process of identification. The mirror image offers the child a picture of physical unity and motor co-ordination of a kind that the child does not truly possess, but with which it identifies. It may seem that, in making this identification, the child has made a free choice and that its successful adoption of the image is a victory in what Lacan calls the Imaginary. Yet neither of these things is true. The child's assumption of the image is, in Lacanian terms, a misrecognition ('méconnaissance'), for the child does not enjoy the independence that the mirror promises. Moreover, as Lacan implies, the child is shown its image in the mirror. Its identification with the mirror image is dictated by the intervention of a third party – the parent, especially the mother – who signals the identification with the words, 'Tu es cela' ('You are that'; 'That's you').[75] The identification is thus enacted in the Symbolic order of language and imposed on the child from without, not chosen from within. And Lacan is clear that the Symbolic order – the rival to the Imaginary – is an order in the sense of a category or a class, but also an order in the sense of a command which is enjoined on the human subject and under which s/he labours. The human being is not a proud nominative designated by a 'je', but an object, a thing, a 'cela'. The subjection of the self to language is clearly evidenced by the mirror stage, but it begins from birth, when the baby is named and so immediately positioned within language.

The process of identification analysed by Lacan will also operate as a metaphor for mimesis, and thus for the assumptions behind one longstanding description of the work of art. The idea that art directly reflects something, or that the reader can simply identify with what is represented within the text, is subverted by Lacanian misrecognition. Kritzman demonstrates, for example, that the writing subject's misrecognition in 'De la diversion' is the source of the essay itself: Montaigne's verbal disquisitions may give a totally illusory, imaginary sense of mastery, yet without the attempt to avoid death through delay, digression, the accumulation of examples and stories, there would be no essay about diversion. Montaigne's whole essay becomes, on that view, not an objective account of the topic it handles, but rather a symptom of the very malady it claims to be diagnosing. In a parallel act of misrecognition, the English lord in *Nouvelle 57* of the *Heptaméron* deludes himself that he can substitute himself for his ideal as the object of the admiring gaze of others.

At issue here is the whole question of desire, as Nancy Frelick declares at the outset of her article. On a Lacanian reading, desire is seen as a lack and the attempt to satisfy this lack is impossible because no one specific object can fulfil desire. Much as Montaigne passes from one anecdote to the next in 'De la diversion' through a dynamics of displacement, so too erotic desire, in Marguerite de Navarre, travels from one object to the next in search of some satisfaction beyond the object, unobtainable because it is in the final analysis 'an idea, a phantasm in the imagination of the lover'. The whole of *Nouvelle 57* of the *Heptaméron*, in Frelick's view, can be viewed as tracing out a series of shifts, following the chain of desire which Lacan compares to the rhetorical figure of metonymy. Like Kritzman, Frelick analyses topological and tropological strategies, in this case those by which Marguerite's English nobleman, in an act of fetishism, effectively replaces the woman who is the supposed object of his affections, by the jewelled glove.

The large-scale analytical narrative which Frelick draws out of *Nouvelle 57* is ultimately centred on that most controversial of objects, the phallus; the story of the English nobleman is the story of the phallus, which is also in some measure the story of Lacanian psychoanalysis. Frelick rightly warns against taking the phallus literally and emphasises its metaphorical status as a symbol of paternal injunction and as a marker of differences, whether linguistic or gender-related. The phallus, Frelick explains, represents the law of the father, which coincides with the father's name ('le nom du père', also echoing 'le non du père'). What Freud had presented as castration, even of an imaginary kind, takes place for Lacan in language: it is the father's interdiction – 'No!', 'Non!' – that cuts the child off from his original source of desire, the (m)other, and dispatches him/her in search of substitutes for that fullness of possession. The shift from the realm of the mother to the law of the father corresponds to the acceptance of the 'emptiness' of language in place of the 'fullness' of purely illusory, imaginary possession. Lacan thus combines the inheritance of structuralist linguistics, which emphasises language as a metaphorical substitute for absent objects, with a properly psychoanalytical concern for the description of the human subject in terms of trauma, castration and dispossession (Lacan's characterisation of the human is as pessimistic as Freud's).

The phallus, Lacanians would argue, is the neutral marker of these psychic events, a symbol which concentrates energies, a 'mobile currency' at once fixed and free that enables the articulation of multivalent levels of signification. Others have been less convinced. Maud Ellmann, for example, draws attention to the contradiction, as she sees it, between the rigidity of values implied by the phallus and the labile fluidity of its positioning in the signifying chain. Stephen Greenblatt, in an article to be discussed later in this introduction, takes issue with the notion that the early-modern self can be defined as a matter of its own psychic history. He sees no continuity between the vocabulary of twentieth-century psychology and the terminology appropriate to the sixteenth century. More gravely still, the very choice of the phallus and its use as a demarcator of gender differences makes it suspect to feminist critics. To these objections we may now turn.


## WRITING WOMEN

All sixteenth-century texts work within the framework of mimesis, specifically the imitation of other texts past and present. One decisive contribution of feminism to this issue is a keen awareness that the issue of imitation is gender marked. The sixteenth-century male writer simply asserted his right to speak, to make himself heard, to write. The female writer can make none of those assumptions. As Carla Freccero shows in her article in this volume, the social, ethical and theological constraints imposed on women converted even the act of speaking into an act of disobedience characteristic of a woman of loose morals. Silence, by contrast, was synonymous with chastity.[76] For Renaissance women writers to speak out of silence was radical enough. More radical still, Freccero stresses, was for a woman writer such as Louise Labé to centre her work 'upon the one area of affect – female erotic desire – most proscribed by the teachings and customs of her day'. When Labé encounters the Petrarchan tradition of writing about love, it is to develop strategies by which to fashion it into a medium fit for the expression of the female voice. It is here that she must manoeuvre most subtly but also more forcefully with the male conventions so as 'to wrest the genre [of love poetry] from its entrenchment in fixed gender roles' (Freccero). Freccero traces the tactics by which Louise Labé accomplishes this operation in her *Elégies*: establishment of a female genealogy which links the poetess to a predecessor, Sappho, whilst at the same time displaying and enhancing that predecessor's work; sympathy with figures such as Semiramis, the unhappy victim of love and an object of vilification in Boccaccio and other male authors; anticipation of criticism, notably from other women (an instance where, as Freccero notes, women collude in their own oppression), followed by an assertion of civic solidarity and class commonality in that section of *Elégie* 3 that Freccero with commendable caution labels 'autobiographical'.

Throughout, Freccero proves that Louise Labé appropriates 'the codes of masculine self-representation' so as to give her own poetic voice greater authority, but – crucially – she inscribes within those codes a 'feminine signature' (Nancy Miller's term quoted by Freccero) or 'les marques du féminin' ('marks of the feminine', Mathieu-Castellani). In the third *Elégie*, that signature is needlework, emblem of the poetess's artistic skill. In other poems, this evidence of a gendered subjectivity emerges in a variety of forms; as one might perhaps expect, the sonnets offer especially striking instances. Thus in sonnet 2, the technique of listing the qualities of the beloved (*enumeratio*) is summarised by the line: 'Tant de flambeaus pour ardre une femmelle' ('So many torches to burn a female'). In the Petrarchan idiom, the beloved was a 'Dame' ('Lady'), but never merely a female. Louise, by selecting this word, points to the bodily experience of the woman as the site of physical suffering and erotic violence, rather than some disincarnate, ethereal self. A similar comment can be made about the much discussed phrase in sonnet 14 where the narrator says she will desire death only when she can no longer 'montrer signe d'amante'. If this odd collocation has a familiar ring for the reader, it is no doubt because it is modelled on a standard expression such as 'signe de vie', but with a purposeful distortion: for the narrator-lover, to live is to love. Yet the expression is far from trite. While it primarily expects the reader to see in it the re-working of a set phrase, it also enables the poetess to claim for herself, publicly, the title of 'amante' ('lover'), in competition with the masculine form 'amant' and in contradistinction to the usual Petrarchan status of the woman as 'bien aimée' ('beloved'). With one short phrase, Louise reverses the standard poetic roles between lover and beloved and stakes a claim for the centrality of love from a woman's perspective. It is in just such ways that her work makes (and marks) a difference – unobtrusive to the casual gaze, significant to the attentive reader. This is precisely 'Petrarchism with a difference'.[77]

The female body is also central to Ann Jones' article in this collection. In the literary genre she considers, the *blason*, gender marking, which is the counterpart of phallic division, is evident from the very fact that the *blason* is predominantly a male genre, fetishising women by treating the parts of the female body as independent units to be dissected and savoured by the male gaze. The male poet (and indeed the male reader) is in the position of a voyeur, luxuriating in the scene created by his gaze and taking place for his own pleasure before his eyes as he describes the female body or reads poetic descriptions of it. Hence the contradiction (and not simply the paradox) that women, supposedly the subject of the poetic universe to which all else is subordinated, are in reality fetishistic objects in a world of male desire. A parallel can thus be established between the scattered female body found in *blason* poetry and 'scattered rhymes', the term by which Petrarch speaks of his own poetic production: male writing of the female body depends upon a visual and verbal fragmentation and is a form of power and control, reinforcing the gender hegemonies that are as prevalent today as they were in the Renaissance. Jones' analysis here draws potently on a number of richly intersecting traditions. The cinema offers ways of understanding the position of the viewer and the angle of vision; Marxism provides instruments for probing the sexual economics and commodification.[78] Above all, Jones makes use of Luce Irigaray, the French feminist writer who, in *Ce sexe qui n'en est pas un* (*This Sex Which Isn't One*), capitalises on the methodologies offered by Marxism and psychoanalysis. Whereas men define themselves as free, sovereign subjects, possessors of power and position symbolised by the phallus, women are described by the inverse of this; in this binary opposition, women are the secondary partners, associated with a lack of the phallus, the absence of autonomy and sovereign rights. On this view, the phallus is assigned a role as the creator and sustainer of a patriarchal society. The phallus is more than a marker of gender difference, or rather the phallus becomes confused with the penis; possession of the phallus puts men on top. Sexual and sociopolitical differences merge. Irigaray's enquiry, quoted by Jones, exposes the flawed ideology of this economic system in which the centre is always the man and his phallus (hence the terms 'phallocentrism' and 'phallocentric'), and in which contrastingly, women are mere commodities, pawns in an network of exchange that reduces individual women to some generalised currency of interchangeable abstractions.

Jones contextualises Louise Labé's use of the *blason* form against the background of Pernette du Guillet's dismissal of the male body and Catherine des Roches' mockery of Neoplatonic praise of women. She follows closely the twists and turns of Labé's sonnets, showing how the poetess overturns the subordination inherent in the *blason*, taking possession of her own body and staking claims on her lover's, until she finally abandons the *blason* for a frank avowal of passion. Jones' article in this volume builds on her earlier study, *The Currency of Eros*, the introduction to which offers fruitful ways of conceptualising the operations perceptible in the work of Louise Labé and the other poetesses she investigates. Adopting recent Marxist theories of negotiation, she explains that this involves 'a range of interpretative positions through which subordinated groups respond to the assumptions encoded into dominant cultural forms and systems of representation'.[79] In the context of Renaissance, this means that women writers can make use of contemporary cultural forms and representations, even agree to be drawn into them and be shaped by those conventions in order to legitimise their aesthetic enterprise, while nonetheless employing them for radically different ends. Thus the 'negotiated' position adopted by the woman writer 'is one that accepts the dominant ideology encoded into a text but particularizes and transforms it in the service of a different group'.[80] All depends on what Marxists term 'situatedness': the particularisation and transformation of dominant ideologies will vary according to class, economic position, political frameworks, religious beliefs, philosophical perspectives.[81] Transformation arises from the conflicts between these different

frames of reference, and thus how women deftly negotiate these conflicts, manage the contradictory determinations of ideological systems. Jones' acute analysis allows us to understand how some women
writers are able to move between several ideological planes at the
same time, while others seem to concentrate on one sphere: all
depends on situatedness. But Jones, like Freccero, underscores that
love lyric proved an especially transgressive genre for a woman writer,
in that it 'centralizes sociosexual differences as no other literary mode
does', enabling 'the woman poet ... to disarticulate and remobilize the
sexual economy of her culture'.[82] The risk incurred by this strategy is
acute, as Jones goes on to state: an implicit correlation was made
between art and prostitution, between the 'body' or corpus of literature on sale to the reading public and the body of the woman on sale
to all comers. When Calvin called Louise Labé a 'common prostitute'
('plebeia meretrix'), it carried more than a moral censure or historical
reproach; it embodied a legal charge, and one from which women in
Renaissance France could easily be the victims.

Jones is right to insist, however, that to see Renaissance women
just as victims, or to have them endlessly repeat 'a timeless story of
individual suffering', would be to impoverish their achievement and
reduce them to disempowerment. In her article here on feminist theories of the gaze, as in her book, she wishes to read women's history
as 'a process of struggle and creative accommodation to social realities and cultural forms'.[83] Eros then becomes a form of instrumenta-
tion by which women can effect change rather than just suffer it and
rail against it. In the hands of Renaissance women writers, Eros is a
flexible currency, facilitating mobility between different planes of
enunciation and different levels of ideological engagement. This
accounts well for the rapid changes of register and position in Labé's
sonnets, varying between lament (sonnet 5) and desire (sonnets 13
and 18), irony (sonnet 23) and celebration (sonnet 10), with, always,
an eye to the female audience now enlisted as sympathetic listeners,
now addressed as potential critics (see especially sonnet 24). By pitch-
ing the debate in women's writing in terms of the theoretical principles with which it engages, Jones opens a further perspective on the
issue raised by Freccero when the latter deftly balances the 'autobiographical' section of *Elégie* 3 against the 'feminine signature'. The
issue concerns the connection between women's writing and women's
lives. To look at this question purely from the standpoint of mimesis
as such (women's writing as a direct reflection of women's lives) is,

Jones implies, to address the problem from the wrong angle. The female 'je' is not the sign of private, fully interiorised individual giving direct and spontaneous expression to her own experience. It is, rather, a designation of an historical subject (in the sense Lacan would understand this) whose 'je' is the meeting point of conflicting and overlapping frames of reference; it is the site of ideological dissonances and incompatibilities which are precisely open to negotiation in the way Jones and Freccero describe. The 'je' is 'overdetermined'; it articulates a 'situatedness'. We do not go to Louise Labé or any other Renaissance woman writer looking for a direct link between the writing and the life, but for evidence of engagement with the intertextual structures of writing and the gender ideologies these convey. What matters is not some putative biography reconstructable from the literary work, but the writer's engagement and negotiation with the rhetoric of literary language, for 'language is both the concrete manifestation of ideology – the categories in which speakers are authorized to think – and the site of its questioning or undoing'.[84] Jones' situated subject and Freccero's gendered subjectivity, with their rich strands of feminism, psychoanalysis and Marxism, provide insights into precisely this.

## A POETICS OF HISTORY AND CULTURE

The concept of negotiation likewise plays a central role in another theoretical movement, New Historicism.[85] This movement is connected principally with the names of Stephen Greenblatt, Louis Montrose, Catherine Gallagher and Jonathan Goldberg, and their associated journal, *Representations*. Although these scholars work largely in the field of English Renaissance studies, their influence has been such as to warrant consideration here. Broadly speaking, for our purposes, two constituent strands can be distinguished in the make-up of New Historicism. The first derives from Hayden White's scrutiny of historiography published in his influential if controversial works *Metahistory* and its sequel, *Tropics of Discourse*.[86] In the first of these books, White's premise, reduced to its essentials, is that historiography is not the realm of the impartial reporting of actual past events. Rather, history is textualised; like novelists, historians tell stories. These stories about the past are not to be taken as reliable guides to 'what actually happened'; they are constructions of the past, often persuasive constructions, but in the end, narratives, 'representations', fashioned by us from the texts we have available from the very past we are endeavouring to account for; we cannot step outside these texts or our own historical situation and see the past in some utopian pure form. In *Tropics of Discourse*, White argues, following a Derridean line, that the discourse of philosophy is governed by figurative discourse, and notably the four tropes metaphor, metonymy, synecdoche and irony; philosophy does not give unmediated access to the truth, but shapes the object of its quest out of rhetorical devices. In short, not just history, but other disciplines too are textualised, which then calls into question the boundary lines between history, literature and these other textual forms, however seemingly distant (e.g. medicine, the law). In principle, there is no reason why a large range of disciplines should not be seen from the same angle as White applies to history. Serious problems attend the detailed working out of White's hypotheses, but a greater contrast with the older scholarly outlook of a Tillyard or a Lewis could hardly be imagined. History was being reinvented in post-structuralist mode, one that mistrusted grand narratives ('les grands récits', as Lyotard was to call them) and saw history as a disconnected series of localised stories rather than – as in Tillyard – a continuous pageant in which each part was linked to the next through an overarching metaphysical paradigm.

The second major strand in New Historicism is provided by Foucault. This is less the Foucault of *Les mots et les choses* than the Foucault of *Histoire de la folie*, *Surveiller et punir* and *Naissance de la clinique*, in other words the Foucault who investigated the processes of ideological power through the institutions which embodied and exercised such power. For Foucault, ideology works through 'discursive formations', by which he means the rules and constraints governing what it is permitted to think and say. The rules compose the cultural Unconscious within which we live and think, and they operate by regulation and exclusion: we cannot think independently of this cultural Unconscious, and what falls outside or in defiance of discursive formations is consigned to madness, silence, prison, hospital. What Foucault is analysing is thus the exercise of power through discourse, discourse which is not just the effect of signfiers but has actual, measurable impact on people's lives. Political hierarchies, ruling elites, entrenched values, all depend for their authority and influence on the successful manipulation of the discursive formations and the tools of government, regulation and restraint they employ.

As a group, New Historicists make some or all of the following claims, expressly or not: no discourse can give access to unchanging truths about ourselves; literary and non-literary 'texts' have permeable boundaries and circulate within and between each other; critical methodologies are caught up in the political or cultural systems they expose or critique.[87] These ideas can be felt strongly in the work of Stephen Greenblatt, whose numerous works, beginning with *Renaissance Self-Fashioning*, evolve a number of identifiable concepts and procedures which have become synonymous with New Historical method.[88] Foremost among these, we have said, is negotiation; to these can be added circulation and exchange. In his well-known essay, 'Towards A Poetics of Culture', Greenblatt acknowledges that his work has been sustained by observation of modern capitalism which, he maintains, has encouraged 'the pattern of boundary making and marking, the oscillation between demarcated objects and monological totality'.[89] He continues:

> ... the work of art is the product of a negotiation between a creator or class of creators, equipped with a complex, communally shared repertoire of conventions, and the institutions and practices of society. In order to achieve the negotiation, artists need to create a currency that is valid for a meaningful, mutually profitable exchange. It is important to emphasize that the process involves not simply appropriation but exchange, since the existence of art always implies a return, a return normally measured in pleasure and interest.[90]

Contemporary theory must accordingly situate itself 'not outside interpretation, but in the hidden places of negotiation and exchange'.[91] Greenblatt's later essay, 'The Circulation of Social Energy', re-states these ideas partly in point form, making a securer link with the processes of literary representation by asserting 'mimesis is always accompanied by – indeed is always produced by – negotiation and exchange', that there are various kinds of cultural capital, of which money is only one, and that individuals are both the agents and products of exchange.[92] Greenblatt's favoured focus for illustrating his ideas is the Elizabethan theatre. He frequently shows how the theatre gave release to the voices of dissent, expression to the subversion latent in Renaissance English society. But – and this is Greenblatt in his moments of Foucaultian influence – this expression of subversion does not ultimately have the effect of overturning the authority that leases the theatre for such an expression; dissent is permitted, only to be absorbed back into the power structures that use the radicality of Elizabethan drama as a way of discharging the turbulent emotions of society; the well-demarcated realm of aesthetic pleasure and questioning can exist only through coercion, discipline, control. Thus when Greenblatt examines *Twelfth Night*, he cites the disturbing use of cross-dressing, covert homoeroticism and sexual heat that the play exhibits and then compares and contrasts this with social discourses on the body, notably with medical views of hermaphroditism and the terrible punishment that was inflicted by Renaissance secular authorities on proven cases of transvestism and transgendering.[93] Greenblatt quotes two instances recorded by Montaigne (one in essay 1.21 – the case of Marie Germain – and another in the Travel Journal) as part of his argument that early-modern sexual identity is thus composed not only of differing competing texts (medical, legal, religious, ethical), but of the friction between a fiction of distinct genders and strong enforcement of gender distinctions where a socio-sexual code is held to be infringed. The circulation of these rival versions and the exchanges, compromises, tug-and-play between them, their speculative power and the coercion to which they are subjected illustrates precisely what Louis Montrose terms 'the historicity of texts and the textuality of history'.[94]

Greenblatt amplifies these points further, and from a complementary direction, when he devotes an essay to Martin Guerre, a famous case of imposture in Renaissance France mentioned (among many others) by Montaigne in his essay 3.11, 'Des boyteux' ('Of Cripples').[95] Greenblatt's starting point is his querying of the idea that a person's psychic life, the basis of psychoanalysis, might be held to be the source of the conflictual 'identity' that universally characterises the human being. Rather the case is the other way round: psychoanalysis is a belated explanation of the tangled, contradictory cultural strands at whose intersection the early modern subject is situated. These strands are so tangled and primeval, Greenblatt claims, that they are not easily narratable according to a single interpretative paradigm such as psychoanalysis would provide. The story of Martin Guerre is an unusually vivid instance of this claim:

> In the judicial murder of the imposter we witness in tiny compass part of the process that secures our concept of individual existence. That existence depends upon institutions that limit and, when necessary, exterminate a threatening mobility; the secure possession of one's body is not the *origin* of identity but one of the consequences of the compulsive cultural stabilizing unusually visible in this story.[96]

This 'compulsive cultural stabilizing' takes a particular form, moreover. The appropriation of another's identity controverts the equivalence between person and property that Greenblatt sets at the heart of the difference between Renaissance and modern conceptions of personhood: 'what most matters in the literary texts, as in the documents that record the case of Martin Guerre, are communally secured proprietary rights to a name and a place in an increasingly mobile social world'.[97] Greenblatt then reverts to his initial argument, to infer that this does not mean we should dispense with psychoanalytical interpretations of Renaissance texts, but rather historicise what such an approach might entail. Quoting Hobbes, for whom person is *persona*, a mask or a disguise, Greenblatt concludes in that regard that, for the Renaissance, 'identity is only possible as a mask, something constructed and assumed'.[98] Modern psychoanalysis strips away the mask in order to reveal the underlying substrata; but, says Greenblatt, early modern identity has no underlying substrata, for it is an identification with a *persona* secured by a title to an artifice. Fiction is thereby placed centre stage, as the instrument used by French Renaissance authority for legitimacy and constraint. This emphasis on mask may, as Greenblatt admits, appear oddly flimsy and insubstantial to us; but the story of Martin Guerre shows how the infringement of the authority of fiction results not in its dissolution, but in powerful reprisals exacted against anyone who exposes it for what it is.

Not surprisingly, New Historicism has elicited a variety of responses to its position. One common objection is that, with its emphasis on the recuperative nature of power, it is too deterministic and pessimistic in its views.[99] English Cultural Materialism, centred on Kate Belsey, Terence Hawkes and the journal *Textual Practice*, has attempted to combat this view by emphasising that the subject need not accept the social, economic, political or sexual positions sketched out for him/her.[100] Another objection, for which New Historicism seems to have no ready answer, is that it suppresses questions of gender and gender difference, as well as race. In truth, as already indicated, the debate over the value of New Historicism is part of a larger problem over the status of history as such: can history be considered the realm of objectively stated and impartially judged facts, or is it composed of narratives, stories which try to make sense?[101] This still open debate impinges on Renaissance Studies partly because New Historicism campaigns vigorously in favour of the latter view, and partly because a similar outlook is endorsed by influential social historians such as Natalie Zemon Davis.[102] The dismantling of the previously strictly partitioned areas of history and literature has brought in its wake a further set of questions such as the relationship between high culture and popular culture or interdisciplinary topics such as the body. The effects of the interpenetration of literature, history and cultural studies, of which New Historicism is in fact a symptom rather than the first cause, may be felt in work as varied as Lisa Jardine's study of ostentatious 'capitalist' consumption in the Renaissance, *Worldly Goods*, in the so-called 'New Erudition' of scholars such as Carlo Ginzburg and Anthony Grafton, and in the recent work of Terence Cave on money and exchange in Rabelais.[103] One underlying theme in these approaches, whether explicit or not, is the alterity of the Renaissance, the fact that it is not a culture which we can simply appropriate and treat as an offshoot of our own, but that it has its own peculiarities that make the sixteenth century both part of our living legacy and a culture now past, resistant to easy comprehension in some important respects. In other words, our study of early modern culture requires that we attend to our own negotiations and transactions with it, quite as much as that culture's transactions with its own component parts. Greenblatt's subsequent focus on the New World in *Marvelous Possessions* and *New World Encounters* likewise chimes happily with the interest in postcolonialism and subaltern studies (i.e. the study of the subjection of native peoples under the ideologies of imperialism); Lestringant's enormous output on voyages of discovery and cannibals falls into a parallel category.[104]

## DU RESTE (MORE OVER)

The cumulative effect of theoretical methodologies in French Renaissance studies has been not only an enrichment of literary discourse, but its gradual pluralisation and a corresponding pluralisation of interpretation as an activity. This is clear from the contributions to this collection: some essays exploit the resources of a single theoretical outlook, while others draw on aspects of several or find compatibilities between different approaches. To end this Introduction, it will be salutory to examine one contribution which invites its readers to scrutinise the act of interpretation itself and thereby asks us to re-assess the methodologies by which we engage with the sixteenth-century French text. Michel Jeanneret's 'The Pitfalls of Methodology' tackles a semiotic analysis of Panurge's consultation scenes in Rabelais' *Tiers Livre*. On the face of it, these are standard episodes in deciphering signs. The authorities consulted provide their own read-ings of the evidence, while classical texts act as a grid against which interpretations can be set. These interpretations are derived by trans-ferring the new data provided by Panurge to the figurative plane. The results all point to the same answer: Panurge will be cuckolded if he marries.

Yet Jeanneret claims that this solution must omit too much of the textual detail to be a satisfactory interpretation. This is not in itself new: any interpretation is bound to leave out elements which either appear irrelevant or do not readily fit with its working hypotheses. Jeanneret's objection goes further than this. He makes two especially important claims. First, he maintains that it is a constitutional part of academic criticism to be satisfied with comfortable hypotheses. 'Many commentators ... tame and conceptualise the text of Rabelais, they look for – and find without trouble – the expression of a moral and religious intention, a lesson in psychology, an entire repertoire of ideas'. Alternatively, critics (and Jeanneret counts his own previous work among them) have celebrated the play and power of the lin-guistic sign in Rabelais, the ambiguities of language, the slippages of meaning. In either case, these approaches demonstrate a 'will to mas-tery' which occults the text's resistance to ultimate interpretation, to a self-assured metadiscourse. Phrased another way, whatever the per-tinence or dexterity of any particular interpretation, there is always a leftover (*un reste*), always something over and above what has been interpreted, always more over (*du reste*). Like Rigolot in a parallel context, Jeanneret thus highlights the problem of the leftover, the ele-ment or elements that cannot be readily assimilated and put up resis-tance to the methodological tools the critic, the theorist or the historian bring to bear. And it is precisely this leftover that gives rise to new, in this case unsettling readings of Rabelais' text.

This brings Jeanneret to his second major claim, which occupies his article in this volume. Against the dryness of academic discourse, he sets 'the troubling images and the psychological aggressions launched by [Rabelais'] text'. In particular, he points to the level of textual violence repressed in any reading which sees Panurge's con-sultation as producing the same result: what is omitted in standard readings is the strength of affectivity, especially the emotional reac-tions of the protagonists, notably Panurge. By extrapolating to a 'higher' plane, we neglect the incarnate, very material dimension of Rabelais' work. The preference for mind over body in critical interpretation of Rabelais is parallel, for Jeanneret, to the preference for theoretical abstraction over the concrete reality of a text that refuses to fit easily into a single mould. The aim, Jeanneret points out, is not simply to restore the emotional force of Panurge's utterances, but to expose the wild fantasms, the unsettling strangeness of Panurge's desires.[105] Animal transformations, bestiality, rape, incest and cannibalism, dreams of potency and sexual satisfaction are all conveyed by the classical myths which Panurge evokes and uses as expressive instruments. The Renaissance science of dreams developed sophisticated interpretative grids and laws so as to read such fantasies. But, in Jeanneret's view, Panurge refuses to adhere to the regulatory system which the science of dreams implies. He does not analyse his own dreams simply as the expression of the desire to get married, but luxuriates in their content; he is less concerned with the result than with the fantasmagorical processes of dreamwork. In other words, Panurge's Unconscious is centrifugal and plural, an irrepressible bundle of desires that keep insistently returning and refuse to be placated by the messages delivered by a variety of consultants or domesticated by the unitary meaning which these consultants affix to Panurge's predicament. Against a reassuring hermeneutics – one that finds the same meaning in every episode – Jeanneret thus finds in these scenes a wild semiology, an over-production of signs in excess or defiance of conventional interpretation.

Elsewhere in his work, Jeanneret relates this problem with signs to a crisis of interpretation in sixteenth-century France.[106] In his present article, he links this problem of signs, of symbolic suggestion, to the 'enigma' of the human, especially the affective and the imaginative, which he regards structuralism and post-structuralism as having neglected.[107] Thus he finds in the behaviour of the Sibyl, for instance, 'neither a metaphysical revelation, nor a moral lesson, nor some abstract truth … but the complex laws of the biological and the psychical, the extravagances of the imagination'. Similarly, by contrast with Pantagruel who consistently (but also narrowly) seeks the higher, abstract point, moral or lesson, Panurge's activity challenges the transparency of sign and referent, focuses on the libidinal, contingent and phantasmatic, and 'seizes the subject at the intersection of the physiological and the psychical, and places it at the centre of his discourse'. Pantagruel's technique of allegorisation has a clear name and a well-defined area of investigation; Panurge's has no such reassuring label. Materialism? Biologism? Marginality? It has no name because it is composed not of one distinct field of enquiry, but of a series of left-overs, leftovers that are hyperbolical, wayward, affectively charged, opening out onto areas of investigation that are usually repressed or strictly controlled, both in academic discourse and in the psychic life. Jeanneret's reading of this episode in the *Tiers Livre* aims not just (or even principally) to alert us to a new field of intellectual investigation, but rather to underscore the 'affective and communicative dimension of language',[108] recalling that one of the prime functions of rhetoric for the French Renaissance was the impact it made on the reader and listener. 'In these conditions, reading is no longer merely a mode of knowing, but a mode of feeling, and even a mode of being.'

Jeanneret's terms of reference need attention here. What is notice-able about his analysis as a whole is that, like the text it handles, it draws on several critical modes. The psyche, unconscious drives and dream; semiology and sign production; textual plurality and prolifer-ation; questions of the body and the subject: all of these are involved in his reading of the fabric of these episodes from the *Tiers Livre*. Yet this versatility in critical approach and suggestiveness is not the result of the haphazard juxtaposition of different analytical vocabularies. On the contrary, Jeanneret is being entirely consistent with the per-spectives he has developed in other contexts. One such perspective is conveyed by the group of terms *brassage* ('mixing'), *bariolage* ('medley') and *bricolage* ('do-it-yourself').[109] These terms frequently underscore, for Jeanneret, the heteroclite character of the materials that make up sixteenth-century French literature. These terms are, in turn, indebted to the notion of polyphony derived from the Russian theoretician, Mikhail Bakhtin, whom Jeanneret has elsewhere put to profitable use.[110] In the present context, polyphony applies particu-larly well to the restless, ex-centric nature of Panurge's enterprise, drawing in diverse, fragmented elements from a variety of normally distinct spheres. Such polyvocality helps explain, indeed, the rapid shifts between kaleidoscopically varied components of which the con-sultation episodes are composed. At the same time, polyphony can also be said to characterise the critic's own discourse, attentive to the strangeness of Rabelais' text, and responsive to the violent twists and turns it takes. Concomitant with the text it examines, Jeanneret's methodology puts its confidence in improvisation, conceptual inven-tiveness, theoretical pluralism. Rather than relying on a single critical model, it implements a contingent re-appropriation, assimilating and adapting as it goes along. The resulting enquiry is certainly heuristic;

but it is not random. It maintains an acute sense of the innovative, without supposing that its own methodology has absorbed its object without a leftover.

## THE TIME OF THEORY

If all the contributions in this volume have one thing in common, it is that they contribute to a permanent enquiry into representation. Or rather, as Lyons and Nichols explain in their introduction to *Mimesis: From Mirror to Method*, late twentieth-century theoretical methodology has witnessed a transition from representation to representing, that is to say a movement away from representation as a static entity with its own aesthetic framework and philosophical underpinning, and towards representing as a process which 'describes the dismemberment of an epistemological continuum or compromise which had permitted ethics, epistemology, rhetoric, political theory, and natural history to enjoy considerable discursive cohesion'.[111] One result of this shift, these authors explain, is that 'mimesis has come to imply not simply depiction of phenomenal reality, but also the incorporation into the figurative act of the problematics of portrayal; that is, how the sheer fact of reproducing the world as sign, the world as language, may expose and call into question precisely those conventions meant to systematize and objectify representation'.[112] All the contributions in this current volume would amply illustrate this statement: the constructed nature of literary representation is at issue in the critical theories and practices employed by the scholars here. That principle might be embodied in deconstruction or, at its most extreme, would break down into a series of heuristic languages, such as Michel Jeanneret discusses in his essay.

The second principle that Lyons and Nichols perceive is a pattern of resistance: the 'persons and events that constitute the subjects of mimesis' display 'resistance to the identities assigned by such cognitive sciences as history and literary criticism'.[113] This is a salutary reminder that the identity of any area of enquiry – let us call it sixteenth-century French literature – is at least as much a construction, and at worse a fabrication, of our activity five hundred years after the event. In this volume, these concerns surface in a variety of forms: at its broadest, is it possible to apply twenty-first-century critical vocabulary to a sixteenth-century text? If so, can one do so without leftover or remainder? How can the problem of anachronism be dealt with? Can one actualise without modernising? The type-case here might well be Martin Guerre, that imposter whose identity was never more than a scandalous fiction. How did Arnaud Du Tilh maintain his imposture for so long and so successfully, even when faced in the Parlement de Toulouse with the real Martin Guerre? The sources for the story frequently suggest that it was black magic, or that Arnaud had met Martin when they were on campaign together. The same sources tellingly admit that it had since become known that Arnaud and Martin never met.

The case of Martin Guerre highlights with particular clarity the zones of opacity that shadow our study of the French Renaissance. To expect to abolish those obscurities would somehow be to abolish the differences between that historical epoch and our own. Indeed, our sense of the Renaissance's difference from us (and our difference from it) is a crucial ingredient of that spectrum of differences that make up our vision of the past and which are symbolically represented in this collection by the diverse readings given of sixteenth-century French literature. That same 'pathos of historical distance'[114] was, we know, enacted by the Renaissance itself in respect of classical antiquity: 'this sense of historical mortality is the pathos of the past and the price of understanding it'.[115] Thus the very vulnerability of our cognitive tools, the contingency of the means we employ to understand the object of our quest, are inexorably written into our enterprise.

And yet ... And yet, if historical distance is the price we pay for understanding the past, nonetheless our search for that past is guided by a spirit of adventure, and a belief that critical investigation, however time-bound, need not inevitably lead to a poetics of despair. To adapt a finely telling phrase of Terence Cave, our intellectual enquiries compose a 'discovery structure', 'a network of experimental connections' between ourselves and the French Renaissance texts we explore, albeit guaranteeing no more than a heuristic coherence.[116] From that standpoint, the essays in this volume are to be understood in Montaigne's sense of that term – a series of try-outs, soundings, provisional adventures in a terrain that invites our attempts at understanding even as it recedes ever further from our grasp. And paradoxically the self-consciousness that these essays embody is an advantage rather than a disadvantage, in that it enables them to foreground both their own theoretical assumptions and, more significantly, those of the Renaissance. Problems of sign systems, the intractability of desire, the position of the reader and the interpreter, the gendering of the text, all these recur as motifs in the articles contained here. They recur also in the Renaissance texts they treat. The works and authors studied in *Distant Voices* display with representative intensity the resistances, the manoeuvres, the distances and differences of sixteenth-century literature, and moreover presented in highly complex patterns already conceptualised and theorised to varying degrees. Modern literary theory does not therefore encounter an object devoid of theoretical ambitions, but one in which those theorised strands may be densely packed, half-submerged or obscure. How the critic disentangles those strands depends, of course, on his or her adventurousness as an interpreter, in both senses of the word 'interpreter': someone who exhibits a skill in analysing, but also a skill in translating from the codes and conventions of the sixteenth century into those of the twenty-first, while respecting the traces of alterity that will inevitably remain. In terms that Montaigne would have recognised, the interpretative enterprise to which French Renaissance literature gives rise is pre-eminently a domain of enquiry, that is a domain where definitive truth and finality are suspended in favour of seeking, involving a weighing of judgement and a balancing of critical discriminations.[117] It is precisely these encounters between two historical moments (now and then) and two historical modes (literature and exegesis) that represent, for us in our time, the testing time of theory.

# Notes

1 Michel Foucault, *Les mots et les choses: Une archéologie des sciences humaines*, Paris, Gallimard, 1966, pp. 32–59.

2 Mark Cousins and Athar Hussain, *Michel Foucault*, London, Macmillan, 1984, p. 15.

3 Jean-Claude Margolin, 'L'homme de Michel Foucault', *Revue des sciences humaines*, vol. 128, 1967, pp. 497–521. For a recent critique of Foucault, see Ian Maclean, 'Foucault's Renaissance Episteme Reassessed: An Aristotelian Counterblast', *Journal of the History of Ideas*, vol. 59, 1998, pp. 149–66.

4 E. M. W. Tillyard, *The Elizabethan World Picture*, London, Chatto and Windus, 1952; Arthur Lovejoy, *The Great Chain of Being*, Cambridge (Mass.), Harvard University Press, 1936; C. S. Lewis, *The Discarded Image: An Introduction to Medieval and Renaissance Literature*, Cambridge, Cambridge University Press, 1964.

5 While sixteenth-century writers do not themselves use the term 'Renaissance', they do use parallel terms such as 'to restore', 'to reinstate', 'to rekindle'.

6 *Poétique*, vol. 103, 1995, pp. 269–83.

7 Cf. Rigolot's characteristically elegant and paradoxical formulation of this point, p. 271: 'Nous sommes donc voués en tant que lecteurs à rechercher un horizon de lecture qui éclaire l'oeuvre tout en nous obligeant à douter de sa pertinence' ('As readers, we are obliged to seek out a framework for reading which illuminates the work while compelling us to doubt its suitability').

8 Roland Barthes, 'De l'oeuvre au texte', in *Le bruissement de la langue*, pp. 69-77, now collected in *Roland Barthes: Oeuvres complètes*, 3 vols, Paris, Seuil, 1993–1995, vol. 2, pp. 1211–17.

9 Jean Paris, *Rabelais au futur*, Paris, Seuil, 1970; Michel Beaujour, *Le jeu de Rabelais*, Paris, L'Herne, 1970.

10 François Rigolot, *Le texte de la Renaissance, des rhétoriqueurs à Montaigne*, Geneva, Droz, 1982, p. 255.

11 Rigolot (1982), pp. 261–62.

12 Not all would accept these arguments. Quentin Skinner, for example, followed by scholars such as Ian Maclean, refuses any non-sixteenth-century vocabulary to speak of the sixteenth century: see *Meaning and Context: Quentin Skinner and his Critics*, Cambridge, Polity Press, 1988.

13 For shrewd comments on the implications of the 'linguistic turn' for Renaissance studies, see Neil Kenny, 'Interpreting Concepts After the Linguistic Turn: The Example of *Curiosité* in *Le Bonheur des Sages/Le Malheur des Curieux* by Du Souhait', *(Ré)Interprétations: Etudes sur le seizième siècle*, ed. John O'Brien, *Michigan Romance Studies*, vol. 15, 1995, pp. 241–70.

14 See Tullio de Mauro (ed.), *Ferdinand de Saussure: Cours de linguistique générale*, Paris, Payot, 1985, and for a fuller account than is possible here, Jonathan Culler, *Saussure*, London, Fontana, 1976.

15 See Gray's *Rabelais et l'écriture*, Paris, Nizet, 1974; *La balance de Montaigne: Exagium/essai*, Paris, Nizet, 1982; *Rabelais et le comique du discontinu*, Paris, Champion, 1994; and the introductions to his recent critical editions of Rabelais' *Gargantua*, Paris, Champion, 1995, and *Pantagruel*, Paris, Champion, 1997. For Glauser's work along similar lines, see his *Rabelais créateur*, Paris, Nizet, 1966; *Le poème-symbole: De Scève à Valéry*, Paris, Nizet, 1967; *Montaigne paradoxal*, Paris, Nizet, 1972; and *Fonctions du nombre chez Rabelais*, Paris, Nizet, 1982.

16 See Roland Barthes, 'La mort de l'auteur', collected in *Roland Barthes: Oeuvres complètes*, vol. 2, pp. 491–95; Michel Foucault, 'Qu'est-ce qu'un auteur?', *Bulletin de la société française de philosophie*, vol. 63, 1969, pp. 73–104; Wolfgang Iser, *The Implied Reader: Patterns of Communication in Prose Fiction from Bunyan to Beckett*, Baltimore, Johns Hopkins University Press, 1974, and *The Act of Reading: A Theory of Aesthetic Response*, Baltimore, Johns Hopkins University Press, 1978.

17 Roland Barthes, 'Introduction à l'analyse structurale des récits', in *L'aventure sémiologique*, Paris, Seuil, 1985, pp. 167–206; also contained in *L'analyse structurale du récit*, 'Points', Paris, Seuil, 1981, pp. 7–33.

18 Terence Cave, *The Cornucopian Text: Problems of Writing in the French Renaissance*, Oxford, Clarendon Press, 1979, p. xix.

19 Terence Cave, 'The Mimesis of Reading in the Renaissance', in *Mimesis: From*

*Mirror to Method, Augustine to Descartes*, ed. John D. Lyons and Stephen G. Nichols, Hanover, NH, and London, The University Press of New England, 1982, pp. 149–65; p. 154. Cave's whole essay repays careful study.

20 For the phrase, see Jonathan Culler, *Structuralist Poetics: Structuralism, Linguistics and the Study of Literature*, London, Routledge and Kegan Paul, 1975, pp. 113–30. What constitutes such competence and how it is constituted are thorny difficulties in Culler's account.

21 'Un suffisant lecteur': *Les 'Essais' de Montaigne*, ed. Pierre Villey and V.-L. Saulnier, Paris, Presses Universitaires de France, 1965, 1.24, p. 127A; 'l'indiligent lecteur': *Essais*, 3.9, p. 994C.

22 Thomas Greene, *The Light in Troy: Imitation and Discovery in Renaissance Poetry*, New Haven and London, Yale University Press, 1982.

23 Cf. the outstanding chapter by Michel Jeanneret, '*Imitatio/Mimesis*', in *Des mets et des mots: Banquets et propos de table à la Renaissance*, Paris, Corti, 1987, pp. 249–72, where Jeanneret deftly shows the complex interdependency of *imitatio* (imitation of classical predecessors) and *mimesis* (imitation of nature).

24 For the term and its application, see Gérard Genette, *Palimpsestes: La littérature au second degré*, Paris, Seuil, 1982; and for a specific application to French Renaissance literature, see André Tournon, 'Palimpsestes, échos, reflets: Le dédoublement dans la poétique de Ronsard', in *Aspects de la poétique ronsardienne*, actes du colloque de Caen, publiés sous la direction de Philippe Lajarte, Caen, Université de Caen, 1989, pp. 27–40.

25 Antoine Compagnon, *La seconde main ou le travail de la citation*, Paris, Seuil, 1979; Terence Cave (1982), 'The Mimesis of Reading'; and 'Problems of Reading in the *Essais*' in *Montaigne: Essays in Memory of Richard Sayce*, ed. Ian D. McFarlane and Ian Maclean, Oxford, Clarendon Press, 1982, pp. 133–66. The critical positions of Mathieu-Castellani and Tournon are discussed below. For further studies in the problematics of reading, see, representatively, Cathleen Bauschatz, 'Montaigne's Conception of Reading in the Context of Renaissance Poetics and Modern Criticism', in *The Reader in the Text*, ed. Susan Suleiman and Inge Crosman, Princeton, Princeton University Press, 1980, pp. 264–91; Steven Rendall, 'In Disjointed Parts/*Par articles décousus*', *New York Literary Forum*, vols 8–9, 1981, pp. 71–83; and Richard Regosin, 'Conceptions of the Text and the Generation(s) of Meaning: Montaigne's *Essais* and the Place(s) of the Reader', *Journal of Medieval and Renaissance Studies*, vol. 15, 1985, pp. 101–14.

26 Gisèle Mathieu-Castellani and François Cornilliat, 'Intertexte phénix?', in 'La farcissure: Intertextualités au XVIe siècle', *Littérature*, vol. 55, 1984, pp. 5–9; p. 6.

27 André Tournon, 'L'intertextualité de la Renaissance: Notes sur quelques problèmes de méthode', in *Les méthodes du discours critique dans les études seiziémistes*, actes présentés par Gisèle Mathieu-Castellani, révisés par Jean-Claude Margolin, Paris, SEDES, 1987, pp. 25–36; p. 27.

28 Cf. Michael Worton and Judith Still, *Intertextuality: Theories and Practices*, Manchester, Manchester University Press, 1990, p. 25, on objections to Riffaterre's theory of intertextuality.

29 Mathieu-Castellani and Cornilliat (1984), p. 7, acknowledge this debt.

30 Tournon (1987), p. 33 for the terms, and p. 139 for the statement: 'Ce que j'ai dit est largement tributaire de Riffaterre qui a travaillé dans ce sens et s'est dis-

tingué dans les analyses de ces marques en quasi-métalangage' ('What I have said is broadly indebted to Riffaterre who has worked on this area and has made a significant contribution to the study of these quasi-metalinguistic marks'). Tournon also refers to the important article by Laurent Jenny, 'La stratégie de la forme', *Poétique*, vol. 27, 1976, pp. 257–81.

31 Worton and Still (1990), p. 25.

32 Francis Goyet, '*Imitatio* ou intertextualité? (Riffaterre revisited)', *Poétique*, vol. 71, 1987, pp. 313–20.

33 The notion of presupposition is also proposed by Jonathan Culler, 'Presupposition and Intertextuality', in *The Pursuit of Signs: Semiotics, Literature, Deconstruction*, London, Routledge, 1981, pp. 100–18. Culler argues cogently that intertextuality should be 'less a name for a work's relation to particular prior texts than a designation of its participation in the discursive space of a culture: the relationship between a text and the various languages or signifying practices of a culture and its relation to those texts which articulate it for the possibilities of that culture' (p. 103). Using criteria derived from linguistics, speech act theory and Barthes, Culler then elaborates presupposition, which places sentences in contact with each other as 'constituents of a discursive space from which one tries to derive conventions' (p. 117).

34 See Worton and Still (1990), p. 26.

35 The expression is from Goyet (1987), p. 319.

36 See Michael Riffaterre, 'Un faux problème: L'érosion intertextuelle', in *Le signe et le texte: Etudes sur l'écriture au XVIe siècle en France*, ed. Lawrence D. Kritzman, Lexington, French Forum Publishers, 1990, pp. 51–59; and for an example of how Riffaterre's theory might work in French Renaissance literature, see Sarah Alyn-Stacey's essay on Marc-Claude de Buttet, 'Intertextualité mythologique: Erosion et interprétants', *Michigan Romance Studies*, vol. 15, 1995, pp. 55–75.

37 Worton and Still (1990), p. 27.

38 *Les 'Essais' de Montaigne*, ed. Villey and Saulnier (1965), p. 146. The English translation is from Donald Frame, *The Complete Essays of Montaigne*, Stanford, Stanford University Press, 1976.

39 Cave (1979), p. 272. This book now exists in French translation: *Cornucopia: Figures de l'abondance au XVIe siècle*, Paris, Macula, 1997.

40 Cave (1979), 'Introduction', p. xvi.

41 Cave (1979), p. 321.

42 Cave (1979), p. xviii.

43 Cave (1979), p. 334.

44 Gérard Defaux, *Marot, Rabelais, Montaigne: L'écriture comme présence*, Paris and Geneva, Champion–Slatkine, 1987, p. 21.

45 Defaux (1987), pp. 45–46.

46 For a discussion of the idea, see Gérard Genette, *Mimologiques: Voyage en Cratylie*, Paris, Seuil, 1976, especially chapter 1, 'L'éponymie du nom', pp. 11–37; and, for a particular application, François Rigolot, 'Cratylisme et Pantagruélisme: Rabelais et le statut du signe', *Etudes Rabelaisiennes*, vol. 13, 1976, pp. 115–32.

47 Defaux (1987), p. 47.

48 Defaux (1987), p. 104, quoting Cave (1979), p. xx.

49 See Edwin Duval, 'Interpretation and the *Doctrine Absconce* of Rabelais's Prologue to *Gargantua*', *Etudes Rabelaisiennes*, vol. 18, 1985, pp. 1–17.

50 Defaux (1987), p. 123. In his article in this volume, Rigolot refers to a further exchange over the prologue to *Gargantua* by Gérard Defaux, 'D'un problème l'autre: Herméneutique de l'*altior sensus* et *captatio lectoris* dans le Prologue de *Gargantua*', *Revue d'histoire littéraire de la France*, vol. 85, 1985, pp. 195–216; reply by Terence Cave, Michel Jeanneret and François Rigolot, 'Sur la prétendue transparence de Rabelais', *RHLF*, vol. 86, 1986, pp. 709–16; rejoinder by Gérard Defaux, 'Sur la prétendue pluralité du Prologue de *Gargantua*', *RHLF*, vol. 86, 1986, pp. 716–22. Defaux's work in *L'écriture comme présence* picks up on the debate.

51 Terence Cave, 'Afterwords: Philomela's Tapestry', *Michigan Romance Studies*, vol. 15, 1995, pp. 271–78; p. 276.

52 Barbara Johnson, 'The Critical Difference: BartheS/BalZac', in *The Critical Difference: Essays in the Contemporary Rhetoric of Reading*, Baltimore and London, Johns Hopkins University Press, 1980, pp. 3–12; p. 5.

53 Cave (1995), p. 274. Cf. Johnson, 'The Critical Difference', p. xi: 'The "deconstruction" of a binary opposition is thus not an annihilation of all values or differences; it is an attempt to follow the double, powerful effect of differences already at work within the illusion of a binary opposition'.

54 Cf. Rigolot, *Le texte de la Renaissance*, p. 63, who sees two types of intentionality at work in Renaissance writing: generic (transtextual), an intention to write according to the laws of genre, and existential (extratextual), covering socio-economic imperatives (to flatter a protector or receive a payment) or psychological motives (to reply to a rival or achieve poetic glory).

55 Defaux (1987), p. 104. The allusion to the text in excess of its glosses is also a reference to *The Cornucopian Text*, p. 100. For a parallel debate, see the exchange between John Monfasani and Richard Waswo in *Journal of the History of Ideas*, vol. 50, 1989, pp. 309–23 and pp. 324–32 respectively. The dispute concerned Waswo's book *Language and Meaning in the Renaissance*, Princeton, Princeton University Press, 1987. Montfasani disputed Waswo's claim that Valla could be said to prefigure twentieth-century problems of linguistic philosophy in any significant way.

56 Thomas Greene, 'Introduction', p. xix for the praise of Cave and, for the Danaids' passage, 'Dangerous Parleys – Montaigne's *Essais* 1:5 and 6', in *The Vulnerable Text: Essays on Renaissance Literature*, New York, Columbia University Press, 1986, pp. 116–39; p. 138.

57 Thomas Greene, 'Erasmus' "Festina lente": Vulnerabilities of the Humanist Text', *The Vulnerable Text*, pp. 1–17; p. 11.

58 Greene, 'Vulnerabilities', p. 12.

59 Greene, 'Vulnerabilities', p. 13.

60 Greene, 'Vulnerabilities', p. 13.

61 Greene, 'Vulnerabilities', p. 14.

62 Greene, 'Vulnerabilities', p. 15.

63 Greene, 'Introduction', p. xiii.

64 Greene, 'Vulnerabilities', p. 17.

65 Thomas Greene, 'History and Anachronism', in *The Vulnerable Text*, pp. 218–35; p. 221.

66 Greene, 'History and Anachronism', p. 223.

67 Jacques Lacan, *Les quatre concepts fondamentaux de la psychanalyse*, *Le Séminaire*, vol. 11, Paris, Seuil, 1973, p. 45; trans. Alan Sheridan, *The Four Funda-*

*mental Concepts of Psychoanalysis*, Harmondsworth, Penguin, 1977.

68 Cf. notably Lawrence Kritzman's *The Rhetoric of Sexuality and the Literature of the French Renaissance*, Cambridge, Cambridge University Press, 1991; Nancy Frelick, *Délie as Other: Towards a Poetics of Desire in Scève's 'Délie'*, Lexington, French Forum, 1994, and '"J'ouïs-sens": Thaumaste dans le *Pantagruel* de Rabelais et le "sujet supposé savoir"', *Etudes Rabelaisiennes*, vol. 30, 1995, pp. 81–97.

69 Indeed, Lacan re-writes this dictum as 'je pense où je ne suis pas, donc je suis où je ne pense pas' ('I think where I am not, therefore I am where I do not think'), and then offers other re-formulations: 'je ne suis pas, là où je suis le jouet de ma pensée; je pense à ce que je suis, là où je ne pense pas penser' ('I am not wherever I am the plaything of my thought; I think of what I am where I do not think to think'). Lacan, 'L'instance de la lettre dans l'inconscient ou la raison depuis Freud', *Ecrits*, Paris, Seuil, 1966, p. 277, trans. Alan Sheridan, 'The Agency of the Letter in the Unconscious or Reason since Freud', *Ecrits: A Selection*, New York, W. W. Norton and Co., 1977, p. 166.

70 Respectively, *Les quatre concepts fondamentaux*, p. 23 and *Ecrits*, p. 379.

71 This is therefore an extension of Rigolot's point in *Le texte de la Renaissance* that we may legitimately supply a theoretical vocabulary or framework which sixteenth-century texts invite, but lack as such.

72 Cf. Patricia Parker, 'Deferral, Dilation, *Différance*: Shakespeare, Cervantes, Jonson', in *Literary Theory/Renaissance Texts*, ed. Patricia Parker and David Quint, Baltimore and London, Johns Hopkins University Press, 1986, pp. 182–209.

73 Lacan (1973), p. 97.

74 Lacan, 'Le stade du miroir comme fonction du Je telle qu'elle nous est révélée dans l'expérience psychoanalytique', *Ecrits*, pp. 89–97; trans. Sheridan, 'The Mirror Stage as Formative of the I as revealed in Psychoanalytic Experience', *Ecrits: A Selection*, pp. 1–7.

75 See the picture in *Roland Barthes par Roland Barthes*, Paris, Seuil, 1979, p. 25, of Barthes as a baby being shown his reflection in the mirror by his mother, with the legend: 'Le stade du miroir: «Tu es cela»' ('The Mirror Stage: "That's you"').

76 For the background on Renaissance conduct books, see Ruth Kelso, *Doctrine for the Lady of the Renaissance*, Urbana and Chicago, University of Illinois Press, 1956 (reprint 1978); Ian Maclean, *The Renaissance Notion of Woman: A Study in the Fortunes of Scholasticism and Medical Science in European Intellectual Life*, Cambridge, Cambridge University Press, 1980.

77 The title of Ann Jones' contribution to *A New History of French Literature*, ed. Denis Hollier, Cambridge (Mass.) and London, Harvard University Press, 1994, pp. 213–16. Cf. Jones' article, 'Assimilation With A Difference: Renaissance Women Poets and Literary Influence', *Yale French Studies*, vol. 62, 1981, pp. 135–53.

78 See, for a complementary perspective, Carla Freccero, 'Economy, Woman, and Renaissance Discourse', in *Refiguring Women: Perspectives on Gender and the Italian Renaissance*, ed. Marilyn Migiel and Juliana Schiesari, Ithaca and London, Cornell University Press, 1991, pp. 192–208.

79 Ann Rosalind Jones, *The Currency of Eros: Women's Love Lyric in Europe, 1540–1620*, Bloomington, Indiana University Press, 1990, p. 2.

80 Jones (1990), p. 4.

81 Jones thereby guards against the idea that the sixteenth century saw an

unequivocal improvement in the status of women or a gradual release from the bonds of patriarchy; see further the now classic essay of Joan Kelly, 'Did Women Have a Renaissance?', in *Women, History, and Theory: The Essays of Joan Kelly*, Chicago, University of Chicago Press, 1984, pp. 18-50.

82 Jones (1990), p. 7.

83 Jones (1990), p. 9.

84 Jonathan Culler, *Literary Theory: A Very Short Introduction*, Oxford, Oxford University Press, 1997, p. 60.

85 See further Jeremy Hawthorn, *Cunning Passages: New Historicism, Cultural Materialism and Marxism in the Contemporary Literary Debate*, London, Arnold, 1996; Kiernan Ryan, *New Historicism and Cultural Materialism: A Reader*, London, Arnold, 1996; H. Aram Veeser, *The New Historicism*, London, Routledge, 1989, and *The New Historicism Reader*, London, Routledge, 1994; Richard Wilson and Richard Dutton, *New Historicism and Renaissance Drama*, London, Longman, 1992. Further bibliographies can be found in these books.

86 Hayden White, *Metahistory: The Historical Imagination in the Nineteenth Century*, Baltimore, Johns Hopkins University Press, 1973; *Tropics of Discourse: Essays in Cultural Criticism*, Baltimore, Johns Hopkins University Press, 1978. For a more detailed analysis of White than is possible here, see Hawthorn (1996), pp. 36–47.

87 The formulation of these points is indebted to Veeser (1989), p. xi.

88 Stephen Greenblatt, *Renaissance Self-Fashioning, From More to Shakespeare*, Chicago, University of Chicago Press, 1980; *Shakespearean Negotiations: The Circulation of Social Energy in Renaissance England*, Oxford, Clarendon Press, 1988; *Learning To Curse: Essays on Modern Culture*, London and New York, Routledge, 1990.

89 Greenblatt, 'Towards A Poetics of Culture' in Veeser (1989), pp. 1–14; p. 8.

90 Greenblatt, 'Towards A Poetics of Culture', p. 12. He adds: 'the society's dominant currencies, money and prestige, are invariably involved, but I am here using the term "currency" metaphorically to designate the systematic adjustments, symbolizations and lines of credit necessary to enable an exchange to take place. The terms "currency" and "negotiation" are the signs of our manipulation and adjustments of the relative systems.'

91 Greenblatt, 'Towards A Poetics of Culture', p. 13.

92 Greenblatt, 'The Circulation of Social Energy', in Greenblatt (1988), pp. 1–20; p. 12.

93 'Fiction and Friction' in Greenblatt (1988), pp. 66–93.

94 Montrose, 'Professing the Renaissance: The Poetics and Politics of Culture', in Veeser (1989), pp. 15–36; p. 23; cf. Montrose's 'The Elizabethan Subject and the Spencerian Text', in Parker and Quint (1986), pp. 303–40. Montrose's essays are important statements of New Historical views on history, the human subject and the aims of New Historicism as a 'movement'.

95 Greenblatt, 'Psychoanalysis and Renaissance Culture', in Parker and Quint (1986), pp. 210–24. The standard work on this story is Natalie Zemon Davis, *The Return of Martin Guerre*, Cambridge (Mass.), Harvard University Press, 1983; Harmondsworth, Penguin, 1985. Davis returned to the Martin Guerre case and registered her disagreement with Greenblatt's position in 'On the Lame', *American Historical*

*Review*, vol. 93, 1988, pp. 572–603. See also Terence Cave, *Recognitions: A Study in Poetics*, Oxford, Clarendon Press, 1988, pp. 12–17, and Elizabeth Guild's two articles, 'Et les interpréter là où elles n'exhibent que leur mutisme', *Michigan Romance Studies*, vol. 15, 1995, pp. 133–50, and 'Adultery on Trial: Martin Guerre and his Wife, from Judge's Tale to the Screen', in *Scarlet Letters: Fictions of Adultery from Antiquity to the 1990s*, ed. Nicholas White and Naomi Segal, London, Macmillan, 1997, pp. 45–55.

96 Greenblatt (1986), p. 218. Italics are Greenblatt's.

97 Greenblatt (1986), p. 221.

98 Greenblatt (1986), pp. 222–23.

99 Greenblatt has attempted to answer some of the most common charges against New Historicism in the first part of his article 'Resonance and Wonder', in *Literary Theory Today*, ed. Peter Collier and Helga Geyer-Ryan, Ithaca, Cornell University Press, 1990, pp. 74–90.

100 For a debate on the nature of cultural materialism, between Catherine Belsey, Alan Sinfield and Jonathan Dollimore, see *Textual Practice*, vol. 3, 1989, pp. 159–72, and vol. 4, 1990, pp. 91–100. The characteristics of this movement are dealt with in the books by Hawthorne and Ryan cited above note 85.

101 On this hotly debated issue, see e.g. Dominick LaCapra, 'Intellectual History and Critical Theory', in *Soundings in Critical Theory*, Ithaca, Cornell University Press, 1989, pp. 182–209 (pp. 190–96 for New Historicism); Peter Burke, *Varieties of Cultural History*, Cambridge, Polity Press, 1997, pp. 162–82 (on history of mentalities) and pp. 183–212 (on unity and variety in cultural history).

102 Natalie Zemon Davis, *Society and Culture in Early Modern France*, Stanford, Stanford University Press, 1975; *Fiction in the Archives: Pardon Tales and Their Tellers in Sixteenth-Century France*, Stanford, Stanford University Press, 1987. Cf. also the exchange between Davis, 'A Renaissance Text to the Historian's Eye: The Gifts of Montaigne', *Journal of Medieval and Renaissance Studies*, vol. 15, 1985, pp. 47–56, and François Rigolot, 'A Literary Critic's Response to a Social Historian: The Gifts of Montaigne', *Journal of Medieval and Renaissance Studies*, vol. 17, 1987, pp. 111–18.

103 See Lisa Jardine, *Worldly Goods: A New History of the Renaissance*, London, Macmillan, 1996; for the label 'The New Erudition', see Randolph Starn in *Representations*, vol. 56, 1996, pp. 1–7, referring e.g. to Carlo Ginzburg, *The Cheese and the Worms: The Cosmos of a Sixteenth-Century Miller*, Baltimore, Johns Hopkins University Press, 1980; and Anthony Grafton, *Forgers and Critics: Creativity and Duplicity in Western Scholarship*, Princeton, Princeton University Press, 1990, and *Defenders of the Text: The Traditions of Scholarship in an Age of Science, 1450–1800*, Cambridge (Mass.), Harvard University Press, 1991; Terence Cave, 'L'économie de Panurge: «Moutons à la grande laine»', *Réforme, Humanisme, Renaissance*, vol. 37, 1993, pp. 7–24, and '«Or donné par don»: Echanges métaphoriques et matériels chez Rabelais', in *Or, monnaie, échange dans la culture de la Renaissance,* actes du 9e colloque international de l'Association Renaissance, Humanisme, Réforme, ed. A. Tournon and G.-A. Pérouse, Saint-Etienne, Publications de l'Université de Saint-Etienne, 1994, pp. 107–17.

104 Stephen Greenblatt, *Marvelous Possessions: The Wonder of the New World*, Oxford, Clarendon Press, 1991, and *New World Encounters*, Berkeley, University of

California Press, 1993. Among Frank Lestringant's numerous publications, see in particular *Le Huguenot et le sauvage*, Paris, Aux Amateurs de Livres, 1990, and *Ecrire le monde à la Renaissance: Quinze études sur Rabelais, Postel, Bodin, et la littérature géographique*, Orléans, Paradigme, 1993.

105 For Jeanneret's work on the notion of the 'étrange', see notably 'La crise des signes et le défi de l'étrange', in *Le défi des signes: Rabelais et la crise de l'interprétation à la Renaissance*, Orléans, Paradigme, 1994, pp. 89–99.

106 This is a recurrent theme in Jeanneret (1994).

107 See also Jeanneret (1987), p. 258: 'Le tort de la modernité a été d'ignorer la puissance de l'imagination' ('Modernism's mistake has been to ignore the power of the imagination').

108 Victoria Kahn, 'Humanism and the Resistance to Theory', in Parker and Quint (1986), pp. 373–96; p. 375.

109 See Jeanneret (1987), pp. 259 ('vaste brassage de pièces centrifuges'), 261 ('grand brassage des idées et des voix'), 262 ('bariolage linguistique et stylistique'), 267 ('bricolage textuel'), 269 ('bricolage').

110 Bakhtin's two most influential works are *Rabelais and his World*, trans. Hélène Iswolsky, Cambridge (Mass.), MIT Press, 1968, and *Problems of Dostoevsky's Poetics*, trans. Caryl Emerson, Manchester, Manchester University Press, 1984. For Jeanneret's use, see Jeanneret (1994), especially 'Polyphonie de Rabelais: Ambivalence, antithèse, ambiguïté', pp. 133–46. Jeanneret (1987) is also informed by Bakhtinian views of the body and food.

111 Lyons and Nichols (1982), p. 15.

112 Lyons and Nichols (1982), p. 3.

113 Lyons and Nichols (1982), pp. 3–4.

114 Nietzsche's phrase cited by Eugene F. Rice, Jr. and Anthony Grafton, *The Foundations of Early Modern Europe, 1460–1559*, second edition, New York, W.W. Norton and Company, 1994, p. 81.

115 Rice and Grafton (1994), p. 81.

116 Terence Cave, 'Travelers and Others: Cultural Connections in the Works of Rabelais', in *Rabelais: Critical Assessments*, ed. Jean-Claude Carron, Baltimore and London, Johns Hopkins University Press, 1995, pp. 39–56; p. 55.

117 A fine example of this use of theory-as-*essai* is now to be found in Terence Cave, *Pré-histoires: Textes troublés au seuil de la modernité*, Geneva, Droz, 1999. This book alludes delicately to several critical discourses, for example in its use of the idea of faultline, deriving from the work of Alan Sinfield, yet without owing allegiance to any.

# CHAPTER 1

# The Highs and Lows of Structuralist Reading: Rabelais, *Pantagruel*, chapters 10–13

*François Rigolot*

> Beati Dunces, quoniam ipsi stumblaverunt
> *Pantagruel*, chapter 11[1]

Rabelais' work seems one of the privileged testing grounds for the theoretical problems which have been exercising the 'cerveaulx à bourlet' (Rabelais p. 403) ('curled-up brains') of literary critics for the last thirty years. Here is not the place to rehearse the current divisions of Rabelaisian criticism following the well-known exchange of articles nearly ten years ago in the columns of the *Revue d'histoire littéraire de la France*.[2] The arguments for and against the presence of a clear, univocal meaning, intended by the author and written into his work, have continued to accumulate. They have recently been taken up again during the conferences held in 1994 to celebrate the (putative) five-hundredth anniversary of Rabelais' birth.[3]

   In this article I plan to re-examine two or three basic texts which in the 1960s gave rise to the so-called 'structuralist' reading. By contrast with the idolising tendency which once gave linguistics the final say in matters of critical truth, my intention will be not so much to confer a privileged status on these theoretical texts (I shall avoid making them 'keys' for deciphering Rabelais) as to take them, so to speak, the other way round and cast an ironical eye over them by re-reading some particularly obscure chapters of *Pantagruel*.

   For analytical convenience we shall first re-read some now classic articles published by Roman Jakobson between 1956 and 1960; they were collected in his *Essays in General Linguistics*. With all the admirable enthusiasm of new converts, the young Turks of

Structuralism considered they now possessed 'reliable' critical tools. Had they not been supplied by an eminent linguist who was able to explain the functioning of the 'literary object' beyond *history* and *the subject*, cleansed of any interpretative leanings? In its splendid semiotic isolation, the Text now opened up to critical scrutiny with the unshakeable guarantee of scientific rigour. The workings of the Text might now escape the vagaries of time and inhabit the utopia of Structure, far from the disciplines of Humanism. It was, to be sure, a foolish belief in an illusory timelessness, and has been debunked by François Dosse in his masterly *Histoire du structuralisme* (*History of Structuralism*).[4]

This enthusiasm was considered all-too-naive by the followers of Deconstruction, New Historicism and Postmodernism; but should we class it along with the outdated dreams of utopian recovery based on an anachronistic belief?[5] Or can it still preserve some scientific plausibility in the ever-changing field of literary ideology? For example, what validity can one grant Jakobson's distinctions, seemingly so clear, as he attempts to catalogue the various functions of language from the factors which inevitably go into the production of the message? These are the questions which I shall try to answer in this article in respect of Rabelais, since with this great conjurer of language, the production of the message is never simple – it always poses problems of meaning which linguistics, supported by history, could help us solve.

In his well-known article 'Linguistics and Poetics', which first appeared in English in 1960, Jakobson gave an overview of the factors which make up any act of linguistic communication.[6] The production of a verbal *message*, he observed, cannot take place without the presence of an *addresser* and an *addressee* who engage in physical and psychological *contact* with each other. The *message*, formulated in a *code* common to both parties, necessarily refers to a *context* (or *referent*) which, at least in theory, is understandable by the addressee. Now these six 'factors inalienably involved in verbal communication' (Jakobson (1981) p. 22) – addresser, addressee, message, contact, context and code – are the counterparts of six different linguistic functions which can be summarised as follows:

> 1) the *referential* function (cognitive and denotative) which bears on the *context*; 2) the *emotive* function, focused on the *addresser*, which conveys 'the speaker's attitude toward what he is speaking about' (Jakobson (1981) p. 22); 3) the *conative* function, which is directed at the *addressee*, and is often

expressed by the imperative and the vocative; 4) the *phatic* function, bearing on the *contact* between the parties, which helps 'check whether the channel works' (Jakobson (1981) p. 24); 5) the *metalinguistic*[7] function, focusing on the *code*, which concerns any query about the language of the communication (Jakobson (1981) p. 25); 6) and last of all, the *poetic* function, for which Jakobson reserves the lion's share, which attends to the *message* by playing on phonic and semantic equivalences (Jakobson (1981) p. 25).

In the light of these definitions, some Renaissance specialists, bitten by the structuralist bug – and I won't hide the fact that I was one of them – wondered how an interpretation of Rabelais might gain from a knowledge of the major factors governing linguistic communication. If one concentrates on the episode of Baisecul (Kissass) and Humevesne (Sniffshit) (*Pantagruel*, chapters 10–13), what help could Jakobson's analysis be in interpreting this 'controverse merveilleusement obscure et difficile' (Rabelais p. 270) ('marvelously difficult and obscure controversy', Frame p. 167)? At the outset, it seems that one can at least identify the predominance of certain factors and certain functions, even though the precise sense of the speeches remains ungraspable as a whole. The question that remains is to what extent these discoveries can illuminate the episode in question, structuralism being by definition hostile to the hermeneutic process.

Everyone knows the storyline: Pantagruel, whose learning has become universally famous, is called upon to adjudicate a 'grand different' (Rabelais p. 275) ('great difference of opinion', Frame p. 170) which perplexes the most eminent lawyers. He summons the two disputants, the Lords Baisecul and Humevesne, and decides to hear their case. At the beginning, nothing seems clearer in the plaintiff's exposition:

> Donc, commença Baisecul en la matiere que s'ensuyt: – Monsieur, il est vray que une bonne femme de ma maison portoit vendre des oeufz au marchez ... (Rabelais p. 276)

> So Kissass began in the following manner: 'My Lord, it is true that a grammer of my household was taking some eggs to sell in the market ...' (Frame p. 170)

The criterion of truth, designated by Pantagruel in the previous chapter as essential to justice ('Contez moy de poinct en poinct vostre affaire selon la verité', Rabelais p. 275) ('tell me your business point by point and in truth', Frame p. 170), seems to be applied in an easily verifiable manner (cf. the expression 'il est vray que'; 'it is true that'). But things start to go wrong as soon as Pantagruel interrupts the speaker and invites him to put his hat back on:

– Couvrez-vous, Baisecul, dist Pantagruel.
– Grand mercy, Monsieur, dist le seigneur de Baisecul. Mais, à propos, passoit
entre les deux tropicques, six blancs vers le zenith et maille par autant que les
mons Riphées avoyent eu celle année grande sterilité de happelourdes, moyen-
nant une sedition de Ballivernes meue entre les Barragouyns et les Accourciers
pour la rebellion des Souyces, qui s'estoyent assemblez jusques au nombre de
bon bies pour aller à l'aguillanneuf le premier trou de l'an que l'on livre la
souppe aux beufz et la clef du charbon aux filles pour donner l'avoine aux
chiens. (Rabelais p. 276)

'Do put your hat on, Kissass,' said Pantagruel.
'Many thanks, my Lord,' said Kissass. 'But to come to the point, there was
passing between the two tropics six half-sous toward the zenith and a half-
penny, inasmuch as the Riffian Mountains that year had had a great sterility of
boobytraps, resulting from the sedition of Fiddlefaddles arisen between the
Gabblers and the Accusianists favoring the rebellion of the Swiss, who had
assembled up to the number of a good angle to go handseling on the first hole
of the year, when you give a sop to the oxen and the key to the charcoal to the
maids for them to give the oats to the dogs.' (Frame p. 170)

All too clearly, whatever the reader's degree of erudition, the text suddenly offers astonishing resistance to deciphering.

Many critical studies have been devoted to this episode. I shall
only recall here some of the most stimulating. From the point of view
of Gérard Defaux, Baisecul and Humevesne are 'des agents de la perversion du langage et de sa fonction' ('agents of perversion of language and its function').[8] John Parkin insists by contrast on the
parodic non-satirical aspects of the speeches: the two Lords are
'simply clownish mouthpieces for [Rabelais'] "fatras"'.[9] We are back
to slapstick. In the attractive esoteric hypothesis of Claude Gaignebet,
'ces plaidoiries sont les "Causes Grasses" d'un procès de Carnaval où
il est parlé précisément du souffle anal' ('these speeches are the
"Causes Grasses" of a Carnival trial which is all anal wind').[10] I myself
analysed these chapters 11, 12 and 13 of *Pantagruel* elsewhere, some
twenty-five years ago. But at that time my analysis was influenced by
the Roland Barthes of the *Critical Essays* rather than the Roman
Jakobson of the *Essays in General Linguistics*. And my descriptive
model borrowed its tools more from rhetoric and logic than from linguistics.[11]

To what extent can the linguistic model Jakobson proposes be
applied to the gobbledygook spoken by the first litigant? The *referential* function of discourse, which reigned supreme in the first sentence,
is seriously disrupted in the following sentences. Nothing was more
readily understandable than this image of a farmer's wife going to sell
her eggs at market. But in what region of France do cattle drink soup

and dogs eat oats? Furthermore, in what mythical geography of places as diverse as the 'Riffian Mountains', the 'Gabblers' and the 'Swiss' do they co-exist? Information abounds but for the reader it is empty of denotative and cognitive value; and this is all the more worrying in a litigant who has been invited to recount the facts to prove his rights ('donnez vous garde de adjouster ny diminuer au narré de vostre cas' (Rabelais p. 275) ('take good care not to add or subtract anything in the account of your case', Frame p. 170), Pantagruel commands him at the beginning).

If the *referential* function is problematised in the litigants' speeches, the same is not true however for the other functions of language which preserve their entire validity in the production of the message. Thus the attitude of the litigants towards what they are talking about remains entirely functional. They lose their tempers, shout insults at each other and use interjections to show their mood: 'Ha, messieurs, Dieu modère tout à son plaisir ...; Sa, Dieu gard de mal Thibault Mitaine!' (Rabelais p. 277) ('Ah, gentlemen, God moderates all things at his pleasure ...; So, God keep from harm Thibaut Mitaine!', Frame pp. 170–71). The judge even has to call them to order when they get carried away by their emotions:

> Alors dist Pantagruel:
> – Tout beau, mon amy, tout beau, parlez à traict et sans cholère. J'entends le cas, poursuyvez. (Rabelais p. 278)

> Then said Pantagruel: 'Easy now, my friend, easy, speak quietly, without anger. I understand the case, so go on.' (Frame p. 171)

The *emotive* function thus plays its full role, despite the aberrations of the informative content.

Likewise, the litigants never lose sight of the presence of the addressee ('Monsieur, il est vray ... Grand mercy, Monsieur ... Or, Monsieur ... Pour ce, Monsieur', Rabelais pp. 278-80) ('My Lord, it is true ... Many thanks, my Lord ... Now, my Lord ... Therefore, my Lord', Frame pp. 170–74): the *conative* function remains intact. They try to sustain the communication between them by each attracting the public's attention with appropriate expressions ('Voyant doncques ... Pour tant ... Et voylà ...', Rabelais pp. 278–79) ('Seeing therefore ... Whereby ... And so ...', Frame pp. 170–72): the *phatic* function is therefore working normally. They go to great lengths to ensure that their speeches are centred on a common code. They both allude to 'ladicte bonne femme' ('the said grammer') at the beginning (Rabelais

p. 278 and p. 282; Frame p. 171 and 174) to point up the 'logic' of their words despite appearances: the *metalinguistic* function also has a full part to play. Finally, by all sorts of echoes of rhythms and sounds, the litigants demonstrate that they are able to manipulate the message. Distortions of proverbs, spoonerisms, deliberate slips of the tongue, various plays on words contribute to the centrifugal effervescence of meaning. By a simple reversal of letters, the worthy Humesvesne confuses 'jouer du luc' ('play the lute', Frame p. 173) and 'sonner du cul' (Rabelais p. 281) ('sound off with the tail', Frame p. 173), thereby concertinering, through an arresting anagrammatical shortcut, the most elevated tone and the lowest style, the sublime and vulgar registers of language: the *poetic* function similarly remains entirely operative in Rabelais' text. All well and good: but can we take the analysis further?

I have already amply noted the rich suggestiveness that the most basic tools of linguistics bring to the reading of a text which is recognised as being particularly recalcitrant. The next stage will be to ask what kind of response Jakobson's structuralist analysis can bring to the question of the apparent disappearance of the referential function of language. To that end, I shall refer to the essay 'Two Aspects of Language and Two Types of Aphasic Disturbances', published in 1956 in *The Fundamentals of Language*.[12] In this famous clinical study of language disorders, the founder of modern phonology classifies two main types of verbal defects which he was able to observe in mental patients. I shall quickly review them.

In aphasics suffering from 'similarity disorder', Jakobson observes that the operations of substitution are affected whereas the ability to combine verbal units is preserved. Patients can complete sentences using connectives, but are unable to fill in the blanks between syntactical links; their speech is an empty framework. By contrast, in aphasics suffering from 'contiguity disorder', the deficiency occurs in the context. Patients are unable to link together linguistic units; they are reduced to using analogies, to having recourse to substitutions; their speech is a heap of material without a framework.

As is well known, so as to describe the phenomena thus observed on the paradigmatic axis (*in absentia*) and the syntagmatic axis (*in praesentia*) of language, Jakobson had to draw on the terminology of traditional rhetoric. The terms 'metonymy' and 'metaphor' were, he thought, suitable to characterise the two basic aspects of aphasia which for him reflected the 'bipolar structure' of all language (Jakobson (1971), p. 93). He went on to identify selection disorder with the *metaphoric process* and contiguity disorder with the *metonymic process*: 'metaphor,' he wrote, 'is alien to the similarity disorder, and metonymy to the contiguity disorder' (Jakobson (1971), p. 90). He added that in other so-called 'normal' beings, the two processes were 'continually operative' although preference might be given to one of the processes over the other 'under the influence of a cultural pattern, personality, and verbal style' (Jakobson (1971), p. 90).

We may therefore ask how far this Jakobsonian theory of metaphor and metonymy could illuminate the linguistic imbroglio in the famous controversy between Baisecul and Humevesne in *Pantagruel*. When the speeches and the final verdict are read out loud, it becomes clear that the two lords are suffering from precisely the clinical problems which Jakobson describes under the name of aphasia and that the same defects can be found, now subject to parody, in the verdict Pantagruel pronounces at the end of the episode. Let us re-read the beginning of Baisecul's speech:

> Mais, *à propos*, passoit entre les deux tropicques, six blancs vers le zenith et maille *par autant que* les mons Riphées avoyent eu celle année grande sterilité de happelourdes, *moyennant* une sedition de Ballivernes meue entre les Barragouyns et les Accourciers pour la rebellion des Souyces, *qui* s'estoyent assemblez jusques au nombre de bon bies *pour* aller à l'aguillanneuf le premier trou de l'an *que* l'on livre la souppe aux beufz et la clef du charbon aux filles *pour* donner l'avoine aux chiens. (Rabelais p. 276; my italics)

> 'But *to come to the point*, there was passing between the two tropics six half-sous toward the zenith and a halfpenny, *inasmuch as* the Riffian Mountains that year had had a great sterility of boobytraps, *resulting from* the sedition of Fiddlefaddles arisen between the Gabblers and the Accusianists favoring the rebellion of the Swiss, *who* had assembled up to the number of a good angle *to* go handseling on the first hole of the year, *when* you give a sop to the oxen and the key to the charcoal to the maids for them *to* give the oats to the dogs'. (Frame p. 170; my italics)

The connecting links emerge clearly in the litigant's speech. Syntax is respected perfectly. The litigant wants to prove his case and uses all the connectives necessary to the *onus probandi* ('burden of proof'). Admittedly, the reader does not understand the meaning of the arguments, but the piling up of consecutive and final clauses reflects the drama of the litigant, a drama of justification.[13]

We may note that the weakening, if not the disappearance, of the *referential function* only operates on one level of communication: that of the author and the reader, or to use more precise terminology, the narrator and narratee. Indeed, it is as if the litigants and their judge perfectly understood the point of this 'obscure and difficult controversy'. There are several pointers in the text to remind us of this. Thus, when Baisecul begins to get worked up by coming out with exclamations which seem incoherent to us, Pantagruel calms him down by saying: 'J'entends le cas, poursuyvez' (Rabelais p. 278) ('I understand the case, so go on', Frame p. 171). Likewise, when Humevesne in turn gets excited when listening to his opponent's speech, it becomes clear that he understands the meaning of a logic which escapes us:

> Icy voulut interpeller et dire quelque chose le seigneur de Humevesne, dont luy dist Pantagruel:
> – Et, ventre sainct Antoine, t'appertient-il de parler sans commendement? Je sue icy de haan pour entendre la procedure de vostre different, et tu me viens encores tabuster? Paix, de par le diable, paix! Tu parleras ton sou quand cestuy cy aura achevé. *Poursuyvez*, dist il à Baisecul, et ne vous hastez point. (Rabelais p. 278; my italics)

> Here Lord Sniffshit tried to interrupt and say something, so Pantagruel said to him:
> 'Here, by Saint Anthony's belly, is it for you to speak without command? Here I am sweating and straining to understand the way your disagreement comes about, and you still come pestering me? Peace, in the devil's name, peace! You'll talk all you like when this man has finished. *Go on*,' he said to Kissass, 'and don't hurry.' (Frame p. 171; my italics)

Finally when, in chapter XIII, Pantagruel gives his verdict in gibberish which is just as incomprehensible, the two litigants consider that their case has been heard and judged equitably:

> [Une fois la] sentence pronuncée, les deux parties departirent toutes deux contentes de l'arrest, qui fust quasi chose increable: car venu n'estoyt despuys les grandes pluyes et n'adviendra de treze jubilez que deux parties, contendentes en jugement contradictoires, soient esgualement contentez d'un arrest diffinitif. (Rabelais p. 287)

> This decision pronounced, the two parties departed, both content with the verdict, which was an almost incredible thing: for it had not come about since the great rains and will not happen for thirteen jubilees that two parties, both contending in contradictory judgment, should be equally contented with a definitive verdict. (Frame p. 177)

It is as if the litigants and their judge shared the same odd mode of speech, in other words, the same *idiolect*. Or rather, what seemed to the reader at first sight like the *idiolect* of asocial individuals turns out to be the *sociolect* of a linguistic micro-society which shares the same code but to which the reader feels an outsider. This proves Jakobson right when he writes: 'There is no such thing as private property in language: everything is socialized [...], and idiolect proves to be a somewhat perverse fiction'.[14] One might virtually say that the reader has to play the role of a mental patient who has lost the ability to 'commute' the linguistic codes:

> As long as he does not regard another's speech as a message addressed to him in his own verbal pattern, he feels, as a patient of Hemphil and Strengel expressed it: 'I can hear you dead plain but I cannot get what you say ... I hear your voice but not the words ... It does not pronounce itself.' He considers the other's utterance to be either gibberish or at least in an unknown language.[15]

In this respect, the reader (or rather the narratee – the distinction is crucial here) is akin to the 'presidens, conseilliers et docteurs' of the law (Rabelais p. 285) who attend the trial but do not understand the first thing about it. Pantagruel, however, never gives the impression that he is faced with 'gibberish'. When called upon to pronounce about the quarrel between the two lords, he calls out:

> – Eh bien, Messieurs, [...] je ne trouve le cas tant difficile que vous le faictes. (Rabelais p. 285)

> 'Well, gentlemen, [...] I do not find the case as difficult as you do.' (Frame p. 176)

He will give his verdict using the same code, 'pensant qu'il falloit à chascun faire droict, sans varier ny accepter personne' (Rabelais p. 285) ('thinking that he must do right by each and every one, without differentiating or favoring anyone', Frame p. 176); and everyone will go away perfectly content with the admirable 'prudence' ('wisdom') of their judge (Rabelais p. 287; Frame p. 177).

The 'structuralist' model, as I have described it and applied it up to this point, thus offers a number of advantages, if only because it supplies a series of concepts which enable us to describe and analyse a set of particularly complex linguistic practices. Yet what this model cannot account for is the cultural context which allows us to decide on the likely interpretation to give the message. Superficially, there is nothing to distinguish the 'gibberish' used by the judge from the linguistic aberrations of the litigants. Only an extra-textual intervention by the readers will enable them to measure the extent of the playfulness, irony or mockery which goes into Pantagruel's intervention as he satirises the legal manners of his time.

Furthermore, a Jakobsonian analysis of the litigants' language does not allow us to distinguish between the level of functions and the level of contents. Indeed when Jakobson speaks of speech 'disorders', he is only concerned, strangely enough, with the intelligibility of the meaning produced and not with the workings of the sense-producing mechanism. Looked at from the standpoint of *signifieds*, the aphasics are undoubtedly afflicted by a glaring disorder: they seem incapable of selecting a vocabulary which would make their speeches intelligible. However, looked at strictly from the standpoint of *signifiers*, the litigants are not afflicted by any 'disorder': they are quite capable of producing metaphors, and of substituting and selecting as much as they please. Quite the opposite, they are brilliant experts at verbal juggling. Paradoxal though it may seem, with them the sign system works to admirable perfection – but without our being able (at least up till now) to give a coherent meaning to the message produced by this system. In other words, it is the readers and not the litigants who are afflicted by psycho-motor disorders, because they cannot find their way around the linguistic system of these legal speeches.

One cannot therefore speak about 'aphasia', in the clinical sense Jakobson uses it, except if one applies it solely to the *semantic* dimension of discourse. Now, structuralism only ever claimed to be interested in the workings of structures *outside* of any consideration of meaning. Paradoxically, an analysis of our aphasics is valid only if it goes against the basic principle of structuralism which it is supposed to implement. From a strictly semiotic standpoint, the speeches and the verdict look like a coherent coded narrative. Admittedly, we do not know the code; but in theory it is not out of the question that some more knowledgeable reader might some day propose a definitive matrix of meaning. This is the case, for instance, with that other enigmatic text which virtually opens *Gargantua*: 'Les Fanfreluches antidotées' ('the antidoted Frigglefraggles', Frame p. 9).[16] Indeed, does not one of the principles of Rabelais' fiction and parodic power lie in presenting a text as an *allegory* which cannot be tied down to any definitive, hard-and-fast solution?[17]

In the episode of the argumentation by signs (*Pantagruel*, chapters XVIII–XX), Thaumaste the great English scholar, sweating heavily and 'ravy en haulte contemplation' ('transported in lofty contemplation', Frame p. 199), will cry out: 'Ha, j'entens [...], mais quoy?' (Rabelais p. 322) ('Ah, I understand! ... but then what?', Frame p. 200). This seems to be the fate awaiting all 'très illustres et très chevaleureux champions' (Rabelais p. 215) who undertake to read the 'horribles faictz et prouesses de Pantagruel' (Rabelais pp. 218–19) ('horrible deeds and exploits of Pantagruel', Frame p. 134). They understand its signs; but can they be so sure that they understand its meaning? The signification of a text depends to a large extent on the process of decoding applied to it. As theoreticians of reception criticism remind us, meaning can only emerge by the intersection of two vectors: the text properly speaking – the signifiers on the page – and the historical, philological or ideological context that readers bring with them, allowing for the fact that this context can vary according to the types of reading favoured by criticism.

Thus structuralism cannot offer an entirely reliable method for reading Rabelais. Its idealistic presuppositions put forward a smooth, rounded theory whose therapeutic function it is to claim to explain the inexplicable. Its power of attraction derived, in a different age from our own, from the semblance of luminosity which it sought to throw on texts, bringing them a comforting serenity. With the help of appropriate descriptive models, the most wayward contradictions seemed at last to yield their secrets. Trusting readers, fascinated by the apparent rigorousness of a comforting technical language and a transcendent theoretical order, believed they could 'devour' Rabelais without leaving any 'remainder'.[18] They projected onto the most undecipherable texts a desire for mastery whose cathartic role might save them from the terrors of a writing out of control. When faced with this beautiful Apollonian image, the uncanniness of Rabelaisian fiction disappeared. The 'abysme de science' (Rabelais p. 261) ('abyss of knowledge', Frame p. 161), when re-appropriated by the semi-scientific belief of the new scholars, lost its unsettling, vertiginous character. The fact is that structuralism, like the historicism of yesteryear, wanted to 'make works speak', whatever the cost, rather than 'let them speak' in the silence or the dislocation of meaning.

At the same time, perhaps we are wrong nowadays to want to wrest Rabelais from his tranquillity in a comforting critical order so as to picture him engrossed by his own 'melancholy'.[19] Though wrong-headed and reductive, Structuralism will have at least made us look at Rabelais' text as a *set of signifiers* whose function can only be described by taking account of the act of linguistic communication it presupposes. Thereby, Structuralism – at least in its Jakobsonian form – will have helped highlight certain aspects of the work which had frequently been obscured by the excessive referentialism of traditional criticism. Admittedly, there is no question of defending nowadays the totalitarianism of a method which, under the apparently objective guise of description, in fact spread the illusion that interpretation could be dispensed with. But criticism at the start of the twenty-first century, faced with the doubts besetting it from all sides about the validity of its approach, might do well to look back indulgently on a method which at least had the advantage of attempting to elucidate literary texts with a modestly 'pedagogical' aim in mind.

As we all know, the word 'pedagogy' has a bad press nowadays, especially since Michel Foucault made use of it to slate Jacques Derrida's unsettling reading of another great text, Descartes' *Meditations*.[20] Yet we must remember the importance Renaissance Humanists gave education. For them, human beings were essentially malleable creatures and the whole purpose of 'upbringing' consisted of giving them a 'form', in other words an appropriate training. 'Homines non nascuntur, sed finguntur' ('humans are not born, they are made'), Erasmus wrote. This pregnant formula lies at the very core of Renaissance Humanism.[21]

However, the Humanists, and Rabelais among them, were always suspicious of the influence exercised, often to excess, by pedagogues. In particular, they never failed to voice doubts about the merits of strict regulatory systems, finding them not only unwarranted, but literally useless. They were to react against the stifling straitjacket of scholasticism which they likened to monstrous 'Ignorance'. Whether we are dealing with Erasmus, Castiglione or Machiavelli – the masters from whom Rabelais drew his sustinence – the tendency always seems to have been to reject speculative thought. Thus in Erasmus, the theory of 'copious' discourse depends less on the need to classify the rules for amplifying language than on the practical application of the generative potential of discourse.[22] Likewise, in the author of *Il Cortegiano*, abstract rules for education prove powerless to 'form' the gentleman who is unable to interiorise the artless art of 'sprezzatura'. Again, in Machiavelli, a political idealism based on an outdated science will be contrasted with the 'verità effetuale' of a practice based on actual experience that works. In all these well-known cases, we can observe a distrust of, if not a concerted 'resistance' towards, theory's influence over the 'pierres vives' ('living building blocks') of discourse.[23]

Humanism thus invites us to maintain a healthy distrust of any method of enquiry which claims to have all the answers. If we use over-subtle speculative methods, we may well lay ourselves open to the accusations Rabelais himself levelled at the Sorbonne: 'et telle est l'opinion de Maistre Jehan d'Escosse' (Rabelais p. 59) ('such is the opinion of Master Duns Scotus'). However, as we have seen, a text seemingly as off-putting as the legal speeches in the *Pantagruel* loses some of its 'undecidability' when it is put back in the context of the practical modalities of communication. It is to the credit of Jakobsonian structuralism that it has given us the means to translate this text into a quite different language (in fact, a 'meta-language') so that we can indirectly restore to it the economy of its 'copia verborum', the charm of its 'sprezzatura' and the efficacity of its 'verità effetuale'.

All in all, with some thirty years' hindsight, while criticism remains divided over allegorical interpretation of Rabelais, and while the invitation to set off in search of the 'plus hault sens' ('deeper meaning') continues to arouse fierce controversy, it is perhaps time to re-adopt a more 'accommodating' (and more realistic) attitude towards a critical and ideological movement which, in spite of its definite inadequacies, was sometimes able to update old texts and restore to them their urge to signify. No doubt its success was uneven and incomplete; no doubt there were hasty generalisations, pointless tautologies and unbearably ponderous moments in structuralist discourse. But as readers of *Pantagruel*, we know one thing for certain: faced with the unfathomable mystery of Rabelais' text, are we not all reduced to being dunces, stumbling around and making others stumble too? Rabelais saw this all too clearly when he showed us, through parody, that this is perhaps our only chance of survival in the vagaries of time: *Beati Dunces, quoniam ipsi stumblaverunt.*

*Translated by John O'Brien*

# Notes

1 *Pantagruel* in Rabelais, *Oeuvres complètes*, Paris, Garnier, 1962, vol. 1, chapter 11, p. 277. All references in French, henceforth incorporated in the text, are to this edition. English translations are taken from Donald Frame, *The Complete Works of François Rabelais*, Berkeley, University of California Press, 1991, with occasional help from Urquhart. References to Frame are henceforth incorporated in the text.

2 Cf. Gérard Defaux, 'D'un problème l'autre: Herméneutique de l'*altior sensus* et *captatio lectoris* dans le Prologue de *Gargantua*', *Revue d'histoire littéraire de la France*, vol. 85, 1985, pp. 195–216, and the response of Terence Cave, Michel Jeanneret and François Rigolot, 'Sur la prétendue transparence de Rabelais', *Revue*

*d'histoire littéraire de la France*, vol. 86, 1986, pp. 709–16, itself followed by Defaux's riposte, 'Sur la prétendue pluralité du prologue de *Gargantua*', *Revue d'histoire littéraire de la France*, vol. 86, 1986, pp. 716–22.

3  For a summary of these arguments with critical bibliography attached, see François Rigolot, 'Interpréter Rabelais aujourd'hui: Anachronies et catachronies', *Poétique*, vol. 103, September 1995, pp. 269–83.

4  François Dosse, *Histoire du structuralisme*, 2 vols, Paris, La Découverte, 1991–92. On this subject, see the insightful article by Thomas Pavel, 'De l'esprit de conquête chez les intellectuels', *Le Débat*, vol. 73, January–February 1993, pp. 11–16.

5  Pierre V. Zima, *La déconstruction: Une critique*, Paris, Presses Universitaires de France, 1994.

6  Roman Jakobson, 'Linguistics and Poetics', in *Selected Writings III: Poetry of Grammar and Grammar of Poetry*, ed. Stephen Rudy, The Hague, Mouton, 1981, pp. 18–51. All references in the text are to this version. The French version is contained in *Essais de linguistique générale*, translated and introduced by Nicolas Ruwet, Paris, Minuit, 1963, pp. 209–48.

7  The published English translation gives 'metalingual'; 'metalinguistic' is the more usual term used today.

8  *Pantagruel et les sophistes: Contribution à l'histoire de l'humanisme chrétien au XVIe siècle*, The Hague, Nijhoff, 1973, p. 150.

9  'Comic Modality in Rabelais: Baisecul, Humevesne, Thaumaste', *Etudes Rabelaisiennes*, vol. 18, 1985, pp. 57–82; p. 67.

10  *A plus haut sens: L'ésotérisme spirituel et charnel de Rabelais*, 2 vols, Paris, Maisonneuve et Larose, 1986, vol. 1, p. 92.

11  *Les langages de Rabelais*, Geneva, Droz, 1972, pp. 41–48; second edition, Geneva, Droz, 1996.

12  Roman Jakobson and Morris Halle, *The Fundamentals of Language*, second, revised edition, The Hague, Mouton, 1971. The French version is translated by A. Adler and N. Ruwet in *Essais de linguistique générale*, pp. 44–67.

13  In my study of these speeches twenty-five years ago, my aim was to spotlight Rabelais' linguistic play with its contrasts between 'form-words' ('synsémantiques') and 'full-words' ('atosémantiques'). Cf. *Les langages de Rabelais*, pp. 41–48.

14  *The Fundamentals of Language*, p. 82.

15  Op. cit., pp. 82–83. French version in *Essais de linguistique générale*, pp. 54–55.

16  *Gargantua*, chapter 2, ed. cit., vol. 1, p. 14 ff.

17  This principle sustains a whole critical outlook. It was, in particular, the approach of V.-L. Saulnier in *Le dessein de Rabelais*, Paris, SEDES, 1957, and in his posthumous sudy on the *Quart* and *Cinquième Livres* (*Rabelais dans son enquête*, Paris, SEDES, 1982). Faced with persecution by hypocrites ('cagots'), the humanist had to take precautions; he had to veil his message, for want of anything better. Cf. my review in *Revue d'histoire littéraire de la France*, vol. 83, May–June 1983, pp. 462–64.

18  In a recent work, Michel Jeanneret shows that the problem of meaning in Rabelais has to be put back in the context of what he calls the 'exegetical malaise' at the beginning of the sixteenth century. The questioning of allegorical practices spreads disquiet in clerical circles: there is hesitation about the levels of meaning and

the relative priority of the literal and the metaphorical. The debates over transubstantiation will be the extreme illustration of this. Cf. *Le défi des signes: Rabelais et la crise de l'interprétation au XVIe siècle*, Orléans, Paradigme, 1994.

19  The following remarks are inspired largely, albeit distantly, by the late Sarah Kofman's book, *Mélancolie de l'art*, Paris, Galilée, 1985.

20  Cf. the postface to *Madness and Civilization* in the 1972 edition in which Foucault replies to Derrida's attack by accusing him of being motivated by 'petty pedagogy' (p. 603).

21  Erasmus' phrase is quoted and commented in Thomas Greene's article, 'The Flexibility of the Self in Renaissance Literature', in *The Disciplines of Criticism*, ed. P. Demetz, T. Greene and L. Nelson, Jr., New Haven, Yale University Press, 1968, p. 249.

22  On this topic, see Terence Cave, *The Cornucopian Text: Problems of Writing in the French Renaissance*, Oxford, Clarendon Press, 1979, pp. 3–34. Revised French version: *Cornucopia. Figures de l'abondance au XVIe siècle: Erasme, Rabelais, Ronsard, Montaigne*, Paris, Macula, 1997.

23  Cf. Victoria Kahn's essay, 'Humanism and the Resistance to Theory', in *Literary Theory/Renaissance Texts*, ed. P. Parker and D. Quint, Baltimore, Johns Hopkins University Press, 1986, pp. 373–96.

# CHAPTER 2

# Rabelais' Strength and the Pitfalls of Methodology (*Tiers Livre*, chapters 7–18)

## *Michel Jeanneret*

The works of Rabelais specialists are like a two-edged sword. They elucidate zones which are obscure and draw out the text's hidden logic; in teaching as in research, their objective is to understand, to order, to rationalise; scholarly commentary implies, by definition, a will to mastery. I do not doubt the necessity of this activity: the more we know about the possible meanings of Rabelais' work, the better; moreover, scholarly research is the normal response to a text that, by its enigmas, solicits this type of investigation. But the danger is in thinking that scholarly metadiscourse can overcome all resistance and dissipate all opacity. Proud of their knowledge, scholars risk forgetting that Rabelais' work does everything to evade, that it plays tricks on the reader to provoke his curiosity, to frustrate his/her certitudes. Where it allows itself to be explained without anything being left over, where it ceases to produce new readings, it dies; well, it wants to live, and it does live – the proof is in our curiosity and our meeting here, in the pages that I have written and that, if all goes well, you will read.

To maintain his work in motion, Rabelais exploits diverse strategies. I would like to signal one of them here, which, because it is by nature incapable of recuperation by scholarly criticism, has been neglected, or even repressed.[1] It concerns a certain category of signs that defy codes, escape rational explanation and open onto a bizarre and troubling world, which is normally censured. They are at once incongruous and inevitable, they penetrate into layers of the psyche where their impact provokes uncontrollable reactions. Knowingly, Rabelais liberates in his reader demons which invade the deepest zones of affectivity. I would like to illustrate this process using a sequence from the *Tiers Livre* – the *Tiers Livre* which, more than any other text of Rabelais, has been subjected to learned and edifying interpretations, and read according to a normative grid. The pages that follow present themselves, on the contrary, as a homage to subversion, to strangeness, and to him who incarnates them, Panurge. It is thanks to him that the bizarre infiltrates the text, that what has been repressed by received wisdom returns, and that the narrative, by the disquieting strangeness of its representations, awakens our phantasms, in such a way that it never ceases to intrigue us.

The sequence opens in chapter seven. Panurge wants to get married and he adopts an ensemble of vestimentary signals to express the fact that he is preparing himself for conjugal life. Thus begins a series of episodes which, according to a scenario destined to invade the *Tiers* and then the *Quart Livre*, will modulate the question of the sign and its interpretation. Panurge's accoutrements, according to his own commentary, refer back to five coded messages: (a) he will wear a ring set with a flea in his ear; explanation: to have 'la pusse en l'aureille' ('a flea in one's ear') signifies 'je me veulx marier' ('I want to get married'); (b) he makes his gown out of coarse dark brown cloth, thus indicating that he will be thrifty and 'mesnaiger parfaict' ('a perfect householder'); (c) in addition to the choice of the cloth, the gown itself, by its resemblance to a classical toga, manifests his desire to belong henceforth to civil society rather than to the army; (d) Panurge renounces breeches and a codpiece, because one goes with the other, and the codpiece is a part of military uniform and he no longer wants to go to war; (e) he 'attacha des lunettes à son bonnet' ('attached spectacles to his bonnet'), so that he resembles a Dominican friar.

Such are the signs revealed by Panurge, so as to show that he wants to get married. But the principal recipient, Pantagruel, is not sure that he understands: he 'trouva le desguisement estrange' ('found the disguise strange'), so much so that 'n'entendent (…) ce mystere, le interrogea, demandant que praetendoit ceste nouvelle prosopopée' ('since he did not understand this mystery, he questioned him, asking what this new disguise meant'). Panurge will then furnish explanations without, however, dissipating the malaise. Wherein lies the difficulty? The interpreter is troubled because s/he perceives contradictions between Panurge's intention and the message implied by his costume. 'Je grezille d'estre marié' ('I'm sizzling to be married'), he repeats, but the words and the visual signs do not say the same thing.

The gown and the spectacles make him look like a monk; the absence of a codpiece effaces the marks of virility even more and the entire outfit does not correspond to that of 'gens de bien et de vertus' ('men of quality and virtue'). Pantagruel does not fail to note the contradiction: 'Ce n'est la guise des amoureux, ainsi avoir bragues avalades (...)' ('this is not the attire of lovers, thus to have breeches at half-mast'), and later another witness will recognize without fail the attire of a cuckold in Panurge's clothes.[2]

What is happening? Panurge appears to use a language that he does not control; the code that he adopts is too personal, too eccentric to assure a correct interpretation of the information. That is what Pantagruel reproaches him with: 'Seulement me desplaist la nouveaulté et mespris du commun usaige' ('Novelty and disdain for common usage alone displease me'). Panurge thought he would be able to construct a new system of signs, without understanding that any system of semiotics rests necessarily on a collective convention. As it has often been said, he is a modern man, a singular individual who no longer adheres to traditionally-established protocols. Because he thinks he can improvise his own language, a breach opens between what he wants to say and what he says in effect, such that an unexpected meaning, an involuntary message, and a disturbing admission slip into his discourse. This unforeseen meaning, uncontrolled and troubling, I propose to call, after a term that Rabelais uses often, 'the strange' ('l'estrange').

Thus with chapter seven a sequence begins that thematises the dispersal or the disruption of signs. It is true that the following episodes – those that I will comment on: the interpretation of the Virgilian lots, the explanation of the dream, the visit to the sibyl of Panzoust, then those that I will not have the space to treat: the consultation of the mute Nazdecabre and of the poet Raminagrobis – no longer illustrate the surprises of encoding, but those of decoding. The problem, however, remains that of signs which free themselves from received hermeneutics to generate strange values. The perturbation of the semiotic system, as I have said, essentially concerns Panurge, as Pantagruel has a proven method at his disposal, which aims to rationalise and domesticate divinatory images. It is true that this distribution of roles is sometimes uncertain,[3] but it matters little, since we are interested less in the psychology of the characters than in a certain type of signs and the surprises of reading.

Panurge wants to get married, but will he be happy, or will his wife make him a cuckold? To settle his hesitation, he embarks upon a series of consultations, and begins by having recourse to different divinatory techniques. The first method consists of opening at random the work of Virgil and looking for an answer in the passage upon which he chances to fall. Three fragments, all of which come from ancient myth, are examined and commented on one by one. The problem that is found throughout chapter 12 is thus that of the interpretation of fables. This question is not a new one, and refers to a methodology of traditional mythographies – those that were in use at the end of the Middle Ages and those that the Italian humanists, beginning with Boccaccio,[4] bequeathed to the learned public of the Renaissance. Differences aside, one guiding principle underpins all these works: they treat myth as allegory and discover hidden lessons by transferring the stories, through a figurative reading, into the registers of morality, faith, natural philosophy. The ancient gods thus survive thanks to a conversion; subjugated to the values of religion, of heroism, or of science, they gain a new respectability. In this way, the moralisation of myth camouflages the bizarreness and the crudity of primitive narratives. The spirit has triumphed over the letter.

Here then we have Panurge and his friends who open up Virgil, the scholar and sage *par excellence*. What will they find there? Scabrous tales, insanities, an incredible catalogue of erotic phantasms. The figures of the classical pantheon recover their primitive violence, their frenetic sexuality. Previously attenuated, intellectualised, myth becomes once again the most audacious expression of the obscure contents of the unconscious.

The tendency displays itself right from the beginning of the chapter. The first excerpt of Virgil is from the fourth Eclogue and, as such, involves the paradigm of the Golden Age, the return to original innocence. The commentary itself evokes thunder-darting Jupiter and the Giants' attack on Olympus – the Giants who, according to Ovid's *Metamorphoses* (I, 150 ff.), are figures from the Iron Age. They symbolise, moreover, brute force, the battle of heaven and earth, of mind and nature, of beauty and ugliness. Immediately the reader is confronted with one of the most sombre representations of mythology: the triumph of violence and evil. Two images, a little later, complete the picture of this monstrous race and the evocation of the cosmic upheavals at the dawn of time: the lame and deformed effigy of

Vulcan, the subterranean blacksmith, then that of Atlas, the Colossus who strains under the weight of the heavens.

The disquieting strangeness of this primitive universe becomes even more accentuated by a series of references to metamorphoses which, playing on the mutual transformation of the divine and the animal, imply an unfinished world, where the various species are still indistinct or interchangeable. For example, that curious retinue of 'déesses desguisées en beletes, fouines, ratepenades, musaraignes' ('goddesses disguised as weasels, martens, bats, shrew-mice'), or the litany of the avatars of Jupiter, who transforms himself 'en cycne, en taureau, en satyre (...), en aigle, en belier (...), en serpent (...), en pusse' ('into a swan, a bull, a satyr (...), into an eagle, into a ram (...), into a snake (...), into a flea'). This same Jupiter, Panurge recalls, was 'nourry par une truie' ('nursed by a sow'), unless it was by a goat, and, later the slave of the worst sexual instincts, merits being compared to a pig, a goat, a ram. Add to this the memory of Lycaon changed into a wolf, complete it with the apparition of several horned gods,[5] and you will obtain a fairly astounding, condensed version of bestiality.

Finally this crude mythology lavishes images of sexual deviation. We have, for example, the transposition of the sexes, with Minerva, 'déesse puissante, fouldroiante' ('a powerful goddess, thunder-darting'), and Camilla, the Amazon of the *Aeneid*,[6] both of them virile warriors who disconcert the reader. Incest also has its place, with Jupiter who 'depucella Juno sa sœur' ('deflowered his sister Juno') and Lucus of Thebes, who raped his niece. Still concentrated in the same chapter 12, the list of perversions continues with two examples of castration, Uranus and Attis, and two allusions to scenes of cannibalism, Lycaon who served Jupiter the flesh of a child, and Cambles, king of the Lydians, who devoured his wife.

Obviously, this parade of curiosities is radically opposed to edifying interpretations of myth. Some forays into the fourteenth- and fifteenth-century versions of the *Ovide moralisé* tell much about the disparities between the two methods. Let us consider the rape of Europa. According to chapter 12 of the *Tiers Livre*, Jupiter 'belina pour un jour la tierce partie du monde, bestes et gens, fleuves et montaignes' ('for one day's stint he rammed out the third part of the world, beasts and men, rivers and mountains'); curious vision of the god turned bull who, in raping the young girl, makes love to an entire continent. To this unbridled sexuality corresponds, in the allegorical version of the *Metamorphoses*, the assimilation of Jupiter to Christ:

the transformation into a bull, explain the versions of the *Ovide moralisé*, is the figure of the Incarnation and the symbol of the sufferings of the Passion.[7] Earlier in chapter 8, Panurge had already interpreted another myth in his own way: the codpiece, he maintains, is the 'piece premiere de harnois militaire' ('the first piece of military harness'), because the testicles are, according to Galen, 'le germe conservatif de l'humain lignage' ('the preserving germ of the human line'). I would gladly believe, he adds, that the balls 'sont les propres pierres moyennans les quelles Deucalion et Pyrrha restituerent le genre humain aboly par le deluge' ('are the very stones of which Deucalion and Pyrrha restored the human race, abolished by the deluge'). The moralisation of the fourteenth century was as different as possible, since stones signified at that time the sin that one throws behind oneself, in the fear of God and love for one's fellow man.[8]

One can, of course, consider these inversions as parodies and see in them a simple literary exercise, just one more example of burlesque debunking. To do so would be to ignore the scope of the project. One would first point out that the enterprise, although scabrous, corresponds to an eminently philological gesture. Going beyond censures and sublimations of all kinds, it gives back to myth its real face, it restores its primitive force. To bring sex, metamorphosis, the chthonic powers to the forefront is to deploy the heritage of the ancients in all its enormity, to restore to the text of fable its original vigour and its extraordinary power to defamiliarise. But the return of the repressed operates on two levels. If going back to origins permits a restoration of myth in its purity, it liberates as well the language of phantasms which is usually repressed. Rabelais' text gives voice to the desires and deliriums buried in the unconscious. Far from being simply retrospective, his philology is also turned toward the reader, in whom it strikes such sensitive chords that their vibrations are still perceptible.

It is logical, in this perspective, that the exploration of dream should succeed that of myth (chapter 14), as if Rabelais had perceived the affinity between the two languages. As before, two methods are confronted: the figurative interpretation neutralises the oniric images, while the reading at the literal level exhibits their strangeness.

Panurge recounts his dream: he had a beautiful and affectionate wife; she planted horns on his forehead; he seemed to change into a drum and she into an owl. For Pantagruel, the reason is understood: 'vous serez coqu, vous serez battu, vous serez desrobbé' ('you will be

a cuckold; you will be beaten; you will be robbed'). He has at his disposal a key to dreams, which permits him to interpret the meaning of
the signs and thus efface all incongruity. He insistently denies, moreover, the apparent content of the images: 'vostre femme ne vous fera
realement et en apparence exterieure cornes on front' ('your wife will
not actually, and to outward appearance, plant horns on your forehead'); 'aussi ne sera de vous faicte metamorphose en tabourin (...) ne
d'elle en chouette' ('you will not be metamorphosed into a drum (...)
nor she into an owl').

For his part, Panurge also allows a divinatory value to dream but,
inversely, ascribes to it an erotic content: the desire for bliss and for
potency, sensual pleasure and a zest for depravity, this is what his
dream reveals. First vision: my wife 'me traictoit et entretenoit
mignonnement, comme un petit dorelot. (...) Elle me flattoit, me cha-
touilloit, me tastonnoit, me testonnoit, me baisoit, me accolloit' ('was
treating and entertaining me sweetly like her little darling. (...) She
was caressing me, tickling me, feeling me, smoothing my hair, kissing
me, hugging me'). Understand: I was like a baby, my spouse was like
a mother to me, which comes to the same as a nice little Œdipal phantasm. Then come the horns which, Panurge insists, give him the air of
a satyr: a libidinous fawn, half animal, and of course, oversexed: 'ainsi
auroys-je eternellement le virolet en poinct et infatigable, comme
l'ont les satyres' ('thus I'd eternally have my gimlet at the ready and
indefatigable, as the satyrs have'). The evocation of several horned
gods, in passing, comes to reinforce the imaginary alliance of the
human and the bestial. But the representation becomes even more
pointed when Panurge, in his dream, asks that the horns be planted
'au dessoubz des œilz, pour mieulx veoir ce que j'en vouldroys ferir'
('under my eyes, the better for me to see what I'd like to butt with
them'). The learned reference to Momus in no way reduces the
bizarreness of the portrait: here we have Panurge who takes on the
appearance of a rhinoceros or some fabulous animal. And the threshold of monstrosity will really be crossed with the double metamorphosis into a drum and an owl; here are sketched the phantasms of the
man-instrument and the woman-bird, that we will find again, amply
illustrated, among the crossbred bodies of the *Songes drolatiques de
Pantagruel*.[9]

Once more, Panurge refuses the pious deviations of the hermeneutic tradition. The famous classic of the key to dreams, the *De somnium
interpretatione* of Artemidorus, invoked by Pantagruel, furnishes

however the appropriate explanations to attenuate the crudity of the images: to see oneself grow horns, the treatise says, 'indicates the decapitation of the dreamer'; as for nocturnal birds like the owl, they 'represent adulterers or thieves or those who work at night'.[10] François Berriot confirms that the general tendency, in the dream interpretation manuals of the time, is to de-dramatise the horror of nightmares, to gloss over lewd visions: 'Sexuality thus loses as well (...) its burden of anxiety: to steal a kiss is to acquire a belonging, to possess the body of another is to exercise economic domination, to see the male sex organ is the portent of social ascension, and if nudity announces poverty to come, the dream of incest is itself asepticised'.[11] Now Panurge does exactly the contrary. He denies the dream the transcendent origin, the objective value, and the complex symbolism ascribed to it by divinatory science. He is not content either to find there the simple and inoffensive expression of his desire to get married. For him, the dream opens onto the uncertain space of phantasmagoria, it brings to light the unspoken voice of the psyche.

The chapter that follows (chapter 15) inserts into the story one of the breaks where Panurge and Frère Jean, wearied by the difficulties of the inquiry and the fervour of the debates, take a little holiday and give themselves some time off. To ensure the quality of his dreams, Panurge has fasted for a long time; now it is he who invites the monk to feast, and the two friends to evoke together the pleasures of monastic life as well as the savours of 'la marmite claustrale' ('the claustral cooking pot'). For them also, the moment has come to attend to the satisfaction of the body. A deliberate pun on the the word 'cabale' indicates the change in priorities. At the end of the preceding episode (chapter 14), with regard to the prophecies of the dream, Pantagruel had invoked the authority of the 'Caballistes et Massorethz interpretes des sacres letres, exposans en quoy l'on pourroit (...) cognoistre la verité des apparitions angelicques' ('cabalists and massoretes, interpreters of Holy Scripture, explaining in what way one could make out the truth (...) about angelic apparitions'). The title of chapter 15, which immediately follows, announces an 'exposition de cabale monasticque en matiere de beuf sallé' ('exposition of the monastic cabala in the matter of salt beef'), and the term will be taken up several times to designate the gastronomical secrets of monks. To the hermeticism of Jewish doctors corresponds the sensuality of *bons vivants*.

Must we then understand that this chapter, dedicated to the defence of corporeal pleasures, concludes the two preceding episodes, where Panurge made the voice of carnal desire be heard? It is, on the contrary, the difference that is striking. Between the innocence of the monastic festivities evoked here and the strangeness of the phantasms displayed before, the contrast is telling. Listening to the libido and the liberation of sexual drives unveil energies that are far more troubling than the avowal of gluttony. The adventure which follows, the consultation of the sibyl of Panzoust, offers, moreover, some new variations on the disturbing and ambiguous spectacle of the body prey to obscure forces.

Panurge will thus consult an old woman who has the gift of telling the future. The latter listens to his question, abandons herself to inspiration, then delivers four enigmatic prophecies (chapters 17–18). Pantagruel thinks he can settle the question by an authoritarian exegesis, but, once again, his allegories do not succeed in damming the flow of Panurge's erotic visions, all the more inspired and eloquent because the words of the alleged sibyl were fragmentary. The discourse of desire, in chapter 18, modestly opens with the desire to get married and to procreate, but soon slips toward the strange idea of double birth. Panurge imagines coming into the world a second time, carried by his wife; his wife would thus be his mother – we have already encountered this phantasm.[12] He adds to this a fellatio scene and a portrait of furtive couplings, the more voluptuous in that they are clandestine, then ends his ramblings with the theme of the woman as flayer, with scabrous allusions to castration and circumcision.

Nothing new on this account. It is the other partner in this episode who merits our interest; the character of the old woman, with her aberrant conduct, reinforces the opacity of signs and confirms their displacement into the register of individual destiny.

The visit to the sibyl, in chapter 17, is at first striking due to the abundance and the detail of the description. There is a good dose of local colour. The peasant surroundings and the objects of everyday life, the thatched cottage of the old woman[13] and her gesticulations, the offerings of Panurge and the unfolding of the ritual, all of this mobilises our attention without apparent reason. Rather than simply establishing the scene of the consultation, the material environment intervenes. The concrete should serve as a vector, relatively indifferent, in the search for truth; but it resists and diverts our curiosity towards itself. The circumstantial installs itself in the centre, the vehicle becomes the message and leaves the reader with an enigma: what should s/he do with this plethora of objects?

The parallel with the description of the Cumean sibyl in the *Aeneid*,[14] reveals that this profusion of accessories was not necessary. Though the desolate landscape, the trance and a few more details are the obligatory *topoi* for marking the transcendental dimension of the scene, Rabelais adds still more; the strangeness of the surroundings, in the hovel of Panzoust, is neither justified nor sublimated by the descent of the god. Something else is at stake here, immanent, mysterious or mystifying, which escapes received codes but which nevertheless solicits interpretation.

The character of the sibyl herself accentuates the malaise. Here again, the description serves as a screen: 'La vieille estoit mal en poinct, mal vestue, mal nourrie, edentée, chassieuse, courbassee, roupieuse, langoureuse, et faisoit un potage de choux verds avecques une couane de lard jausne et un vieil savorados' ('The old woman was ill-favoured, ill-dressed, ill-nourished, toothless, bleary-eyed, hunchbacked, runny-nosed, languid; and she was making a green cabbage soup with a rind of bacon and some old broth from a soup bone'). If the encounter begins with the nauseating spectacle of this decrepit body, it ends on the foul vision of an obscene body: she 'leur monstroit son cul' ('showed them her tail'). Neither the parodic project nor the carnivalisation of the sacred exhaust this scene, which is much more powerful than a simple reversal of the high and low. The traditional signs of ecstasy are not completely effaced, but they suggest instead madness, dehumanisation, the slide of old age toward an animal condition: 'Que signifie ce remument de badiguoinces? Que pretend ceste jectigation des espaulles? A quelle fin fredonne elle des babines, comme un cinge demembrant escrevisses?' ('What's the meaning of this movement of her chaps? What's the point of this shrugging of her shoulders? To what purpose does she quaver with her lips like a monkey dismembering crayfish?'). The poor old woman is probably just crazy, a senile mind, a would-be magician, and, instead of a sibyl, a witch who has been overwhelmed by her humours.[15]

Once again, the mystery has been displaced from the supernatural toward the human. What to do with the aberrant conduct of the old woman? If there is a secret to explore, it resides probably in the avidity, in the sexuality, in the babblings of this grotesque figure. The scene is saturated with meaning, symbolic suggestions abound, but what presents itself to be found is not what one was expecting: neither a metaphysical revelation, nor a moral lesson, nor some abstract truth, according to the dualistic logic of allegory, but the complex laws of the biological and the psychical, the extravagances of the imagination.

The triple structure of the episodes – a message then the commentaries of Pantagruel and Panurge – contains the seeds of a reflection on the status of signs. Each time Pantagruel settles the question in a few words; the terms of divination being fixed, he recognizes the hidden meaning of images and, so as to undercut the disturbing value of their strangeness, he assigns them a second value. He applies the proven method of moralisation.

Many commentators work in the same manner. Compelled by the same seriousness as Pantagruel, they tame and conceptualise the text of Rabelais, they look for – and find without any trouble – the expression of a moral and religious intention, a lesson in psychology, an entire repertoire of ideas. The narrative, like the predictions, is translated into clear notions, into edifying principles. And so we have Rabelais ordered *ad usum delphini*, his text sublimated – but proportionally weakened. The violence of allegorical reading and the censure that it exerts, although denounced at the very heart of his work, have never ceased to be used.

If Rabelais only wanted to denounce Panurge's sophisms, would he grant him such a large place in the text? If he only wanted to treat marriage, or self-knowledge, or concupiscence, would he need to repeat the same demonstration so many times? To read the *Tiers Livre* in the same spirit as Pantagruel reads predictions is to amputate one of its essential dimensions and reduce it to an anaemic fable. Already at their first encounter (*Pantagruel*, chapter 9), Pantagruel was incapable of conceiving that Panurge was hungry; his thought was too elevated to come to terms with such contingencies, that is to say, too narrow to envision the whole person. In refusing to let himself be forced into the intellectual frameworks or the ideological choices of his master, Panurge denounces the captive minds of a system that excludes one aspect of the real – or of the novel.

It is true that Panurge is also haunted by fixed ideas, that he is dishonest and mistaken in his interpretation of the predictions. From the point of view of morals and of rational truth, he has it all wrong. But to his credit he attempts to explore a territory that is little known and of ill repute. Awkwardly and crudely, he flushes out the libidinal repressed that is hidden in myths, in dreams, and even in everyday actions. He lifts the veil from biological contingencies and phantasmatic activity, he seizes the subject, at the intersection of the physiological and the psychical, and places it at the centre of his discourse. Engaged in this research, he can do nothing but challenge the binary system, in its allegorical version, which postulates that signs can be cleanly translated and which replaces ignorance with knowledge and the latent with the evident. To the determinate method of Pantagruel is opposed a hermeneutic that is looking for its own identity, that defines its instruments and its objects hesitantly, uncertainly. An undefined and uncharted space opens itself up to be discovered, and an exploration begins, for which suitable tools are lacking.[16]

The strange text of Rabelais has offered and continues to offer academics inexhaustible opportunities to deploy their erudition and give reign to their sagacity. But this type of commentary risks impoverishing or adulterating works that are infinitely richer and more powerful than what academic discourse retains of them. The danger takes on multiple forms. On the one hand there are those who, through recourse to history, the elucidation of learned references, the identification of intertextual echoes, through an entire body of information which has not, moreover, lost any of its legitimacy or its necessity, help us to understand the text. This danger similarly threatens interpreters who question the meaning or meanings of the narratives – be these moral or spiritual values, reflections on knowledge, or even (we are seeing more and more of this) matters of linguistic and literary importance. But the temptation of academicism also menaces another category of commentary (under which most of my own work falls): those who, exploiting the hermeneutical defiances of Rabelais, insist on the ruses of his writing and the uncertainties of meaning – ambiguities, polyphonic fragmentation, conflicts of the serious and the comic – to conclude that the message is fundamentally unstable. If I do not have the intention to burn here what I have adored, I must, nevertheless, concede that this approach, more than any other, confines Rabelais to a strictly intellectual debate. It recognizes that the text is infinitely productive, but risks limiting its performance to pure mental gymnastics – the identification of the acrobatics of the discourse, the games of language, the fascination of slippages of meaning. But from the moment that reading fixates on textual mechanisms and the accidents of communication, a new scholasticism is put into place – a culture of schools and a debate of scholars, which drain the work of its force and censure its disquieting strangeness.

The reading that I am defending here advocates neither naïveté nor ignorance, but attempts to restore the place and dignity of imagination and affectivity. It exposes itself to the provocation of a savage symbolics and, without looking to rationalise its effects, records the impact of the troubling images and the psychological aggressions launched by the text.

It would be wrong to think that this conception of reading as an emotional or instinctual event is anachronistic. For many Humanists, the great works of antiquity create precisely this type of experience: they touch and destabilise, they speak to the profound layers of sensibility and leave profound marks. When you read the classics, says Du Bellay, it is as if you were on 'l'ardente montaigne d'Aethne' ('the burning mountain of Etna'): '... ilz vous engendreront telles affections, voyre ainsi qu'un Prothée vous transformeront en diverses sortes' ('... they will create such emotions in you, that truly they will transform you just like Proteus into different states').[17]

Reading the Bible properly – the living Word of God – says, for example, Erasmus,[18] is an existential experience that induces an upheaval of one's entire person. As much as, or even more than, bringing in outside knowledge and intellectual analysis, it requires an intimate adhesion, an understanding by means of the heart and an intuitive grasp. The legitimate perception of the Gospel is based on an act of love and is guided by enthusiasm, such that the reader, inspired by Grace, lets her/himself be possessed and regenerated. It is, of course, incongruous to compare the spiritual impact of the divine Word, according to Erasmus, and the disquiet caused by the strange scoria of the imagination, according to Rabelais. I am only looking to indicate that reading, as it is often conceived during the Renaissance, plays itself out on a stage that is one of empathy and affectivity just as much as one of rational analysis.

To this is added the fact that Humanists were extremely interested in the effects of art on temperament and paid the greatest attention to psychological changes induced by aesthetic experience. The work of art speaks to the soul, it diffuses shock waves, and, by the force of its language – the sounds, the rhythms, the images – brings about intense reactions. Saying is thus the equivalent of doing, a violent performance, an intrusion into the intimacy of the subject, a way to take power:

Celuy sera veritablement le poëte que je cherche en nostre Langue, qui me fera indigner, apayser, ejouyr, douloir, aymer, hayr, etonner, bref, qui tiendra la bride de mes affections, me tournant ça et la à son plaisir.

He will truly be the poet that I am looking for in our Language, he who will make me indignant, pacified, delight, suffer, love, hate, wonder, in brief, who will hold the reins of my emotions, turning me here and there at whim.[19]

Du Bellay copies this definition of the true poet from that of the orator, as he finds it, for example, in Cicero.[20] Eloquence consists of pleading one's cause by arousing emotions, by exploiting all of the sentimental chords in order to move the audience and to dispose it favourably; Quintilian treats at length the importance of *movere* in discourse and defines the appropriate techniques for inspiring *pathos* (*affectus* in Latin) in the listener.[21] Now rhetoric, as we know, has numerous affinities with other arts and furnishes them with both ends and means. Tragedy, for example, must profoundly touch the spectators, inspire terror and pity in them, make them share in the anger, the hate, the jealousy of its characters; its success is based on its psychological impact; if it neglects to move the audience, it betrays its calling.

Whether it attempts to appropriate the powers of eloquence or draws its inspiration from other models – notably the Greek theory of musical modes, taken up widely in Neo-Platonic circles[22] – poetry also claims this influence for itself, to the point of distinguishing the specific effects particular to each form. By the magic of style, by its sonorous presence and its evocatory force, it reaches the soul and modifies its affectivity. This language, says Montaigne, 'est plein et gros d'une vigueur naturelle' ('is full, pregnant with a sustained and natural power').[23] It was conceived in enthusiasm and, by the force of its radiance, it communicates this enthusiasm; sublime, supernatural, it overwhelms the reader and gives him/her access to a radically different order of experience. To read Virgil or Lucretius is, for Montaigne, an existential event. The poetic encounter is of the same order as the amorous encounter: love at first sight, the coming together of two partners who emerge transformed.

The magical effect that he feels when in contact with the great authors, why wouldn't the modern writer, in turn, try to make his own readers feel this? Poets, orators, and, from time to time, Rabelais himsef, want to move their audience. They claim to intervene in people's lives to change their moods, bend their will and, by the efficacity of their words, ensure that the reader is no longer, after reading, the same as before. Literature, as they conceive it, is neither a simple diversion nor the neutral vehicle of just any message, but a force that acts upon the emotions, in this zone where the physical and the psychical, interdependent, influence each other reciprocally. In these conditions, reading is no longer merely a mode of knowing, but a mode of feeling, and even a mode of being. The good reader appropriates the message for her/himself by transporting it into a personal sphere; s/he feels it like a presence and a power. An event takes place, one which cannot be taken into account by scholarly dissertation.

This is why it is important to put methods in their place and to measure their limits: to recognise their necessity, but refuse their hegemony. On two counts at least they risk inhibiting the emotional shock of reading. First, they only mobilise rational faculties; this is, moreover, their goal: to ensure a rigorous analysis, in order to escape the fuzziness of personal impressions. Second, they follow precise aims and can only find what they are looking for; they focus attention, orient reading, and thus lose in their ability to listen what they gain in clarity.

Thus the risk is that methods function like a quarantine area protecting from the aggressions of the text, reducing the artistic event to an intellectual experience among others. The type of reading postulated by a text like that of Rabelais (and so many others), demands, on the contrary, the greatest receptivity and taste for adventure. Instead of closing itself in behind methodological barriers, it lends a free-floating attention to the work, a curiosity alive to all signals; it exposes itself to surprise. To use literature to assure our comfort and verify our certitudes would be to pass over the essential.

*Translated by Amy Wyngaard*

# Notes

1 I have already argued for the category of the strange in Rabelais' works in 'La crise des signes et le défi de l'étrange' and 'Rabelais, les monstres et l'interprétation des signes', in *Le défi des signes: Rabelais et la crise de l'interprétation à la Renaissance*, Orléans, Paradigme, 1994. The edition of Rabelais used is that of the *Œuvres complètes*, ed. M. Huchon, Paris, Gallimard, Bibliothèque de la Pléiade, 1994. English translations of Rabelais' quotations are borrowed from *Rabelais: The Complete Works*, trans. D. M. Frame, Berkeley, Los Angeles, Oxford, University of California Press, 1991.

2 'Voyez la une belle medaille de Coqu' ('That's a nice picture of a cuckold'), Dindenault mocks (*Quart Livre*, chapter 5). For a concordant analysis of this chapter, see D. Russell, 'Panurge and his new clothes', in *Etudes Rabelaisiennes*, vol. 14, 1977, pp. 89–104.

3 For instance, at the beginning of chapter 12, where Pantagruel invokes several strange myths.

4 Boccaccio, *Genealogia deorum* (about 1350), ed. V. Romano, Bari, 1951.

5 Diana, Bacchus, Pan, Jupiter Ammon, all bearing horns, are evoked in chapter 14.

6 She is evoked indirectly throughout the third passage of Virgil, which concerns Arruns' preparing to kill her.

7 See *Ovide moralisé: Poème du commencement du XIVe siècle*, ed. C. de Boer, vol. 1, Vaduz, Sändig Reprint, 1984; book II, ll. 5103–38, and *Ovide moralisé en prose*, ed. C. de Boer, Amsterdam, North Holland Publishing Company, 1954, pp. 110-11.

8 See the same editions: verse version, book I, ll. 2351–64; prose version pp. 60–61.

9 *Les songes drolatiques de Pantagruel* (1565), ed. M. Jeanneret, La Chaux-de-Fonds, Editions ('wva'), 1989. In it figure precisely a man-drum (fig. 65) and a woman-owl (fig. 11).

10 See Artemidorus, *La clef des songes (Onirocriticon)*, trans. A. J. Festugière, Paris, Vrin, 1975, book I, 39 and book IV, 56, respectively.

11 F. Berriot, 'A propos des chapitres XIII et XIV du *Tiers Livre*: Notes sur quelques manuscrits d'interprétation des songes à la veille de la Renaissance', in *Réforme, Humanisme, Renaissance*, vol. 23, 1986, pp. 5–14; pp. 11–12.

12 See chapter 14.

13 The thatched cottage resembles 'la case de Hireus ou Oenopion, en laquelle Jupiter, Neptune et Mercure ensemble ne prindrent à desdaing entrer, repaistre et loger; en laquelle officialement pour l'escot forgerent Orion' ('the hut of Hireus or Oenopion, in which Jupiter, Neptune, and Mercury did not disdain to enter, feed, and lodge; in which in a pisspot, to pay their way, they forged Orion'). As above, this comparison invokes a preposterous myth: the three gods, in guise of thanks, create Orion from their urine (Ovid, *Fastes* V, 499–536).

14 *Aeneid* VI, 8 ff.

15 'Une Canidie, une Sagane, une phitonisse et sorciere' ('A Canidia, a Sagana, a pythoness and witch': chapter 16). In the intertext of Horace (*Epodes* 5), Canidia and Sagana are hideous figures who have more to do with folly than inspiration.

16 See S. Perrier, 'La problématique du songe à la Renaissance: La norme et les marges', in *Le songe à la Renaissance*, Université de Saint-Etienne, 1990, pp. 13–19.

17 Joachim du Bellay, *La Deffence et Illustration de la Langue Francoyse*, ed. Henri Chamard, Paris, Didier, 1961; I, 5, p. 37.

18 See Erasmus, *Les Préfaces au 'Novum Testamentum' (1516)*, ed. Y. Delègue and J. P. Gillet, Geneva, Labor et Fides, 1990; see also the texts cited by T. Cave, *The Cornucopian Text: Problems of Writing in the French Renaissance*, Oxford, Clarendon Press, 1979, pp. 79–94.

19 Joachim du Bellay, op. cit. (note 17); II, 11, p. 179.

20 See *De oratore* I, 8, 30 and I, 12, 53; *Brutus* 50, 188 and *Orator* 38, 131.

21. Quintilian, *Institution oratoire*, 7 vols, trans. J. Cousin, Paris, Belles Lettres, 1975–80; 6, 2, 8 ff; 12, 10, 59 and *passim.*

22 See D. P. Walker, *Music, Spirit and Language in the Renaissance*, London, Variorum Reprints, 1985.

23 Montaigne, *Les Essais*, ed. Pierre Villey and V.-L. Saulnier, Paris, Presses Universitaires de France 1965; 3.5, p. 873; *The Complete Essays*, trans. M. A. Screech, Harmondsworth, Penguin Books, 1991, p. 987.

CHAPTER 3

# 'Blond chef, grande conqueste': Feminist Theories of the Gaze, the *blason anatomique*, and Louise Labé's Sonnet 6

*Ann Rosalind Jones*

The *blason*, the love poem written in praise of a woman's body, has been centralised in recent Renaissance studies through the work of Nancy Vickers, the first among feminist critics to theorise the psychosocial dynamics of this Renaissance genre.[1] Feminist film theory of the 1970s and 80s, focused on the cinematic forms structured to gratify the male gaze, has also been enlisted to define the impulses driving the poet's 'look' at an iconic female body. The motives and processes of the masculine gaze posited by this psychoanalytically inflected line of thought are generalised across time by Luce Irigaray in her feminist deconstruction of the 'scopic' (visually oriented) sexual economy of Western culture, from Plato to Freud.[2] One way to ground such theory in a specific historical situation is to trace out connections between sixteenth-century poetry and preaching, that is, to analyse lyric as a literary code operating among other discourses in the moralised gender system articulated in Renaissance conduct books for the middle classes, whose writers anxiously attempted to control how both sexes looked and saw. 'Don't look now, or ever' was the counsel of most writers on the proper behaviour of men, and even more, of women.[3] The ideology, or belief system, underlying such advice surfaces in the poetry of the time as well, written by men and women in response – sometimes obedient, often challenging – to the conventions of seeing and being seen.

To understand the *blason* as a literary genre, I propose a composite approach. Beginning with feminist uses of Freud's insights into men's defence mechanisms and Irigaray's critique of a culture domi-

nated by masculine ways of seeing, I will give these perspectives a
local habitation by focusing on the literary texts produced by a bourgeois woman, Louise Labé, composing her sonnets in the merchant
city of Lyons in the mid-sixteenth century.


## CORPS AND CORPUS: THE GENEALOGY OF A GENRE

The most influential Renaissance version of the *blason* was established
in Francesco Petrarca's *Canzoniere*, his collection of sonnets and
songs first printed in 1470. To describe his beloved Laura, Petrarch
composed short poems focused on one of her physical features – her
eyes, or her hair, or her hand. Why this fragmentation, this concentration on one body part as opposed to some representation of the
entire woman? Vickers remarks that what is 'specifically Petrarchan'
about such poems is 'the obsessive insistence on the particular, an
insistence that would in turn generate multiple texts on individual
fragments of the body or on the beauties of women'.[4] She explains this
'insistence on the particular' by pointing out a myth central to
Petrarch's collection: the story, recounted by Ovid in the *Metamorphoses* (III, 138–255) of the hunter Actaeon and the goddess Diana.
Actaeon stumbles unaware upon Diana bathing nude in a forest pool;
angry at the mortal man's stare, she throws water at him and transforms him into a stag, whereupon he is attacked and torn apart by his
dogs.

The male poet's reaction to this violent scenario corresponds to
Freud's narration of how a boy's first sighting of the genitals of the
opposite sex can produce a man whose sexual excitement depends
upon a fetish, that is, an object such as a foot, a shoe or an item of
lingerie on which he focuses his desire. According to Freud, this
replacement of a woman by a part of something associated with
women is a defence mechanism, a way of coping that allows the boy
to overcome his terrified first reaction to the sight of a woman's body,
which he perceives as terrifyingly different from his because he sees
no penis. Interpreting this absence as the result of a castration that
threatens him, too, in a panic he shuts down his vision of the female
body and channels his attention into a part-object instead, some
isolated or displaced feature – a foot, a garment – onto which he can
concentrate his desires because doing so enables him to deny, or
foreclose, the sight of the female 'lack' that has so frightened him.

Vickers reads the Actaeon myth as an oblique narrative of the process leading to poetic fetishism:

> Woman's body, albeit divine, is displayed to Actaeon, and his body, as a consequence, is literally taken apart. Petrarch's Actaeon ... realizes what will ensue: his response to the threat of imminent dismemberment is the neutralization, through descriptive dismemberment, of the threat. He transforms the visible totality into scattered words, the body into signs; his description, at one remove from his experience, safely permits and perpetuates his fascination. (1982, p. 96)

She relates the form of the *Canzoniere*, a loosely organized collection of discrete poems that Petrarch entitled *Rime sparse*, 'scattered rhymes', to the visual and verbal fragmentation through which the male observer attempts to replace the goddess-beloved by representing her in words:

> ... threatened rhymes try to iterate a precious, fleeting image, to transmute it into an idol that can be forever possessed, that will be forever present. But description is ultimately no more than a collection of imperfect signs ... that, like fetishes, affirm absence by their presence (p. 105).

A similar theory about the transmutation of woman into idol was elaborated by Laura Mulvey in her groundbreaking 1975 essay 'Visual Pleasure and Narrative Cinema'.[5] She, too, speculates that the male spectator looks at women in self-protective ways: he either identifies with an on-screen hero who exposes and tames the heroine, or he enjoys the director's construction of a static, dazzling partial feminine image. Mulvey begins with a summary of Freud's work on 'scopophilia', the love of looking shared by children faced with the puzzle of adult sexuality: 'Freud associated scopophilia with taking other people as objects, subjecting them to a controlling and curious gaze' (p. 16). She adds a feminist clarification: 'In a world ordered by sexual imbalance, pleasure in looking has been split between active/male and passive/female. The determining gaze projects its fantasy onto the female figure, which is styled accordingly'. 'Styled' is a usefully flexible term for describing this process: so, too, does the Renaissance poet 'style' his beloved through descriptive close-ups that keep the alarming female body in its entirety out of sight. Mulvey's argument that such close-ups interrupt cinematic realism is equally relevant to the perspective of the Renaissance *blason*:

> Conventional close ups (on the legs of Marlene Dietrich, for example) integrate into the narrative a different mode of eroticism. One part of a fragmented body destroys ... the illusion of depth demanded by the narrative; it gives flatness, the quality of a cut-out or icon, rather than verisimilitude to the screen (p. 20).

Similarly, the *blason*-poet fixes the beloved woman in the familiar, repetitive vocabulary of Petrarchism. Rather than advancing a plot, the *blason* freeze-frames the woman in a close-focused, fragmented image. As Mulvey concludes, 'Fetishistic scopophilia ... can exist outside linear time, as the erotic instinct is focused on the look alone'.

Does this psychoanalytic-cinematic framework illuminate a typical sixteenth-century *blason*? As an example, let us take Eustorg de Beaulieu's praise of the cheek, written for a famous contest, 'le concours du *blason*', organized by the poet Clément Marot, in exile at the court of Ferrara in 1536. Each of the participants in this contest wrote a poem in praise of one part of a woman's body, 'blasoning' it – that is, announcing its merits to the world. Maurice Scève won the prize with a poem on the eyebrow. Eleven poems from the contest were published in the same year with the title *Blasons anatomiques du corps fémenin*. Constantly augmented, the collection was republished five times up to 1543, when it reappeared with thirty-seven *blasons* and twenty-one *contreblasons*, satiric attacks on old and ugly body parts.[6] We are in the realm, then, of a genre that quickly attracted many writers, all men, and, judging from the frequency of publication, many readers (Vickers, 1985). Eustorg de Beaulieu's *blason* in this collection is insistently visual. The poet's eye feeds on the cheek, while he calls attention to his own performance as portraitist:

> *La Joue*
> Très-belle et amoureuse joue
> Sur laquelle mon coeur se joue
> Et mes yeux prennent leur repas,
> Joue faite mieux qu'au compas,
> Joue blanche, ou bien claire et brune,
> Ronde comme un croissant de lune ....
> O joue gaillarde et dehait
> De qui tout amoureux fait fête
> Contemplant ta beaulté parfaite.
>     Joue de qui le seul portrait
> Les plus rusés à soi attrait.
>     Joue que nature illumine
> D'un peu de purpurine
> A mode de fleur de pêcher,
> Pour te vendre aux amants plus cher.

Very lovely and loving cheek / On which my heart delights to play / And my eyes feed themselves / Cheek better shaped than with a compass, / White cheek, or else bright and brown, / As round as a waxing moon /.... Oh, cheek, gay and full of joy / Which every lover compliments / Admiring your perfect beauty. / Cheek, whose description alone / Draws the cleverest men to you. / Cheek which nature brightly lights / With a subtle little crimson hue, / Like the blossom of the peach  tree, / To sell you more dearly to your lovers.[7]

This cheek, so variable that it clearly belongs to no particular woman, takes its value instead from the praises of male admirers, whom Beaulieu mentions four times in these first lines. The curious combination of amorous and commercial language in the last line positions even Nature as a participant in the system of literary exchange through which female beauty is divided up and condensed into topics that excite men to poetic competition.

The poet goes on to contrast ugly cheeks to the perfect one, defining the ideal of naturalness by listing women's potential for falling short of it. Praise turns more frankly to insult in the obscene *contre-blasons* later added to the collection, for example, Marot's denunciation of *Le Tétin* (Charpentier, editor (1983), pp. 168–69), compared to which Beaulieu's denunciation of make-up in *La Joue* is very mild. Even so, this section of his poem centres upon negative alternatives to the beautiful cheek, on the supplement, or lesser half, of an opposition against which the ideal is defined:

> Joue non flétrie ou pendante,
> Point grosse, rouge ou flamboyante,
> Ains tenant le moyen par tout.
>     Joue haïssant – aussi – sur tout
> D'user sur soi d'aultre peinture
> Que de Dieu seul, et de nature.
>     Joue ne maigre, ne trop grasse,
> Mais replète de bonne grace,
> Ne trop pâle, ne noire aussi.

Cheek neither withered nor sagging, / Not at all fat, red or flaming, / But everywhere fitting the golden mean. / Cheek detesting above all / Painting yourself in any way / Except God's own, and Nature's, too. / Cheek not too thin, not too fat, / But entirely full of grace, / Not too pale, and also not too dark.

The final lines put the focus squarely on the poet himself through the self-citation he uses to call attention to his verbal struggles and to name his accomplishments. This is praise for the *blasonneur* more than praise for the lady:

> Joue, tu me mets en souci
> Comment je te don'rai louange,
> For de t'appeler: Joue d'ange,
> Joue d'albâtre, ou cristalline,
> Joue que le naturel Pline

Ne saurait au vrai blasonner,
Ou Joue que – à bref sermonner –
N'as ne ride, tache ne trace,
Et es le plus beau de la face!

Cheek, you drive me to my wit's end / As to how I'll give you praise, / Except by calling you 'Angel's cheek, / Cheek of alabaster or of crystal, / Cheek that Pliny the naturalist / Would be unable to "blason" truthfully', / Or 'Cheek that' – to make the sermon short – / 'Has neither wrinkle, spot nor mark, / And is the greatest beauty of the face!'

One remarkable aspect of this poem, in addition to the supreme confidence of its judgements both positive and critical, is its competitive verve. Eustorg's cheek is praised as superior to every other kind of cheek, his portrait of it celebrated as a lure for all men, his metaphors for it more inventive than anything that even Pliny, the encyclopaedic natural philosopher of Rome, could produce. The single, free-floating female facial feature is the pretext and the summons to a contest among men.[8]

## THE MALE GAZE: THEATRE AND MARKETPLACE

In a later study of the blason focused on the effects of its male performers and male audience, Vickers analyses Shakespeare's *The Rape of Lucrece*, a poem on Lucretia, the Roman noblewoman raped by Tarquin, the son of a usurper king, after he has heard Lucrece's husband Collatine describe her beauty. Committing suicide after the rape, she becomes the rallying point for Collatine's clan and allies, who unite to avenge her and to restore democracy to Rome.[9] The husband's *blason* of his wife's beauty, Vickers points out, generates the envy that causes her rape:

... celebratory conceit inscribes woman's body between rivals: ... she constitutes the field upon which the battle must be fought. For to describe, as *Lucrece* so eloquently reminds us, is ... to control, to possess, and ultimately, to use to one's own ends (p. 181).

This positioning of a woman to serve men's ends is addressed in a broader framework by the French philosopher Luce Irigaray, who defines Western culture as a relentlessly male-dominated field. In 'Ce Sexe qui n'en est pas un', an essay on the phallocentric regime of the male gaze, which privileges the penis as a visible mark of sexual identity, she argues:

> Woman, in this sexual imaginary, is only a more or less obliging prop for the enactment of male fantasies … the predominance of the look, and of the discrimination and individuation of form, is particularly foreign to female eroticism …. Her entry into a dominant scopic economy signifies, again, her consignment to passivity: she is the beautiful object of contemplation. While her body finds itself thus eroticized, and called to a double movement of exhibition and chaste retreat in order to stimulate the drives of the [male] 'subject', her sexual organ represents the horror of 'nothing to see'. (Irigaray (1977), pp. 25/25–6)

Masculine fear of castration, the female body defensively hypostasised as a collection of parts to be seen separately: Irigaray understands the unconscious behind the male gaze much as Vickers and Mulvey do.

Irigaray also argues that women in Western culture are exchanged among men. She combines Lévi-Strauss' analysis of marriage customs and Marx's analysis of the commodity[10] to explain the abstraction that results from phallocentric societies' definition of all women as less than men. In order for men to construct themselves as sovereign subjects (freely choosing individuals) by contrast to the materiality, irrationality, and lack of the phallus that they attribute to all women, one woman serves as well as any other. The parallel Irigaray draws between women and merchandise illuminates both the circumstances of performance of the Ferrara *blasons* and their writers' separation of each 'blasoned' feature from any particular woman's body:

> All the systems of exchange that organize patriarchal societies and all the modalities of productive work in those societies are men's business. The production of women, signs and commodities is always referred back to men … and (women) always pass from one group of men to another. (Irigaray (1977), pp. 171/168)

One consequence of this handing on of women (and of poems describing one part of them) is the creation of a general standard of beauty by which all women can be measured, a standard that effaces the particularities of specific women:

> … when women are exchanged, woman's body must be treated as an abstraction. The exchange operation cannot take place in terms of some intrinsic, immanent value of the commodity. It can only come about when two objects – two women – are in a relation of equality with a third term [the perfect cheek, for example] that is neither the one nor the other. It is thus not as 'women' that they are exchanged, but as women reduced to one common feature …. Woman has value on the market by virtue of one single quality: that of being a product of man's (cultural, poetic) labor. (Irigaray (1977), pp. 171/175)

In the contest of male poets, the *blason* isolates and idealises a particular feature through the verbal skill by which each poet intends to outdo his rivals. Such competition does away with any need for particular women. Anatomised in this way, the Lauras and Délies disappear, distilled into the poet's description of a perfect cheek or eyebrow: 'They all have the same phantom-like reality. Metamorphosed in identical sublimations, all these objects now manifest just one thing: ... (men's) labor has accumulated in them' (ibid).

Irigaray's observation about the contradictory assignment women face in such a culture – 'a double movement of exhibition and chaste retreat' – has particular relevance to Renaissance gender ideology. One consequence of men's demand for women's chastity as a guarantee that their sons were their legitimate heirs was that women in the sixteenth century were constantly scrutinised, at the same time that they were trained to avoid meeting men's looks.[11] Ruth Kelso, in her survey of conduct books, summarises the early modern virtue of 'shamefastness', a central ideal of proper behaviour for a girl, as follows:

> Her face should be grave and her eyes habitually lowered, even to the point, one extremist would go, of leaving no chance for anyone to accuse her of ever having looked in the face of her father, mother and brothers, much less of anyone else, from the age of seven. Downcast eyes are the features most stressed ... because through the eye one's mind is revealed to others, and she is wise who keeps such knowledge for herself; only a little look can discover a great love (p. 50).

The fear that women will seduce men by revealing their attraction to them underlies moralists' many prescriptions for downcast eyes, which assert a radical double standard. The power of the masculine gaze is shored up by the prohibition of women's looks.

One such moralist, Jean Bouchet, in his *Triumphes de la Noble et amoureuse dame et l'art de honnestement aymer* (*The Triumphs of the Noble and Loving Lady and the Art of Loving Honorably*, Poitiers, Jean de Marnef, 1532), recommends chastity equally to men and to women and advises them of four ways to protect it. But when he comes to the topic of the gaze, he presumes that the person who has it is a man. Accordingly, he cites an Old Testament warning from Ecclesiastes 21, which assigns the duty of controlling the look to men:

> Le quatriesme [moyen] est fuyr les choses qui ... induysent les hommes et femmes a se entre aymer de folle amour / qui sont les foulz et impudiques regars ... Et a ce propos dict le saige: Ne regardez les femmes a ce que tu ne tumbes en leurs lacqs. (D3v)

> The fourth method is to flee from the things that lead men and women to love each other in wanton ways / which are flirtatious and immodest looks .... And

in regard to this the wise man says: 'Do not look at women lest you should fall into their traps'.

The logic, or rather the anti-logic here, is revealing. If a man looks at a woman, he will inevitably be corrupted; this is why he must be forbidden to look. But if he nonetheless allows his gaze to fall upon a woman, she is to blame: she lays the traps into which men fall.[12] Bouchet's attempt to assign the same duty to both sexes is incompatible with the Judaeo-Christian axiom that woman has been, and always will be, the source of temptation.[13] Lacking entirely in this mind-set is the possibility that a man might be able to look at a woman and to resist her charm. Rather, a fatal automatism is attributed to men: the male gaze brings on desire and does away with any ability to master it.

As a result, Bouchet assigns the responsibility for chastity almost entirely to women. Predictably, he devotes a large part of his advice about purity to young girls. In his *Epistres morales et familieres du Traverseur* (*Moral and Familiar Letters by the Travelling Preacher*, Poitiers, Jacques Bouchet, 1545), a book of Christian counsel written in ten-syllable couplets, he addresses his *Epistre* 10 'aux pucelles et filles a marier' ('to maidens and marriageable daughters'):

> Aiez tousiours vostre regard bening
> Bas, et honteux, non superbe, et maling,
> Quand vous serez en l'Eglise ou en rue
> Ne jectez pas ca ne la vostre veue.
> La sage dit que fornication
> En femme on veoit a la prolation
> Quand souvent parle, et hault et bas regarde
> Et de travers, donnez vous en donc garde. (E3v-E4)

> Always keep your look benign,/ Lowered and shamefast, not proud and sly, / When you're in church or on the street / Don't shift your glance this way and that. / The wise man says that fornication / Can be seen in a woman's forward speech, / When she talks often, and looks up and down / And sideways; so beware.

In his seventh epistle, Bouchet aims similar advice at married women:

> La femme doit ... se garder ...
> De folz regards, et propos dissoluz,
> Avoir les sens rassis et resoluz, ...
> Garder se doit par ses regards tirer
> Aucun a soy, n'aultruy desirer. (D4v)

> The wife must ... avoid ... / Flirtatious looks and wicked words, / Keep her senses under firm control .... / She must avoid by her glances / Attracting any man, or desiring any other.

But however strictly Bouchet wants to repress men's and women's looks as a path toward wayward desires, he himself represents ideal feminine purity in a form shaped by the judging, particularising gaze of the *blason*. One passage from *Les Epistres* demonstrates that the descriptive formulae of Petrarch and Marot were as firmly entrenched in guides to behaviour as in poetic discourse: to represent the proper behaviour of a young girl in church, Bouchet produces a *blason*. Like the *blasonneurs*, he qualifies his enumeration of virtues with the opposing vices: devout beauty consists in the avoidance of frivolity. His lines focus on the eyes and mouth, standard features of the *blason*, and the *mise-en-scène* is structured by a gaze that travels in a leisurely, approving way up the body of the maiden, imagined at her prayers. The poet's evaluating eye takes possession of the girl, whose lowered glance keeps her unaware of his look:

> Il fait bon veoir une fille devote
> En ung monstier qui ne fait point la sotte,
> Mais prie Dieu de cueur humble et tremblant,
> De bouche aussi sans aucun faulx semblant
> Les yeulx baissez, non par ypocrisie,
> Et sans avoir ailleurs sa fantaisie. (E4v)

> It's good to see a devout girl / In a pew not acting like a fool, / But praying God with humble, trembling heart, / And a mouth also without false pretence / With eyes downcast, not from hypocrisy, / And without having her mind somewhere else.

Bouchet's tracts repay close analysis because his images typify the early modern desire to repress the feminine look and the effort, evidently doomed to failure, to limit the male gaze to moral ends.

Three decades after Bouchet, the demand for feminine modesty appeared in a more popular and paradoxical format, a small book that gave its moral counsel the form of cosmetic advice: *L'Attiffet des Demoizelles* (*The Young Ladies' Beautifier*)[14], published in Paris (Fédéric Morel) in 1575 by Guillaume de la Tayssonnière, a gentleman-poet of Bresse. This is the paradox: the woman must limit her gaze to avoid tempting men, but the moralist also promises that a modest, downward look will make her more beautiful – hence more likely to attract men's admiration:

> Pendant que vous aurez ce tiltre de fillage
> Il ne faut brusquement eslever le visage
> Pour respondre à un mot, moins, ridant vostre front,
> Surhausser le sourcil, comme les sottes font,

Ains moderément bas affichant vostre veuë,
Serez avec douceur de response pourveuë. (p. 12)

As long as you have this title of maidenhood / You must not suddenly lift your face / To answer back; even less, wrinkling your brow, / Raise your eyebrows, as foolish girls do; / But calmly casting your eyes down low, / You'll be sweetly supplied with an answer.

The woman reader is offered exactly the bait she is warned against: to become more alluring to the masculine eye precisely to the extent that she seems to pay no attention to it. Masculine assumptions so deeply inform Renaissance ideology regarding the duties of each sex that it cannot posit a man's gaze free of lust and is completely unable to entertain the possibility of a frank, risk-free look from a woman.

## THE FEMININE 'BLASON': SEIZING THE GAZE

Given the regime of the male gaze in public life, what position could women construct for themselves in relation to it? As unwelcoming as it seems, women poets appropriated the *blason* of beauty for themselves in various ways. In their texts, the *blason* as visual apparatus and verbal formula is refocused, interrogated, and reversed. In spite of its honoured origin in Petrarch and French poets using women's body parts to compete with one another, the genre was open to contestation.

One thing that the reigning system of the male gaze and the prohibition of the female look make it easier to understand is women poets' predilection for Neoplatonic love theory, which, following Plato's *Symposium*, downplayed the body by positing physical beauty merely as a first step upward to the attainment of a blissful union with the super-corporeal ideal of beauty. While a male poet such as Maurice Scève claims to read the perfection of his beloved lady's soul in the perfect semicircle of her eyebrow, his literary partner Pernette Du Guillet, the young wife of a Lyonnais nobleman, in her *Rithmes* (1545) sets the beloved man's body in opposition to the spiritual beauty of his soul.[15] When she recounts her initial inability to see past his physical appearance to his intellect (*Epigramme* 11), she admits: 'à droict l'on me peult reprocher, / Que plus l'ay veu, et moins l'ay sceu cognoistre' ('I can be justly reproached, / That the more I saw him, the less I could truly know him', p. 19). Yet by abandoning the bodily focus of the *blason*, Pernette claims a vision more profound than the descriptive close-ups practised by her male contemporaries. Relinquishing the physical gaze allows her to construct a self-*blason* demonstrating her exemplary understanding of the elite philosophy of love, 'la saincte amitié' ('holy friendship'), so eloquently articulated by her poet-master. Repressing the man's body in favour of his mind, Pernette names herself as the recipient and reader of praises that distinguish the poet who praises her more than good looks could do:

> *Epigramme 17*
> Je suis tant bien que je ne le puis dire,
> Ayant sondé son amytié profonde
> Par sa vertu, qui à l'aymer m'attire
> Plus que beaulté: car sa grace, et faconde
> Me font cuyder la premiere du monde. (p. 25)

> I am so happy I cannot say it, / Having seen the depth of his true affection / In his virtue, which draws me to love him / More than beauty; for his grace and eloquence / Make me think myself the first woman in the world.

Pernette responds to the prohibition of the female gaze by transforming what it sees from body to spirit. But her glance is not at all downcast; rather, it has a certain aristocratic *hauteur*. In contrast to the modest not-seeing of Bouchet's proper maiden, she 'blasons' herself for having attained a supremely elevated vision. As Jan Boney points out, such 'A shift away from the scopic economy gives an advantage to a poet trying to preserve her chastity …. This strategy of privileging the beloved's text over the beloved's body, privileging reading over looking, is a voice-enabling strategy for a female poet'.[16]

Rather than being given a transcendental focus, the *blason* could be treated with outright mockery. In this critical spirit, Catherine des Roches, the daughter and stepdaughter of lawyers, who collaborated with her mother Madeleine des Roches in *Les Oeuvres de Mes-dames des Roches de Poetiers Mere et Fille* (Paris, Abel Langelier, 1578), wrote a dialogue between Sincero and Charite.[17] Sincero is an extravagantly flattering lover whose *blasons* exemplify the idealising descriptions of Neoplatonism, according to which physical beauty in a woman's face is a sign of the spiritual beauty of her soul; Charite, the mouthpiece for Catherine, is the clear-sighted recipient of Sincero's compliments. In response to his *blasons*, praising among other features 'voz beaux yeux soleils de mon ame' ('your beautiful eyes, the suns of my soul'), Charite points out that such praise leaves a woman speechless – a serious consideration for Catherine des Roches as a professional poet. Charite comes into being precisely to the extent that she names and refuses the double bind in which such compliments position her:

> Vous m'estonnez plus de courtoisies que de raisons, depuis que vous avez commencé à me loüer je n'ay sceu quelle contenance je devoy tenir, ny lequel estoit le plus seur pour moy[,] de me taire, ou de parler; si je parle, refusant les loüanges que vous m'attribuez, il semblera que je veuille vous donner occasion de contester d'avantage; si je me tais[,] vous penserez que mon silence avoüe tout ce qu'il vous plaist dire en mon faveur (p. 252).

> You dazzle me more with compliments than with arguments; since you began to praise me, I haven't known what expression I should wear, nor which was safer for me, to be silent or to speak. If I speak, to refuse the praises you give me, it will seem that I want to give you the chance to argue further; if I am silent, you'll think my silence confirms everything it pleases you to say in my favour.

Charite pinpoints one motive behind such 'loüanges': to keep the lady silent so that the lover can keep talking.

She also deflates the intricate Neoplatonic tale that Sincero goes on to recount: his lady, created by Providence following the orders of ideal Beauty and then sent down to earth, was so missed by the gods that they raised Sincero up to heaven to console themselves with the portrait of Charite engraved in his heart. Sincero's conclusion ('et voila, Madame, comment par la faveur de vostre beauté je voisine les Cieux': 'and that, my Lady, is how through the favour won by your beauty, I dwell in Heaven') gives Charite her opening:

> Je croy plustost que par la faveur de voz propos vous portez mon nom au Ciel (Syncero) et que vous l'en raportez quand bon vous semble. Or pource que vous desirez d'estre estimé amoureux et poëte, vous pouvez feindre sans en estre repris, et moy, qui ne pratique ny avec la Poësie, ny avec l'Amour, je puis seurement vous ouyr sans adjouter beaucoup de foy à voz parolles (p. 256).

> I think, rather, that through your flattering words you lift my name up to Heaven, Sincero, and bring it back down when it suits you. But because you want to be admired as a lover and a poet, you can feign without being reproached for it; and I, who have nothing to do with poetry or with love, can certainly listen to you without putting much faith in your words.

This is more than a claim to social decorum. Charite gives her readers a neat exposure of male-authored *blasons* as poetic self-display and a frank appraisal of their limited truth.

In contrast to Pernette's replacement of the male body with male-authored texts and Catherine's mockery of Neoplatonic praise of women, Louise Labé in her *Euvres* (first published in Lyons in 1555, ten years after Pernette's *Rithmes*) 'blasons' both the beloved man and herself in order to establish an identity shared between them. She represents the beloved man and herself as clearly physical beings. Her sonnet 2 opens as if it were a conventional *blason*, but she shifts from the man's physical attractions – his eyes – to his actions, actions that she, too, performs: 'O beaus yeus bruns, ô regars destournez, / O chaus soupirs, ô larmes espandues' (p. 122). Several critics have pointed out the deliberate confusion of agency in these lines:[18] whose glances are turned away, whose tears are shed, whose hot sighs are whose?

In contrast to the distance established between poet and lady by the male *blasonneur*'s assessing gaze, Labé blurs the distinction between lover, beloved and poet: each lover is all three. In the last lines of sonnet 2 she focuses briefly on specific parts of the man's body, but her list soon shifts from his physique to his lute: 'O ris, ô front, cheveus, bras, mains et doits: / O lut pleintif, viole, archet et vois' ('Oh, laugh, oh, forehead, hair, arms, hands and fingers, / Oh, plaintive lute, viol, bow and voice'). The lute, because it is the instrument that Labé claims as another self in sonnet 12, contributes further to the merging of identities: 'Lut, compagnon de ma calamité, / ... Tu as souvent avec moy lamenté' ('Lute, companion in my calamities, / ... you have often joined me in my laments', p. 127).

Labé's fullest *blason* unfolds in sonnet 10, but here, too, physical and social details draw her close to the man: both have blond hair, both are famous for their eloquence. A mirrored pair is assembled by the opening description of sonnet 10 and Labé's self-description in other poems in which she insists upon the qualities she shares with her beloved. Of the man, presented as a poet crowned with a laurel wreath, she writes:

> Quand j'aperçoy ton blond chef couronné
> D'un laurier verd, faire un Lut si bien pleindre,
> Que tu pourrois à te suivre contreindre
> Arbres et rocs: quand je te vois orné,
> Et de vertus dix mile environné,
> Au chef d'honneur plus haut que nul ateindre,
> Et des plus hauts les louenges esteindre .... (p. 126)

> When I see your blond head crowned / With a green laurel, making a lute weep so well / That you could force trees and rocks to follow you; / when I see you adorned / And surrounded by ten thousand virtues / At a peak of honour attained by no one else, / And surpassing the praises of the greatest men ....

Labé, too, is blonde, as her mocking quotation in sonnet 23 of the *blason* dedicated to her by this inconstant man affirms: 'Las! que me sert, qui si parfaitement / Louas jadis ... ma tresse dorée?' ('Alas, what good does it do me / That you once so perfectly praised ... my golden hair?' p. 134). She also claims fame equal to the public praise received by sonnet 10's poet-hero. In her second *Elégie* she reminds him, absent and, she suspects, unfaithful, of her international renown not only as a beauty but as a poet:

> Si say je bien que t'amie nouvelle
> A peine aura le renom d'estre telle,
> Soit en beauté, vertu, grace et faconde,
> Comme plusieurs gens savans par le monde
> M'ont fit à tort, ce croy je, estre estimée. (p. 112)

> Yet I know for certain that your new love / Will hardly have the fame of being the same / In beauty, virtue, grace or eloquence, / As many wise people throughout the world / Have made me, wrongly, I think, be admired.

Labé 'blasons' qualities that identify her with her beloved, whose body she locates in a public space and celebrates for actions – speaking fluently, playing music, winning admiration – which she herself performs. Rather than defining her full subjectivity in contrast to an isolated fragment of a man's body, she asserts a mutuality that elevates both lovers as twinned poets sharing equal renown.

   Irigaray, speculating further about the visual effects of a male-centred culture, suggests that women's sexual pleasure is less scopic and appropriative than men's, more tactile and fusion-seeking: 'Ownership and property are doubtless quite foreign to the feminine. But not *nearness*. Nearness so pronounced that it makes all discrimination of identity, and thus all forms of property, impossible' (Irigaray (1977) p. 50/31). Hearing, a sense that operates in closer proximity to its object than vision can do, is central in Labé's interrogation of the *blason* in sonnet 21. She opens the poem with visual categories, but her questions about the characteristics that define the perfect man move on to qualities of sound belonging to the lute, the attribute she shares with her beloved:

> Quelle grandeur rend l'homme venerable?
> Quelle grosseur? quel poil? quelle couleur? ...
> Quel chant est plus à l'homme convenable?
> Qui plus penetre en chantant sa douleur?
> Qui un doux lut fait encore meilleur? (pp. 132–33)

> What height makes a man worthy of respect? / What weight? What sort of hair? What colour of skin? ... / What kind of song best suits a man? / Who penetrates most deeply as he sings of his pain? / Who improves upon even a well-tuned lute?

Andrea Chan points out the emphasis on aural beauty both here and in sonnet 10: 'the musical talent of the Beloved and the sweetness of the sounds he makes are accorded the same importance as the beauty of his appearance'.[19]

Labé ends the poem by rejecting description entirely, and with it the atomised and commodified body parcelled out in the male-authored *blason*. In her last three lines, she dismisses free choice and artful compliment, the privileges claimed by Ferrara's founding *blasonneurs*, to insist on the power of passion over conventional categories of beauty:

> Je ne voudrois le dire assurément,
> Ayant Amour forcé mon jugement,
> Mais je say bien et de tant je m'assure,
> Que tout le beau que lon pourroit choisir,
> Et que tout l'art qui ayde la Nature,
> Ne me sauroit acroitre mon désir.

> I would not want to say for sure, / Love having swayed my judgment, / But I know well and assure myself of this much: / That all the beauty one could choose / And all the art that assists Nature / Could not increase my desire.

By claiming passion for a man who overwhelms her power to judge or choose, Labé rejects the abstraction of the *blason*. To refuse to answer questions implying absolute standards of beauty is to claim total immersion in love for a particular man, in a 'nearness' foreign to the calculating eye and distancing ritual of the *blasonneurs*' naming of parts. Labé's renunciation of the power to establish descriptive conventions for male beauty is, in fact, a power play of a different kind: it asserts her difference from male poets of praise.

She imagines a much more explicit *prise de pouvoir* in sonnet 6, in which she works out a multiple reversal of roles – who sees, how many see, who is seen? Her *blason* of the man in this poem sets up a drama not only of looking but of smelling, touching, and persuading performed by three allied women, one the poet, the other two goddesses. The sonnet opens by attributing an all-powerful look to the man, figured as a freely moving star (in sonnet 15, similarly, he is called 'mon Soleil', 'my Sun') whose choice of beloved brings her 'honour.' What is imagined here is not private delectation – the woman seen in an intimate space reserved for a single male observer – but a public choice that awards fame to the woman who is the object of the man's look:

> Deux ou trois fois bienheureus le retour
> De ce cler Astre, et plus heureus encore
> Ce que son oeil de regarder honore. (p. 124)

Two or three times blessed the return / of this bright star, and more blessed still / She whom his eye honours by looking at.

The judging gaze of the man opens the poem. But his active, mobile role dissolves as the syntax gradually takes the woman through a reversal of roles which repositions the man as the object of three women's acts – the recipient of the female lover's kiss, a gift given by one goddess, Flora, and the source of a fragrance enjoyed by another, Aurora:

Que celle là recevroit un bon jour,
Qu'elle pourroit se vanter d'un bon tour
Qui baiseroit le plus beau don de Flore,
Le mieus sentant que jamais vid Aurore,
Et y feroit sur ses levres sejour!

What a fine day that woman would enjoy, / How she could brag of a good turn / Who would kiss Flora's fairest gift, / The most fragrant that Aurora ever saw, / And linger there upon his lips!

This is not the exchange of a partial portrait of a woman between men, but the handing on of a desirable man from the goddesses of spring and dawn to a mortal woman – a woman who frankly brags ('se vante') of her triumph. The scene contains something of the public aspect of *blason*-exchange by men: the beloved woman is 'honoured', two female partisans preside over the events leading to the kiss. On the other hand, Irigaray's theory of female erotic pleasure calls attention to the fact that Labé attributes this man's desirability not only to his appearance but to his scent and touch. Labé's allusion to this *odor d'uomo* ('le mieus sentant') reinforces the closeness she imagines in her fantasy of the leisurely kiss she would like to take from the man.

The vocabulary of the sonnet then swerves into the realm of economic exchange: Labé adopts a logic of rights to assert her possession of the elusive man. She has paid the traditional lover's price of suffering, of submitting to the absences and disdain of her 'Star'. Now, through her eloquence and the force of her gaze, she intends to collect what is due her:

C'est à moy seule à qui ce bien est du,
Pour tant de pleurs et tant de tems perdu:
Mais le voyant, tant lui feray de feste,
Tant emploiray de mes yeus le pouvoir,
Pour dessus lui plus de credit avoir,
Qu'en peu de temps feray grande conqueste.

It's to me alone that this good is due, / In exchange for so many tears and so much wasted time: / But seeing him, I would celebrate him so, / I'd use the power of my eyes so much, / To put him further in my debt, / That very soon I'd conquer him completely.

Labé, planning seduction by fair means or foul, declares her confidence in both her words and her look. 'Faire fête à' often means 'to flatter'; she will capture the man with her eloquence. And she describes the effect of her eyes, the 'grande conqueste', by trans-gendering the military metaphors commonly used in Renaissance men's treatment of love as war. In the final line of the woman poet, the female lover as warrior courts and conquers the man.

In contrast to the non-appropriative female eroticism posited by Irigaray, however, Labé's goal is to possess the man once and for all. She uses the word 'crédit' here in a sense very different from the courtly language in which it simply means 'favour'. 'Crédit' carries the same mercantile connotations as did 'créance' (a financial obligation, a literal debt) in the sixteenth century. The definition of the word in Cotgrave's French-English dictionary (1611) ends with two synonyms drawn specifically from the world of banking and commerce:

> Credit: m. Credit; reputation, account, renowne; esteeme in, favour with; ... also, as *Creance*; trust, or credit given; or, a debt entrusted.

This language of debt-collecting, rather than the claim to erotic reward of courtly love poetry, may well be related to Labé's social status as the daughter of a wealthy artisan-merchant, Pierre Charly, and the wife of another ropemaker-chandler, Ennemond Perrin. Educated far above her rank, she played the role assigned by the rising bourgeois fathers of Lyons to certain visibly accomplished women in their families: 'to convert cash into cultural value', as Karine Berriot puts it.[20]

Labé's 'democratising' of literature has been convincingly linked to social change in Lyons by critics whose goal is to articulate the links between socio-economic history and cultural production.[21] Enzo Giudici argues that Labé's merchant city used the French language as it was commonly spoken, in opposition to the Latin reserved for court and professional authorities in Paris, and he proposes that this commitment to the language of the newly rising classes went hand in hand with the growth of feminism in the Renaissance.[22] Berriot discusses at length the interconnection between the elevation of vernacular French and the rise of Lyons' merchant bourgeoisie, arguing that a radically anti-aristocratic political philosophy can be discerned in Labé's prose dialogue *Le Débat de Folie et d'Amour* (Berriot (1985),

p. 165). François Rigolot points out her sense of civic solidarity, which included the women as well as the men of her city (Rigolot, editor (1986), pp. 9–10).

Labé's texts speak for her social group in brief but explicit passages. In her dedicatory epistle, she advises the young noblewoman Clémence de Bourges not to be satisfied with wealth, which she dismisses among the other 'gifts of fortune', but to earn fame and pleasure by working seriously as a writer (p. 42). In her *Débat de Folie et d'Amour* she has Mercury point out the special privileges that aristocrats have built into their own laws, disregarding those of the 'commun' ('common people', p. 86). In her first *Elégie*, Labé insists that women of all classes, whatever their 'hautesse' and 'lignage' ('high rank' and 'ancestry'), are equally at risk of being 'asservies' ('enslaved') by Love (ll. 55–59, 108). Her participation in a bourgeois mentality also helps to account for her unawed treatment of classical myth, as in the off-hand invocation of Flora and Aurora as her assistants early in sonnet 6, and for her literalisation of emotional debt at its conclusion. There, the identity she claims to share with the beloved man breaks down. As long as he is absent, their fusion can only be imagined. Refusing to be a commodity, she insists on keeping accounts.

There is a certain irony, then, in the many *blasons* produced for Labé by the admirers whose twenty-four poems in her praise were published at the end of her *Euvres*. In this 'Hommage', her gaze, which she represents as so bold and effective in sonnet 6, is reduced to a feature to be looked at. Olivier de Magny's sonnet entitled 'Des beautez de D. L. L.', praises, in its second quatrain, 'les rais de cet oeil qui doucement m'enchante' ('the rays from that eye that sweetly enchants me', p. 164). And a bizarre sonnet attributed to Claude de Taillemont focuses on Labé's eyes as they turn upward, half closed (in ecstasy? in prayer? in boredom?), unseeing and therefore all the more alluring:

> Car d'un corps fait au comble de son mieus,
> Du vif mourant contournement des yeus,
> A demi clos tournant le blanc en vuë: . .
> Les regardans en soymesme transmue. (p. 149)

> For from a body brought to its perfection / By the life-in-death movement of her eyes / Half-closed, setting the whites in view, / She transforms the beholders into herself.[23]

Labé herself imagines and does much more than this for her audience. Her insight into the *blason* and her transformation of its capacity to fragment, abstract, and reify the beloved it purports to praise, come into view through the theoretical frame provided by feminist analysis of the psychic defences and will to dominate in men's uses of this form of representation. Her critical clarity toward the *blason* and her erotic expansion of its possibilities in sonnet 6 make available a pleasurable as well as suspicious re-reading of the genre. In Labé's scrutiny and revision of the gaze poem, it can truly be said that her eyes have it.

# Notes

1 N.J. Vickers, 'Diana Described: Scattered Woman and Scattered Rhyme', in *Writing and Sexual Difference*, ed. E. Abel, Chicago, University of Chicago Press, 1982, pp. 95–109; 'This Heraldry in Lucrece's Face', *Poetics Today*, vol. 6, 1985, pp. 171–84. See also, P. Parker, 'Rhetorics of Property: Exploration, Inventory, Blason', in *Literary Fat Ladies: Rhetoric, Gender, Property*, London, Methuen, 1987; P. Fumerton, '"Secret Arts": Elizabethan Miniatures and Sonnets', in *Cultural Aesthetics: Renaissance Literature and the Practice of Social Ornament*, Chicago, University of Chicago Press, 1991, pp. 67–110.

2 L. Irigaray, *Speculum de l'autre femme*, Paris, Minuit, 1974. Trans. as *Speculum of the Other Woman* by Gillian Gill, New York, Columbia University Press, 1985. See also, 'Ce sexe qui n'en est pas un,' in *Ce Sexe qui n'en est pas un*, Paris, Minuit, 1977. ('This Sex which Is Not One' in *This Sex Which Is Not One*, trans. Catherine Porter with Carolyn Burke, Ithaca, Cornell University Press, 1985). The first page number after citations from Irigaray in my text refers to the French edition, the second to the English translation.

3 See R. Dyer, 'Don't Look Now: Richard Dyer examines the instabilities of the male pin-up', *Screen*, vol. 24, 3–4, 1982, pp. 61–73, for an illuminating comparison of the ways contemporary men and women look at each other. He contrasts the feminine 'look' to the masculine 'stare' in ways often relevant to the gazes structuring the Renaissance poems to be analysed here. I am indebted to Nancy Vickers for sending me this article and for her other suggestions about my paper on the *blason* for the English Institute conference at Harvard University in August 1993.

4 Vickers (1982), p. 96.

5 In *Screen*, vol. 16, 1975, pp. 6–18. Reprinted in Mulvey, *Visual and Other Pleasures*, Bloomington, Indiana University Press, 1989, pp. 14–26.

6 A. Saunders, *The Sixteenth-Century Blason Poétique*, Bern, Peter Lang, 1981; F. Charpentier (ed.), *Louise Labé, 'Oeuvres poétiques'; Pernette du Guillet, 'Rymes'*, Paris, Gallimard, 1983.

7 Eustorg de Beaulieu, *La Joue*, in *Blasons anatomiques du corps fémenin*, in F. Charpentier, editor (1983), pp. 141–42.

8 For a brilliant analysis of the uses to which women and women characters are

used to establish 'homosocial' relations, often competitive, among men, see E.K. Sedgwick, *Between Men*, New York, Columbia University Press, 1986. Irigaray uses the term 'hommosexuel' to describe the male/male fixation that defines phallocentric culture. Neither theoretician intends a homophobic attack on men who openly avow sexual attraction for one another. It is the covert, hence more powerful effects of the fixation on men's men as agents and as norm that interest them both.

9 See Vickers (1985), p. 173. See also S. Jed, *Chaste Thinking: The Rape of Lucretia and the Birth of Humanism*, Bloomington, Indiana University Press, 1989.

10 For women as objects of exchange among men, see C. Lévi-Strauss, *The Elementary Structures of Kinship* (1949), reprinted Boston, Beacon Books, 1969, and the influential feminist appropriation of his argument in G. Rubin, 'The Traffic in Women: Notes on the "Political Economy" of Sex', in *Toward an Anthropology of Women*, ed. R. Reiter, New York, Monthly Review Press, 1975, pp. 157–210. For Marx on commodities, see *Capital*, I, chapters 1–3.

11 On causes for increased anxiety about women seeing and being seen in early modern Europe, including the shift onto women of the chastity previously assigned to monks and priests, and Protestant intensifications of requirements for modesty as a result of increased attention to the nuclear family, see R. Kelso, *Doctrine for the Lady of the Renaissance*, Urbana, University of Illinois Press, 1956, p. 25; E. Berriot-Salvadore, *Les femmes dans la sociéte française de la Renaissance*, Geneva, Droz, 1990, pp. 45–116.

12 For a study of 'the aggressive eye topos' in classical and Renaissance love theory and poetry, including commentary enabling comparison between men and women poets, see L.K. Donaldson-Evans, *Love's Fatal Glance: A Study of Eye Imagery in the Poets of the 'Ecole Lyonnaise'*, University of Mississippi, Romance Monographs no. 39, 1980. He argues that in Labé's sonnet 6 the final six lines transform the idealised image of the beloved man through 'the Lover's eyeplay, which is dynamic, aggressive and self-serving' (p. 70).

13 In an interesting early history of powers attributed to the eyes, which helps to explain the contradiction between Renaissance idealisation and suspicion of the gaze, Ruth Cline summarises Old Testament views as follows: 'The eye is an evil influence; except for the eye, the heart would follow right principles. The eye is attracted by beauty and the vanity of worldly things' ('Heart and Eyes', *Romance Philology*, vol. 25, 1931–32, pp. 263–97; p. 272).

14 *Beautifier* is my perhaps awkward translation of 'Attiffet', which Huguet defines neutrally as 'ornement, parure' but then cites a passage linking such embellishment to courtisans (E. Huguet, *Dictionnaire de la langue française du seizième siècle*, 7 vols, Paris, Champion, 1925–67). Cotgrave also includes a pejorative synonym in his definition: 'Attires, or tires, dressings, trickings' (*A Dictionarie of the French and English Tongues*, London, 1611. Reprinted Columbia, University of Southern Carolina Press, 1950 and 1968). The modern connotation given by Larousse is also more negative than that of the word as Tayssonnière uses it: 'Attifer: Fam. et péj. Habiller, parer avec mauvais goût ou d'une manière un peu ridicule'. Tayssonnière's text was reprinted in Turin, J. Gray et Fils, 1871.

15 *Les Rithmes et Poesies de Gentile, et Vertueuse Dame Pernette du Guillet Lyonnoise*, Lyons, Antoine du Moulin, 1545. See also, *Les Rymes*, ed. Victor Graham, Geneva, Droz, 1968. My quotations are from Graham's edition.

16 J. Boney, '"Ardeur de veoir": Reading Knowledge in Pernette du Guillet's *Rymes*', *L'Esprit créateur*, vol. 30, 4, 1990, pp. 49–60; p. 59.

17 I quote from the edition by Anne Larsen, Geneva, Droz, 1993.

18 N. Ruwet, 'L'analyse structurale de la poésie' and 'Un Sonnet de Louise Labé', in *Langage, Musique, Poésie*, Paris, Seuil, 1972, pp. 151–75, 176–199; p. 178; Charpentier (editor, 1983), p. 29; F. Rigolot (editor), *Louise Labé: Oeuvres complètes*, Paris, Garnier/Flammarion, 1986, p. 23. References to the work of Labé are to Rigolot's edition.

19 A. Chan, 'The Function of the Beloved in the Poetry of Louise Labé', *Australian Journal of French Studies*, vol. 17, 1, 1980, pp. 46–57; p. 49.

20 K. Berriot, *Louise Labé, La Belle Rebelle et le François nouveau*, Paris, Editions du Seuil, 1985, p. 167.

21 For a brief account of Marxist literary theory, see T. Eagleton, *Marxism and Literary Criticism*, London, Methuen, 1976, especially his account of Pierre Macherey. For marxist-feminist theory, see C. Kaplan, 'Pandora's Box: Subjectivity and Sexuality in Socialist Feminist Criticism', in *Sea Changes: Culture and Feminism*, London, Verso, 1986. On historical links between social orders and love theory, see G. Duby, *The Chivalrous Society*, trans. Cynthia Postan, London, Arnold, 1977. On connections between social conflict and ideologies of gender in Renaissance France, see N.Z. Davis, 'City Women and Religious Change' and 'Women on Top' in *Society and Culture in Early Modern France*, Stanford, Stanford University Press, 1975.

22 E. Giudici, *Louise Labé: Essai*, Paris, Nizet, 1981, p. 14.

23 The gratification of the male gaze by the beauty of a woman who does not look back persists in modern illustrations of Labé's life and poems. A marble bust from Lyons' Musée des Beaux Arts represents a woman in the pose described by Taillemont, head tipped sideways and eyes almost closed. A photo of this unseeing figure is reproduced on the cover of two recent books: François Pedron's fictionalised biography, *Louise Labé, la femme d'amour*, Paris, Fayard, 1984, and François Rigolot's otherwise admirable edition (1986).

# CHAPTER 4

# Louise Labé's
# Feminist Poetics

*Carla Freccero*

Louise Labé is perhaps the most famous female poet of the French Renaissance, although there is relatively little of her work extant: a collection, published in 1555, of 24 sonnets preceded by a dedicatory epistle to Clémence de Bourges, a prose dialogue called *Le Débat de Folie et d'Amour* (*The Debate between Folly and Love*), and three elegies. In addition, there exist numerous poems dedicated to her or written about her, in both praise and blame. She belongs to the great wave of poetic innovation in sixteenth-century France, represented most illustriously by the group of poets known as La Pléiade, which included the poet Pierre de Ronsard and the author of *La Deffence et Illustration de la Langue Francoyse* (*The Defence and Illustration of the French Language*), Joachim du Bellay's manifesto of a new French Renaissance poetics.

These poets – and Labé herself – combined the two Italian Renaissance philosophical and poetic traditions known as Neoplatonism and Petrarchism. Neoplatonism came to France via Marsilio Ficino's translations of Plato's dialogues, which both heterosexualised platonic love and transformed it into a potentially Christian poetics. Thus, Neoplatonism enabled poets to reconcile the erotic and the spiritual on a philosophical level, while it also provided a schema for a poetic practice combining erotics, aesthetics and morality: by loving, humans climb a ladder of affect from the human and the physical toward the transcendent ideals of the Good and the Beautiful. Neoplatonism thus would also enable poets such as Louise Labé to praise erotic passion and argue that the love of a human object was capable of ennobling and refining the human spirit rather than corrupting and degrading it, as the traditional Church would claim. Finally,

Neoplatonism served as a philosophical ruse for a poetic practice that was manifestly idolatrous, as the legacy of Petrarchism amply demonstrates.

Francesco Petrarca's (1304–1374) sonnet cycle, *Rime sparse* (*Scattered Rhymes*), became the paradigm for the sonnet sequence for generations – and indeed centuries – to come. Petrarch's sonnet sequence (or *canzoniere*) constructs a fictional narrative of unreciprocated love for a woman, Laura, and chronicles his sightings of her and the various emotions, thoughts, and moods his love for her occasions in him, until finally he renounces her and turns his love heavenward. Petrarchism thus provided a model combining the atemporality of the love lyric (which focuses primarily on the present moment and does not, strictly speaking, tell a story) with narrative development. The codified conceits of the lover's state of mind and being, clichés of secular love in modern times, are also legacies of Petrarchism. The classic oxymoron is a typical example – 'I freeze and I burn', hyperbolically demonstrated in Louise Labé's sonnet 8 ('Je vis, je meurs: je me brule et me noye'; 'I live, I die: I burn and I drown'). Finally, Petrarch's work makes clear the way in which the beloved object is a pretext for the poet, the figure or symbol of his (or her) stylistic virtuosity; Laura, the name of Petrarch's beloved, is also the *lauro* or laurel, symbol of poetic achievement. Thus we see in the work of the Pléiade that Ronsard unabashedly creates sonnet cycles to not one, but at least three different women, ostentatiously alluding to the incidental or pretextual nature of the identity of the beloved, using the name to mark shifts in stylistic phases of his poetic production. Indeed, Louise Labé does not even name her beloved, thus finally erasing altogether the referential relevance of the object.

What the French Renaissance inherited from Petrarchism was thus a set of formal and thematic guidelines: the Italian sonnet form (an octave, consisting of two stanzas of four lines each, and a sestet, consisting of two stanzas of three lines each, with varying rhyme schemes: *abba*, *abba*, then *ccd*, *eed*; or *cdc*, *cdd*; or *ccd*, *ede*, etc.); the requirement to tell a story; a codified relation of unreciprocated courtly love, whereby the lover desires the lady whom he – pronoun intended – idolises and from whom he receives no satisfaction; a codified pathology of the lover's condition; and a set of poetic conceits, such as the oxymoron mentioned above and the deployment of classical mythology.

Of course, as with any great model, the French poets responded to

Petrarch's *canzoniere* by imitating, parodying, transforming, and also rejecting the form and the content depicted there. In a famous and humorous passage from Ronsard's 'Elégie à son livre' (1556) ('Elegy to his Book'), the poet declares, concerning the Petrarchan requirement to love only one lady and to love her devotedly without receiving any favours in return:

> Réponds-lui je te pri', que Pétrarque sur moi
> N'avait autorité de me donner sa loi,
> Ni à ceux qui viendraient après lui, pour les faire
> Si longtemps amoureux sans leur lien défaire.
> Lui-même ne fut tel, car à voir son écrit,
> Il était éveillé d'un trop gentil esprit
> Pour être sot trente ans, abusant sa jeunesse
> Et sa Muse au giron d'une vieille maîtresse:
> Ou bien il jouissait de sa Laurette, ou bien
> Il était un grand fat d'aimer sans avoir rien.[1]

> Reply to him, please, that Petrarch / Did not have the authority to give me his law, / Nor to those who would come after him, to make them / Love for so long without undoing their ties. / He himself was not like that, for, judging by his writings / He was gifted with too refined a spirit / To have been foolish for thirty years, abusing his youth / And his Muse in the lap of an old mistress: / Either he enjoyed his Laurette, or else / He was a fool to love without getting anything in return.

It is in the context of this simultaneous imitation of, and irreverence toward, the great Italian models that Louise Labé's work will evolve.

Louise Labé (1516/23–1566) has received recent critical attention in part because feminist literary criticism has sought to rediscover women writers of the past and to 'recover' them from critical judgements made through a lens of male chauvinism, sexism, or downright misogyny. Indeed, in her own day she was often vilified as a whore, most famously perhaps by Calvin, who called her a 'plebeia meretrix' ('a common whore').[2] As feminist critics and historians have pointed out, philosophical, medical, legal, educational, and religious traditions combined to shape an ideology that demanded silence, obedience, chastity, modesty, and subservience from women of most classes, but particularly of the upper classes, since many proletarian and peasant women were required to exercise greater agency in cooperation with men to ensure basic survival. As the historian Joan Kelly first remarked, the Renaissance was not an especially progressive time for women.[3] Many aristocratic women, however, benefited from a certain leniency regarding these strictures, as long as they acted within certain specified constraints. Women of the royal line in France, for example, received an extensive education and could write; thus most female writers during the Renaissance were from the noble classes.

Louise Labé was not an aristocrat however; she was a member of the bourgeoisie, the daughter and wife of ropemakers. Her father, who died wealthy, was illiterate, but provided his daughter with the education – formerly reserved for aristocrats – that enabled Louise Labé to become the cultivated intellectual that she was.[4] Indeed, one benefit of the economic transitions in early modernity that gave rise to capitalism and to a growing middle class was that class competition between the nobility and the bourgeoisie promoted literacy and female education. Labé herself makes the argument that it is now possible for women to apply themselves in the domain of learning and encourages other women to do so as well:

> Estant le tems venu, Mademoiselle, que les severes loix des hommes n'empeschent plus les femmes de s'apliquer aus sciences et disciplines: il me semble que celles qui ont la commodité, doivent employer cette honneste liberté que notre sexe ha autre fois tant desiree, à icelles aprendre: et montrer aus hommes le tort qu'ils nous faisoient en nous privant du bien et de l'honneur qui nous en pouvoit venir ... ('Epître dédicatoire', p. 41).

> Since the time has come, Mademoiselle, that the severe laws of men no longer prevent women from applying themselves to the sciences and disciplines, it seems to me that those who can do so must use the noble liberty that our sex so desired in former times, to learn them: and show men the wrong they do us in denying us the benefit and the honour that might accrue to us from these things.

Although one might argue that Labé's words here are somewhat optimistic and that female emancipation was to wait another three hundred or so years, it is nevertheless significant that a lively feminist consciousness makes itself known in her writings, which include a sense of women's collective condition rather than an argument about the exceptionality of the few. Indeed, as Ann Jones and others have argued, Lyon, an active urban centre of trade in sixteenth-century France, fostered a sense of civic identity (Labé often refers to herself and her female addressees as 'dames Lionnoises'; 'women of Lyon'), so that not only were class boundaries (between aristocrat and bourgeois) more fluid, but also gender hierarchies were somewhat mitigated by this sense of civic belonging.[5]

What feminism in general and feminist literary criticism in particular have allowed scholars to understand about the work of Louise Labé is its consciousness of gender as well as class, and its connection to a literary tradition that includes other women writers as well as the debates concerning women and their abilities. These debates in France were known as the *querelle des femmes*, and included as one of their main participants the first European professional female writer and a forerunner of modern feminism, Christine de Pisan (c. 1364–c. 1431). Christine made her living from writing after the death of her husband and dedicated much of her work to counteracting the misogyny of her male intellectual contemporaries and literary antecedents, Boccaccio in particular. Giovanni Boccaccio had written a work in Latin entitled *De claris mulieribus* (*Concerning Famous Women*), in which he catalogued famous women from myth, legend, and history. In the guise of praising their heroic public accomplishments, Boccaccio often painted portraits of female moral – and particularly sexual – depravity, acknowledging that, indeed, women were powerful, but in monstrous ways. Christine wrote a sort of rebuttal to this text, entitled *Le Livre de la cité des dames* (*The Book of the City of Ladies*), in which she undertook to correct the errors Boccaccio and others committed by vilifying history's illustrious women. A century later, both Louise Labé and another French Renaissance female writer, Marguerite de Navarre, also dedicated themselves to setting the record straight with regard to the accomplishments and the reputations of other, prior, famous women. In her dedicatory epistle and her elegies, Labé makes clear to her readers that she writes in part in order to prove that women are capable of the worthy accomplishments of learning for which so many men are known.

What is even more radical about Louise, however, is that her work centres dangerously upon the one area of affect – female erotic desire – most proscribed by the teachings and customs of her day. Here too, feminist criticism enables the critic to focus upon the difference that gender makes, a difference especially relevant for secular lyric love poetry. On the one hand, a female love poet must overcome the strictures imposed by an ideology that dictates that women should be silent and chaste, that they should have or express no sexual desire in order to be considered 'good' women; otherwise they are whores, as Calvin's above-mentioned remark demonstrates. On the other hand, the female love poet must overcome or transform an entire tradition of courtly love and lyric poetry that specifies a male lover/poet who speaks and a female beloved who constitutes the object of the poet's gaze, his meditation, and who is the vehicle – like a muse – of his fame. Thus a doublebind of sorts is created: as the subject of desire, the poet takes on the attributes of masculinity. As object of desire, though, a woman cannot speak at all. In the tradition – and usually within the social order itself – a woman risked either the charge of usurping masculinity in order to act, or she risked being accused of loose morals for exposing herself as object of desire in the public arena. What happens then, when the poet Labé speaks, and when she speaks about her erotic desire? And what happens when she enters a tradition and transforms that speaking subject from a masculine one into a feminine one? What are the strategies she uses to protect herself from slander, on the one hand, and to wrest the genre from its entrenchment in fixed gender roles, on the other, in order to make the genre her own? In a sense Louise Labé's poetry puts into practice the 'gender trouble' that inhabits identity, subjectivity and agency, so eloquently described by Judith Butler.[6]

The opening elegies provide the reader with some of the clearest arguments Labé adopts that then in turn shape a reading of her sonnets, which illustrate the various techniques she uses to speak in her own voice and to deal with the problem of the gendered roles of subject and object of love. In the elegies, she paints a portrait of herself as poet and clearly articulates her consciousness of the difficulties she encounters by being so bold as to speak publicly about her desire. Furthermore, the first and third elegies, as well as sonnet 24, the last in the collection, directly address other women, the 'dames Lionnoises', and thus create a sense of female community in relation to the project of overcoming the obstacles that Louise – and the women of her day – encounter.

As François Rigolot points out, Clément Marot, a sixteenth-century lyric poet, is responsible for the introduction of the elegy as a poetic form in France. Thomas Sebillet, author of another manifesto of poetic practice, the *Art poetique françois* (*French Poetic Art*) (1548), argues that an elegy is an epistle, or versified letter, that deals with love and desire, that chronicles the pleasures and sorrows of the lover's experience with the object of love, but does so simply and without excessive ornament. It is written in decasyllables of alternating masculine and feminine rhyming couplets (Rigolot, p. 15). Louise and her contemporaries used the Latin poet Ovid's *Heroides* as their model, a collection of fictional love letters written by abandoned women of legend and myth, lamenting their condition. Thus already there is a tradition of a sort of poetic letter-writing, specifically aimed at an addressee, that features women's speaking voices. In Louise's case, we might ask what difference does it make when the voice that speaks is a woman's, rather than that of a man posing as one?

> Au tems qu'Amour, d'hommes et Dieus vainqueur,
> Faisoit bruler de sa flamme mon coeur,
> En embrasant de sa cruelle rage
> Mon sang, mes os, mon esprit et courage:
> Encore lors je n'avois la puissance
> De lamenter ma peine et ma souffrance.
> Encor Phebus, amis des Lauriers vers,
> N'avoit permis que je fisse des vers:
> Mais maintenant que sa fureur divine
> Remplit d'ardeur ma hardie poitrine,
> Chanter me fait ... (I, ll. 1-11).

> In that time when Love, conqueror of men and Gods, / Made my heart burn with his flames, / Embracing with his cruel madness / My blood, my bones, my mind and my will: / Still then I did not have the power / To lament my pain and my suffering. / Phebus, friend of the green Laurels / Had not yet permitted me to write verses: / But now that his divine madness / Has filled my intrepid breast with ardour, / He makes me sing ....

The first ten lines of Elegy I describe how, when the poet was first smitten by love, she was incapable of writing about it; the reference in line 7 to the Greek God Phoebus Apollo, whose emblem is the laurel, signals the primary importance to Labé of poetic fame in her endeavour to write about love. The 'fureur divine' or 'divine madness' that animates her to write belongs to neoplatonic theory and refers to one of the kinds of inspiration that can kindle creativity in mortals. Here, in this introduction to her work, she lets the reader know that she is not an epic poet, where the subject matter is war ('... non les bruians tonnerres / De Jupiter, ou les cruelles guerres, / Dont trouble Mars, quand il veut, l'Univers'; '... not the loud thunder / Of Jupiter, nor the cruel wars / With which Mars troubles the Universe when he wishes', ll. 11–13). Instead, in lines 14 and 15 Louise Labé connects her project to that of the recently discovered Sappho, the Greek poetess from Lesbos most famous to us for her lesbian love poems (Rigolot, p. 20). This genealogical connection to a newly recovered female poet reinforces Louise's feminism in some surprising ways: she will not be talking about a female object of desire, but by linking her project to Sappho's, she asserts the female poet's right to speak of desire, that dangerous territory for women, while the mention of another female poet puts female poetic achievement at the centre of the reader's attention.

Labé writes about her love as being in the past, according to a long tradition of 'emotion recollected in tranquillity', to use Wordsworth's description of proper poetic art. In doing so, she sets the stage for her sonnet cycle as a narrative account of a past experience and thus an experience with a temporal dimension to it. She also harks back to Petrarch's references to his own love lyrics as follies of his youth, thus potentially defending herself against charges of present foolishness. And yet she makes continual reference to the ways in which the memory re-evokes for her the pain of the past in order to demonstrate the power of such love, an argument she will use to gain sympathy from the 'ladies' whom she fears will judge her harshly. Thus, unlike Petrarch, Labé does not repudiate love's power or its product, lyric poetry; rather she affirms the status of love as a sufficiently dignified subject to produce poetic power.

Lines 25–43 ironically and humorously invoke her predicament as a female lover who has also been a beloved, an object of love for other lovers:

> C'estoit mes yeus, dont tant faisois saillir
> De traits, à ceus qui trop me regardoient
> Et de mon arc assez ne se gardoient.
> Mais ces miens traits ces miens yeus me defirent,
> Et de vengeance estre exemple me firent.

> It was my eyes, from which I made gush forth / Many arrows toward those who watched me too much / And did not guard themselves enough from my bow. / But those same shafts of mine undid my own eyes, / And made of me an example of revenge (ll. 28–32).

The usual metaphoric sequence of events is as follows: Cupid, the god of Love, shoots arrows that emanate from the eyes of the beloved (in Neoplatonic language these are described as sparks) into the heart of the lover. The lover is pierced by these arrows – smitten, as we say – and falls ill with love. In these lines Labé describes how she was accustomed to causing others to fall in love with her, so much so that she was taken by surprise when, as if in revenge for the sighing and weeping she caused, those very same arrows pierced her own heart and made her fall in love. The poet thus acknowledges her gender and the unusual position she is about to occupy as the poet/lover rather than the object of love. At the same time, these lines boast about her desirability; she advertises herself as a woman who inspires love. References such as these, to herself as a desirable object, may have promoted the scandalous reputation Labé acquired, for the most familiar context for sexual self-advertisement was of course prostitution, and many of the other famous female lyric love poets of Labé's day, notably the Venetian poets Tullia d'Aragona and Veronica Franco, were also courtesans, or high-class prostitutes, and thus advertised both their poetic and erotic power in their verses.[7]

In line 43, Labé addresses her female readers, this time begging their indulgence and advertising her poetic skills by offering to write of their love laments when the time comes for them to fall in love:

> ... Dames, qui les lirez,
> De mes regrets avec moy soupirez.
> Possible, un jour je feray le semblable,
> Et ayderay votre voix pitoyable
> A vos travaus et peines raconter.

> Ladies who will read them [these verses] / Sigh with me over my regrets. / One day it is possible that I will do likewise, / And I will help your pitiable voices / Recount your labours and your woes (ll. 43–47).

While it is traditional, at least since Dante's *Vita nuova*, to address ladies in sonnet cycles, in part to signal that love is the subject matter and that the vernacular, or mother-tongue, is the language being used rather than Latin (because women generally did not know Latin and because Latin was considered the language in which to write 'serious' literature), Labé does not assume that they will listen with a sympathetic ear; rather she tries to persuade them to be on her side. Throughout her work, it is clear that Labé fears censure on the part of other women, the 'moral enforcers' of the community, and thus focuses her argument in self-defence on them. Thus she illustrates, in her work, a common dilemma faced by feminism and by any subversive practice in its confrontation with hegemonic structures: that the oppressed often collude in the enforcement of their own oppression. Labé's response to this dilemma is, at times, ambivalent, in that she will wish harm upon the Ladies who judge her. But here, she invokes a community of interests and adopts the rhetoric of persuasion. Furthermore, in offering to write for them, Louise does something completely different: she establishes her solidarity with women's predicament and advertises her skills as a poet for women.

Arguing that anyone, and especially those most unwilling to be moved, can be conquered by love, Labé presents the example of queen Semiramis. Notorious for having succumbed to incest and vilified by Boccaccio and others, Semiramis is here represented as a competent military ruler and governor, a virago or a woman with a 'coeur viril' (l. 84, 'virile heart'), like those women praised by Jacob Burckhardt (one of the nineteenth-century inventors of the term Renaissance) as the equals of men in his *Civilization of the Renaissance in Italy*.[8] Indeed, 'virile' was the only way of referring to women who exercised power in domains not considered feminine by the customs of the day. Labé's point in describing Semiramis is not to accuse her of unnatural appetites, but to illustrate how even the most 'manly' of women, engaged in enterprises such as war, which are considered to be the opposite of love, could capitulate to Cupid's arrows:

> Semiramis, Royne tant renommee
> ...
> Trouva Amour, qui si fort la pressa,
> Qu'armes et loix veincue elle laissa.
> Ne meritoit sa Royalle grandeur
> Au moins avoir un moins fascheus malheur
> Qu'aymer son fils?

> Semiramis, most renowned queen / ... / Found Love, who constrained her so much / That, conquered, she gave up both arms and laws. / Did not her royal grandeur merit / At least a less grevious misfortune / Than to love her son? (ll. 61, 69–73).

Thus, while seeming to present her as a negative example, Labé in fact rehabilitates Semiramis as a brave and successful ruler who is tragically brought down by love. At the same time, by identifying with Semiramis, Labé also takes on the properties of the virile woman.

Labé concludes the first elegy by deploying a familiar *topos* of the love lyric, the *carpe diem*, most cruelly evoked in Ronsard's poem, 'Quand vous serez bien vieille' ('When you are very old'; 1578). This theme normally sets up a contrast between youth and age and warns the woman not to scorn love now while she is young lest she fall in love when she is old and ugly. In Ronsard's poem, being old and alone is punishment enough, but Louise's point is a different one: the woman will get what is coming to her. Just as she refused love when she was young, so the one she loves will flee from her when she is old. Here she threatens the 'Dames' she addresses in lines 43–54, by painting a portrait of a pathetic old woman who falls in love; there is considerable aggression in the lines that describe the woman vainly attempting to make herself beautiful with cosmetics (ll. 99–106). But finally Labé, unlike her masculine counterpart whose defensive counterattack is designed to coerce the lady into submitting to his wishes, deflects that aggression by offering a general conclusion about love: 'Ainsi Amour prend son plaisir, à faire / Que le veuil d'un soit à l'autre contraire' ('And so Love takes pleasure in making it / So that the wish of one is contrary to the desire of the other'; ll. 113–14), thus ceasing to blame the woman for her youthful recalcitrance and suggesting that it is Love, and not the lady, who is the fickle one.

The third elegy presents an even more forceful justification of Labé's poetic project and demonstrates just how extensively she transforms the masculine love lyric tradition with a self-consciousness about the difference that gender makes in that tradition. She opens the elegy with an even stronger echo of the address to the ladies – 'Dames Lionnoises' – that Dante, Boccaccio, and others use; she also again invokes the Petrarchan *topos* of youthful folly: 'Ne veuillez pas condamner ma simplesse, / Et jeune erreur de ma fole jeunesse' ('Do not wish to condemn my artlessness, / And the youthful error of my foolish youth'; ll. 5–6). As I mentioned before, the address to the ladies often signals the lowliness of the genre, its lack of serious content: the work is written in the vernacular rather than Latin and it treats of love rather than the great epic themes of war and heroism. Meanwhile, in the pens of men, the address to the ladies is also a seductive gesture; the poet suggests that he will move the ladies with his talk of love. Labé creates an entirely different context with her address. First she appeals to civic solidarity and class commonality by referring to the ladies as women of Lyon; thus she produces a virtual solidarity between herself and other women. Second she asks them to pardon the folly of her youth, but immediately undermines the declaration by saying 'Si c'est erreur' ('If it *is* folly'; l. 7), once again embarking on a project to ennoble her poetic enterprise. Indeed, in what follows, she compares her 'error' to a catalogue of far greater sins to point out the foolishness of treating love as a crime.

The 'autobiographical' section of the poem that describes her youth and the origins of her downfall (before the *innamoramento*, or the 'falling in love') paints a portrait of a young amazon of sorts, extending the comparison between herself and Semiramis (Elegy I), but in a more Renaissance vein, in that her childhood included sewing and studying as well as 'military' exercises, exemplifying the Humanist injunction to develop both the body and the mind:

Lors qu'exerçoi mon corps et mon esprit
...
Pour bien savoir avec l'esguille peindre
J'eusse entrepris la renommee esteindre

De celle là, qui plus docte que sage,
Avec Pallas comparoit son ouvrage.
Qui m'ust vù lors en armes fiere aller,
Porter la lance et bois faire voler,
...
Pour Bradamante, ou la haute Marphise,
Seur de Roger, il m'ust, possible, prise.

Then I would exercise both body and mind / ... / To learn well how to paint
with a needle / I would have tried to outdo the fame / Of that one, more
learned than wise, / Who compared her work to that of Pallas. / Whosoever
would have seen me then in proud armour / Carrying the lance and hurling the
spear, / ... / For Bradamante or the proud Marphise, / The sister of Roger, he
would possibly have mistaken me (ll. 30–42).

In this mythical self-portrait, Labé portrays herself as a young, stu-
dious, and athletic woman, 'Mon coeur n'aymant que Mars et le
savoir' ('My heart loving only Mars [war] and knowledge'; l. 44),
whose 'virility' is undone by love. In order to convey love's power, in
other words, Labé masculinises herself, while describing the self-
estrangement brought on by love (see Elegy I) as an effeminisation.
Here then she plays with the codes of masculine self-representation to
lend her speaking voice poetic authority and to distance herself from
the cliché that women are weak and prone to lovesickness anyway.
What is striking is that even in this portrait of her youth, Louise adds
a detail stressing her artistic skill: she compares her needlework to
that of Ovid's Arachne, whose tapestries rivalled the workmanship of
the goddess Athena and who was punished for this by being turned
into a spider. This moment in Labé's poem constitutes what Nancy
Miller has identified as the 'feminine signature' in literature by
women, or 'the embodiment in writing of a gendered subjectivity':
using a metaphor of writing 'proper' to the feminine (needlework),
Labé suggests that she was always a writer and links her endeavour to
that of other female figures whose skills of representation are
practised at the cost of a certain violence to themselves.[9] She also
compares herself to the heroine-warriors of the *Orlando furioso*,
Ariosto's Renaissance romance poem, and thus immediately fiction-
alises and renders 'literary' this autobiographical portrait. Thus,
unlike Semiramis, who is tragically defeated by love, Labé suggests
that she was always a writer, that she will triumph through representation, and that love and its object are secondary to her project of
representation.
    The second half of the poem is a meditation on the effects of time

on love. In a prosopopeia, where a name takes on the properties of a person and speaks, Love challenges the poet, promising that she will fall to his powers (ll. 47–58). Labé then describes how Love overcame her when she was sixteen and how, thirteen years later, she is still in that condition (ll. 59–76). Time, she argues, conquers everything, and puts an end to great monuments; to people great and small, and even to love (ll. 77–88). But the examples of love present two cases of men notorious for their infidelity: Paris, who left his lover for Helen, and Jason, who abandoned Medea. These images thus serve to condemn masculine infidelity rather than confirm the ephemerality of love. Furthermore, they may contain a threat; Medea, it will be remembered, exacted revenge on Jason for his betrayal by killing his children and serving them to him to eat. And although Medea is primarily remembered as a monstrous and mad woman, Labé once again 'rehabilitates' a historically maligned woman by stressing not her act of revenge, but the betrayal that occasioned it, calling Medea and Oenone women who 'meritoient … estre estimees, / Et pour aymer leurs Amis, estre aymees' ('merited esteem, / And for having loved their lovers, [merited] being loved in return'; ll. 89–90).

The examples of Oenone and Medea lead Labé to argue with Love (still personified) and finally pray to him that if she is to be condemned to love until her death, then may he also produce the same passion in the one she loves. Thus rather than simply arguing for a cure, or resignedly accepting her fate, Labé, departing from the tradition that precedes her, argues for a mutually reciprocated love, a commingling of subject and object. Ronsard will do this as well, but whereas Ronsard addresses his beloved directly or describes their mutually reciprocated passionate love, Labé distances herself from the object, addressing the god of Love instead. The images she uses to describe that other – for he is never named – suggest something more sinister: 'Fay que celui que j'estime mon tout, / … / Sente en ses os, en son sang, en son ame, / Ou plus ardente, ou bien egale flame' ('Make it so that he whom I esteem with my all, / … / Feels in his bones, in his blood, in his soul, / Either a more ardent, or else at least an equal flame', ll. 98–102). Bones, blood, soul; these elements of the beloved suggest nothing so much as death. While the tradition of the love lyric includes the *blason*, or celebratory description of the beloved, a description that, as Nancy Vickers has pointed out, consists in a dismemberment of the body of the lady through a catalogue of her parts (hair, eyes, nipples, neck), here not even the body remains, but only the essences: solid, liquid, and spiritual.[10] This is what is left of the beloved when the body is no longer. It may be that, lacking a tradition for producing a *blason* of the male body, the poet resorts to an abstraction; on the other hand, the absence of a name and Labé's own insistence on the primacy of her poetic art suggest yet again that the beloved is a mere pretext, a cipher rather than a person, a collection of essences that contribute to the poet's artistic self-expression. In addition, the use of these particular elements to convey the pretextual sign of the beloved is not merely solipsistic, a reflection of the poet's narcissistic investment, but also deeply aggressive, a death-wish of sorts that 'murders' the beloved (one is reminded of Medea's revenge) as well as immortalises him.

In these readings I have tried to show how a feminist perspective, informed by historical context and literary history, sheds specific light on the poetry of Louise Labé, herself part of the genealogy of feminist literature and of a women's literary tradition. While in Louise's day, women writers of both prose and poetry faced public censure for the expression of passions other than religious, and especially for expressions of their erotic desire, centuries later female writers were praised for directness, immediacy, and unmediated authenticity or sincerity in their passionate expression of love, especially when that writing treated the thematics of abandonment.[11] In other words, one way in which traditional criticism has demonstrated its gender bias is to deny to women writers the same self-conscious linguistic and literary mastery in their work as is assumed to be the mark of a great male artist, particularly when the subject matter involves love. A critical appraisal of Louise Labé from the turn of the century might serve as a typical example:

> Elle aima passionément, voilà tout ce que nous pouvons dire; et c'était la première fois qu'en notre langue la passion s'exprimait en se déchaînant avec cette véhémence et cette naïveté.[12]

> She loved passionately, that is all that we can say; and it was the first time that, in our language, passion was expressed with such unrestrained vehemence and naïvety.

What feminist criticism has permitted us to do then is to evaluate Louise Labé's poetry as the artistic production of a woman who was very aware of her anomalous position *vis-à-vis* the tradition of lyric love poetry and the customs of her day. It has also permitted us to see her as a thoroughly learned and self-conscious poet whose irony, detachment, and skilful use of intertextuality to connect her project to literary, mythic, and historical figures and events of the past, make of her work an even more astonishing lyrical achievement, in that she succeeded in conveying an impression of unmediated and naive passionate expression.

# Notes

1 Pierre de Ronsard, *Les Amours*, ed. F. Joukovsky, Paris, Gallimard, 1974, pp. 157–63; p. 158. All translations are my own, unless otherwise indicated.

2 Louise Labé, *Oeuvres complètes*, ed. F. Rigolot, Paris, Garnier-Flammarion, 1986, p. 272. All citations of Labé's work are from this edition; translations, unless otherwise noted, are my own.

3 J. Kelly, 'Did Women Have a Renaissance?' in *Women, History, and Theory: The Essays of Joan Kelly*, Chicago and London, University of Chicago Press, 1984, pp. 19–50. See also Freccero, 'Gender Ideologies, Women Writers, and the Problem of Patronage in Early Modern Italy and France: Issues and Frameworks', in *Reading the Renaissance: Culture, Poetics, and Drama*, ed. J. Hart, New York and London, Garland Publishing, 1996, pp. 65–74.

4 A.R. Jones, *The Currency of Eros: Women's Love Lyric in Europe, 1540–1620*, Bloomington and Indianapolis, Indiana University Press, 1990, p. 156. My essay owes much to Ann Jones' work on female poetic practice in the Renaissance.

5 See Jones (1990), pp. 155–60, and N.Z. Davis, *Society and Culture in Early Modern France*, Stanford, Stanford University Press, 1965, repr. 1975.

6 *Gender Trouble: Feminism and the Subversion of Identity*, New York and London, Routledge, 1990, especially pp. 1–35.

7 See Jones (1990) for a study of some of the Venetian women poets; also M.F. Rosenthal, *The Honest Courtesan: Veronica Franco, Citizen and Writer in Sixteenth-Century Venice*, Chicago and London, University of Chicago Press, 1992. See also Freccero, 'Gender Ideologies'.

8 See J. Burckhardt, *The Civilization of the Renaissance in Italy*, New York, Harper & Row, 1958, Vol. II, 'The Position of Women': 'To understand the higher forms of social intercourse at this period we must keep before our minds the fact that women stood on a footing of perfect equality with men. ... The highest praise which could then be given to the great Italian women was that they had the mind and courage of men' (pp. 389, 391).

9 N.K. Miller, 'Arachnologies: The Woman, The Text, and the Critic', in *The Poetics of Gender*, ed. N.K. Miller, New York, Columbia University Press, 1986, pp. 270–95; p. 272.

10 N.J. Vickers, 'Diana Described: Scattered Woman and Scattered Rhyme', in *Writing and Sexual Difference*, ed. E. Abel, Chicago, University of Chicago Press, 1982, pp. 95–109.

11 For an interesting exploration of this phenomenon as it applies to the epistolary tradition from the seventeenth century onward in France, see K.A. Jensen, *Writing Love: Letters, Women, and the Novel in France, 1605–1776*, Carbondale and Edwardsville, Southern Illinois University Press, 1995.

12 F. Brunetière, 'La Pléiade française et l'école lyonnaise', in *Revue des Deux Mondes*, December 15, 1900. Cited in Rigolot (1986), p. 252.

# CHAPTER 5

# Reading and Writing in the Tenth Story of the *Heptaméron*

*Floyd Gray*

In privileging the concepts of *écriture* and *lecture*, contemporary theorists have diverted attention from the author as source and the work as object, focusing it instead on writing as a version of the speech act and reading as a subjective activity. When the meaning of a work is seen as the reader's distinctive experience of it, the authority of the author and work is subverted and assumed by the reader. Reading and writing are viewed in this perspective as correlative phenomena, the one participating in the fulfilment and determinacy of the other.

A similar complicity between reader and work seems to obtain in the *Heptaméron*. From the beginning, Marguerite de Navarre abdicates her status as author, first of all through explicit anonymity, inasmuch as the work was originally published without her name, then by displacement, in relinquishing the role of narrator and commentator to others. Not only do the *devisants* narrate the stories, they interpret them as well, reading them according to their own perceptions and prejudices.

The immediate effect of Marguerite's absence from the text is to defer meaning in a play of differences. But this effect, contrary to modern expectations, contributes directly and indirectly to the process of ordering and constructing meaning. Directly, when we react, negatively or positively, to a particular reading by a particular *devisant*; indirectly when, confronted with a series of conflicting readings, we turn back to the story itself, reading it retroactively in an attempt to reconcile the differences arising from their discussion. While Parlamente *tells* the story of Floride and Amadour, Marguerite *writes* it, and it is her writing finally which circumscribes and defines its meaning.

Part of the difficulty in reception which readers of Marguerite have experienced has do with the confused way in which the work was transmitted. The *Heptaméron* is a collection of some seventy stories, the order and number of which varies considerably from manuscript to manuscript. The collection first appeared in print in 1558, edited by the humanist scholar Pierre Boaistuau. This edition was entitled *Histoires des Amans fortunez* and contained sixty-seven stories, arranged idiosyncratically. It omitted the discussions linking the stories as well as the name of the author, deflecting thereby any didactic or moralising intent.

The following year, Pierre Gruget published a new and more comprehensive edition of the collection under the title by which it has been known ever since, claiming to have restored the tales to their proper order and naming Marguerite de Navarre as their author. The seventy-two stories of this edition do not add up to the hundred projected in the prologue, making it fall short of the number completed by Boccaccio in the *Decameron*, Marguerite's acknowledged model. The organising principle is quite regular and systematic: five men and five women alternately tell one story each day; a humorous tale follows a serious one; each day is bracketed by a prologue and an epilogue, and each tale is followed by a conversation between the participants who proceed to disagree about the implications of the story just related. The stories are meant to divert and the commentary to instruct, but these functions are neither always completely separate nor distinct. Scholars have long attempted to establish the historical identity of Marguerite's ten narrators, and it is generally agreed that the names she ascribes them are partially or imperfectly anagrammatic, suggestive of the character or biography of the person in question. Thus Parlamente, the narrator of the tale which concerns us here, may represent Marguerite herself.

A second source of difficulty arises from their originality. The most radical and seminal features of the *Heptaméron*, distinguishing it structurally and ideologically not only from the *Decameron* but also from other previous collections of stories, are, first and foremost, the dialogues of unequal, but increasing, length and complexity accompanying each of the stories and, secondly, the absence throughout of professed authorial intention or intervention. Once the anonymous narrator of the prologue (whom one may or may not be tempted to identify with Marguerite herself) has described the circumstances bringing the group together, recalled the history of an earlier project to produce a French *Decameron*, and prescribed the protocol to be followed at present, there is no longer any clearly identifiable directing voice and, therefore, no fixed point of view.

Although the meaning of a given story may seem self-evident, the discussion it prompts among the various *devisants* tends to multiply and problematise it. Since no single interpretation is privileged and no consensus or conclusion is reached, one can infer, rightly or not, that either Marguerite presumed that her meaning was sufficiently implicit or that the book is unfinished and that, in its completed form, it would have included an epilogue in which the various and conflicting points of view would have been reconciled, making both meaning and moral explicit. As this is not the case, a problem in reading arises: how are we to understand a book that advances a variety of readings without ever choosing among them? In a word, is it possible to cut through the competing interpretations and read Marguerite writing as Marguerite, situating and pre-judging her characters, manoeuvring and manipulating both *devisants* and readers?

In recounting the story of Floride and Amadour, Parlamente tells us something about the way the narrator views it; in writing it, Marguerite tells us something about the way the author views it, and their respective meanings may or may not coincide or be identical. In any event, there is room for play in the space between the writing and the telling, as evidenced first of all by the narrator's relative neutrality, that is, her lack of explicit moralising, even when, as in the rape scenes or in the incident of self-mutilation, she had the obvious opportunity, even responsibility, to do so; and secondly, by the discrepancy between the *devisants* as characters and as commentators. And it is in this indefinite space that Marguerite operates both as author and authority, without interfering directly, that is, pedantically, in the didactic process.

As a preliminary to any proper appreciation of what Marguerite intends her stories to mean, a review of the consequences of the principal conventions governing their selection is in order. First of all, their orality. Conceived and recorded as conversations between a group of *devisants* and, through them, with us, they are to be heard rather than read. When therefore we read them, we receive and perceive them otherwise. Since words evaporate, but writing remains, the reader has the advantage over the *devisants* of a tangible and verifiable record. No longer limited by the fiction of oral presentation, we are able to receive the text as it is written, to *see* how its particular configuration collaborates in the expression as well as the transmission of meaning.

Secondly, the prerequisite that all of the *nouvelles* in the collection be true, either witnessed by the narrator or heard from somebody worthy of belief. Repeatedly the narrator assures the audience of the truth of the story. But what are we to understand by 'true'? That the stories are historical, providing an exact transcription of actual events, or that they merely imitate or coincide with such events, thereby anticipating Balzac's 'All is true'? In either case, the *devisants* are unable to agree on their ultimate meaning because they are not concerned with the facts of the story, but only the consequences of the protagonists' respective situation or conduct.

Finally, the stories are to be contemporary, as the word *nouvelle* implies, as well as entertaining, therefore not too long, enabling the *devisants* to pass the time pleasantly. Thus Oisille's two reasons for finding the Châtelaine de Vergy story unsuitable for inclusion in the collection: 'l'une pour sa grande longueur; l'autre, pour ce que ce n'est pas de nostre temps; et si a esté escripte par ung autheur qui est bien croyable, et nous avons juré de ne rien mectre icy qui ayt esté escript' ('One is that it is a long story, and the other is that it is not a story of our time, and although it is by a reliable author, we have after all sworn not to tell stories from a written source').[1] Parlamente, on the other hand, argues for an exception on the grounds of its newness: 'Il est vray ... mais, me doubtant du compte que c'est, il a esté escript en si viel langaige, que je croys que, hors mis nous deux, il n'y a icy homme ne femme qui en ayt ouy parler; parquoy sera tenu pour nouveau' (p. 400) ('That is true ... but if it's the story I think it is, then it's written in such antiquated language, that apart from you and me, there's no one here who will have heard it. So it can be regarded as a new one', p. 512).

But to what extent are all of the stories oral, new and true? Jourda has shown that some half-dozen are adaptations or near-translations (the Châtelaine de Vergy story is acknowledged as such), fourteen are historically verifiable, six probably so, and perhaps others could be. For the rest, more than half the total, Marguerite undoubtedly drew on personal experience, anecdotes, court gossip, oral tradition and the like. It has been suggested that she collected rather than composed the majority of her stories, which she first heard from friends and acquaintances, and then edited as she wrote them down. While we may choose not to believe, as Brantôme assures us, that she composed most of them while travelling in her litter, writing them as quickly and easily as if she were taking dictation, it remains true, nonetheless, that they are meant to reproduce the spoken rather than the written word.

In fact, despite the priority both editors and readers have afforded the stories, they contribute considerably less to the work's originality than the accompanying discussions. Mostly derivative, if not actual quotations of other stories, then, at least, quotations of stereotypical stories or situations, the *nouvelles* function essentially as a plot or a ploy to capture the reader's interest and attention (which accounts for the prevalence of stories dealing with sex and sexuality), whereas the discussions provide convincingly impromptu performances of Marguerite's dialectical skill and invention.

Insofar as the *devisants* are both narrators and audience, they can be seen as models of the author and her readers, incorporating them figuratively into the text. Each narrator, in prefatory remarks, and each listener, in the subsequent discussions, provides a commentary on the activities of storytelling and critical interpretation. This recourse to self-referentiality could signal a desire to include the excluded, to overcome the distance separating author from reader, to point out that, over and beyond the hermeneutic manipulations of the individual *devisants*, the story has a meaning of its own, inherent in its narrative structure.

Although Parlamente indulges herself as narrator, most noticeably in the plot-retarding monologues, she also is mindful of her audience's pleasure, voluntarily abridging her story in places: 'commencea la guerre grande et cruelle entre les deux Roys, laquelle ne suis deliberé de racompter, ne aussy les beaulx faictz que feit Amadour, car mon compte seroit assez long pour employer toute une journée' (p. 67) ('war broke out between the two kings. It was a great and merciless war. I have no intention of relating the course of events in detail, or even of recounting the many heroic deeds accomplished by Amador, for to tell you all this I should need a whole day', p. 135). 'Je laisseray à dire les voiages, prieres, oraisons et jeunes, que faisoit ordinairement Floride pour le salut de Amadour' (p. 69) ('I shall leave aside for now the pilgrimages, the prayers, the devotions, the fasts, which Florida began regularly to offer for Amador's salvation', p. 137). 'Je vous laisseray à penser les propos que Floride et luy peurent avoir ensemble' (p. 70) ('I shall leave you to imagine the words that passed between him and Florida', p. 139). 'Je n'entreprendz poinct vous dire la douleur que sentoit Amadour escoutant ces parolles'

(p. 75) ('I shall not try to describe Amador's feelings as he listened to these words', p. 143). At the end of her story, she adds: 'Je sçay bien, mes dames, que ceste longue nouvelle pourra estre à aucuns fascheuse; mais, si j'eusse voulu satisfaire à celluy qui la m'a comptée, elle eut esté trop plus que longue' (p. 83) ('I'm afraid, Ladies, that this story has been rather long, and that some of you might have found it somewhat tedious – but it would have been even longer if I'd done justice to the person who originally told it to me', p. 152). While one can detect solicitude for the audience in these disclaimers, one can also read them as rhetorical devices which the narrator uses not only to assure her authority in spite of the rambling and somewhat static nature of her story, but also, and even more importantly, to signal, through its several abridgements, the achievement and complexity of the whole.

If there is something peculiarly Renaissance in Marguerite, is it not her renunciation of the traditional authority of the author and the privileging of personal interpretation through the questioning of the *devisants*? Dialogue, beginning with Plato, is a means of criticism and debate, of questioning accepted values without arriving at an unqualified conclusion, and such is its eventual effect, if not its actual function, in the *Heptaméron*. Marguerite's *devisants*, informed by opinion rather than guided by rule, are unable to come to a common agreement. While her contemporaries would have been perfectly attuned to the ludic propensities of a irreconcilably splintered morality, the modern reader, less didactically-minded, tends to be more concerned with the tragic aspects of interpersonal and gender-related questions.

The tenth *nouvelle* establishes at once a double perspective. As Floride's story, it is an example of victory over heart, body, love and lover;[2] as Amadour's, it is an example of the inadequacy of 'grande hardiesse,'[3] linguistic as well as physical. Initially speech, or its lack, is a substitute for action. Thus, at Amadour's first encounter with Floride, he is reduced to silence: 'là où il estoit estimé le mieux parlant qui fust en Espaigne, devient muet devant Floride' (p. 57) ('He, the most eloquent man in Spain, was speechless before her', p. 124). Young and inexperienced, Floride does not recognise the import of these psycho-physiological signs, and takes pleasure in confiding in him without anticipating any future commitment on her part. Amadour marries Avanturade in order to remain in touch with Floride. Unfortunately, his wife's sudden death deprives him of his sanctioned link to Floride and forces him to abandon his strategy of patience and deferment. Speech having proved insufficient and faced with the prospect of permanent separation, Amadour resolves to chance an early return on his investment: 'se delibera de jouer à quicte ou à double, pour du tout la perdre ou du tout la gaingner, et se payer en une heure du bien qu'il pensoit avoir merité' (p. 72) ('he made up his mind to make one last desperate gamble – to risk losing all, or to gain everything and treat himself to one short hour of the bliss that he considered he had earned', p. 140).

If feminist criticism has been surprisingly slow in discussing the *Heptaméron*, it is no doubt because it has proved difficult to read Marguerite writing as a woman. One such attempt contends that Floride's point of view dominates the tenth story, that, for instance, when she disfigures herself, Amadour does not mention the change in her face;[4] instead, the text describes *her* reaction to *his* face: 'Et, quant Floride veit son visaige et ses oeilz tant alterez, que le plus beau tainct du monde estoit rouge comme feu, et le plus doulx et plaisant regard si orrible et furieux qu'il sembloit que ung feu très ardant estincellast dans son cueur et son visaige' (p. 78) ('His whole expression, his face, his eyes, had changed as he spoke. The fair complexion was flushed with fiery red. The kind, gentle face was contorted with a terrifying violence, as if there was some raging inferno belching fire in his heart and behind his eyes', p. 147).

Actually, this is less a description of her 'reaction' to his face than the narrator's description of the changes which come over *his* face, changes brought on in part by his angry reaction to Floride's willful disfigurement: 'Par Dieu! Floride, le fruict de mon labeur ne me sera poinct osté par vos scrupules' (p. 78) ('Almighty God, Florida, I'm not going to have the just deserts of all my efforts frustrated by your scruples!', p. 147), as he explains more succinctly in a subsequent passage: 'S'il me fault mourir, je seray plustost quicte de mon torment; mais la difformité de vostre visaige, que je pense estre faicte de vostre volunté, ne m'empeschera poinct de faire la mienne' (p. 79) ('If I am to die anyway … then the agony will be over all the sooner! Nor am I going to be deterred because you've disfigured your face! I'm quite sure you did it yourself, of your own volition', p. 148). Rather than proving how the heroine's point of view dominates the narrative, this passage shows the importance the narrator attaches to the interpetation of the play of facial expression (*contenance*) throughout the story as a visible indicator of hidden emotion. In a word, whatever incoherences in behaviour and, consequently, in narrative progression occur, may have less to do with the inability of the female characters to achieve status as subjects within the narrative than with the exigencies of narration itself which, in order to acquire presence and assure renewal, requires the confrontation afforded by successive entanglements and inconsistencies.

It has been said that sex is not much fun in the *Heptaméron*, and this is certainly true of the tenth *nouvelle*. When love is limited to language, there is understanding and subtle pleasure, but when desire enters the picture, it tends to take a violent turn. Those critics who consider Floride exemplary, and the two rape scenes only as illustrations of Amadour's bestiality, have missed the comic relief inherent in their sudden reversal. In both instances, when Amadour's attempts are abruptly suspended by Floride's cries for help, his subsequent confusion and embarrassment are made to seem amusing. At the dénouement of his first unsuccessful attempt, Amadour, utterly despairing, throws himself back on the bed with such violence that the gentleman who came at her call and who thought he had breathed his last is asked by Floride, infinitely more composed, to go and fetch some fresh vinegar. At the second attempt, Floride cries out to her mother, and Amadour, not quite as ready to die as he had just declared, has enough time to gather himself together and, when the Countess enters, he is already standing by the door, with Floride at a distance.

Floride is justifiably angered by what occurs, but this is her anger and not the narrator's, who neither praises her virtue nor moralises its effects. Placed on the defensive by Amadour's attempts to claim the *repos* he feels they have both earned, she decides simply to avoid her former confidant, thus procuring both his anguish and her own unhappiness. Unable to renounce what he feels is the just outcome of his long courtship, and equally unable to obtain satisfaction through persuasion or force, he is finally resolved to put an end to his torment through death: 'vous esperez me tormenter plus en vivant que mille morts ne sçauroient faire. Mais combien que la mort me fuye, si la chercheray-je tant, que la trouveray; car en ce jour-là seullement, j'auray repos' (p. 81) ('you want to keep me alive in order to torture me, and hope thereby to cause me greater pain than a thousand deaths could ever do. Death may shun me, yet I shall seek it out, and I shall find it, for only in death shall I have repose!', p. 151). Though his demise relieves her of any obligation to him, victory for her is hollow. She retires to a convent, never to be heard from again. Thus the meaning of *repos*, the outcome both seek, is translated ironically into privation, namely the end of their story as well as their lives.

Despite Parlamente's ambivalence towards them, critics have tended to praise Floride and condemn Amadour, depicting her as innocent and virtuous and him as calculating and violent. To be sure, Parlamente uses a number of negatively charged words, seemingly portraying him as a kind of Julien Sorel in his relations with Floride. Thus when Amadour, upon first seeing Floride, '*se delibera* de l'aymer' (p. 56) ('His mind was made up. He would love her', p. 123), the verb *se deliberer* has seemed reprehensibly 'deliberate' to critics concerned more with ideology than philology.[5] While the usual meaning of 'se délibérer à', from the thirteenth to the seventeenth centuries, is in fact 'se déterminer à', etymology tells us that one who deliberates is one who ponders (*deliberare: de+libra* = 'scale', 'pound'), and context tells us that the word translates here the musing descriptive of Amadour's initial reaction to Floride's beauty.

Amadour's decision to marry Avanturade has seemed equally duplicitous, especially since the word 'couverture' conveys the impression of stealth and dissimulation: 'il espouza celle dont il estoit plus aymé qu'il n'y avoit d'affection, sinon d'autant que ce mariage luy estoit très heureuse *couverture* et moyen de hanter le lieu où son esperit demoroit incesamment' (p. 60) ('His marriage was no more than a cover, no more than a convenient excuse to enable him to visit her on whom his mind constantly dwelled', p. 127). Calculation seems to determine his subsequent conduct as well: 'Ayant gaingné ce poinct-là de ceste grande estime, se conduisoit si saigement et *froidement*, que mesme celle qu'il aimoit ne congnoissait poinct son affection' (p. 60) ('Having reached these heights in the Countess's esteem, he behaved in such a sensible, such a restrained manner, that even the lady whom he loved so dearly failed to perceive his feelings', p. 127). 'Se delibera', 'couverture' and 'froidement' concur in suggesting a devious seducer, bent upon satisfying his illegitimate desires.

On the other hand, although these words have negative connotations, Marguerite does not always use them negatively, as reference to her other works show. Moreover, Amadour's marriage *was* a fortunate cover, providing him with the means to frequent Floride,[6] allowing him to conduct himself 'froidement', that is to say without displaying the physical effects of his passion.[7] Finally, all three words are clearly judgemental in that they describe the troubled beginnings of a dubious relationship, one requiring that each of the protagonists play an increasingly duplicitious and difficult role.

In the *Heptaméron*, Marguerite frequently depicts characters whose reason is wrong rather than right,[8] who 'deliberate' contrary to all reason, whose jealousy, concupiscence, cruelty and anger lead to treachery, rape and even murder. Yet, again and again, she makes it clear that right can spring from wrong.[9] Amadour is a victim of love, his life and conduct radically changed by his impossible passion for Floride. His love is not calculated nor calculating; rather he is deceived by love into thinking that his love will be returned, and it is upon this premise that he embarks on a troubled and fatal course resulting in eventual salvation for both.

The summary of narrative identifies the sequence of events that constitutes the action of the story. As we have seen, these events are the reality, the 'real' of the story, but we need still to examine the syntax by which the different events are linked together. What narrative there is – and in this story it is reduced essentially to a number of peripeteias and their consequences – serves to provide an order which is sequential and logical to the inception, progression and subsequent destruction of an ambivalent relationship. This is another way of saying that incident is less important in the tenth story than intensification, that Marguerite is less interested in recalling all of the circumstances appertaining to the story of Floride and Amadour than in selecting and developing those elements of their story which directly affect and justify the meaning of its outcome. From the beginning, all of the connections she initiates between the characters are impossible, questionable, contested, denounced. The story of their increasingly tangled relationships is both narrated and figured by the interlacing of a series of irreconcilable strands. All of the characters are inextricably tied together, but there is no link, whether through blood, marriage, love or desire, which is shared or which is in conformity with an accepted norm. The text is a tissue of conflicting perspectives and actions, promoted and aggravated by a number of crises or reversals, which is one of the primordial necessities of the phenomenon of narrative development.

First of all, there is no union which is not a source of discord. The Comtesse d'Arande is a widow who has brought up her daughter Floride according to the strictest codes of virtue and honour. In preferring the Duc de Cardonne as her husband to the Infant Fortuné, because with him her daughter would stay closer to home, she initiates the first link in what is to become a chain of causes and effects. Floride loves the Infant Fortuné, but is married to the Duc de Cadone; Amadour loves Floride but marries Avanturade; Amadour embarks upon an affair with Poline, which she welcomes but which he has no desire to pursue, making her suspicious and Aventurade and Floride jealous. Actions and reactions arise from these unnatural unions, creating a series of inextricable circumstances and moving the narration inexorably towards inevitable catastrophe.

Secondly, the relations between the characters, Floride and the Duc de Cardonne, Floride and her mother, Amadour and Avanturade, Amadour and Poline, Amadour and Floride, are further complicated and modified by deceit and dissimulation. References abound to masks, concealment, studied looks and ruses. There is also the slow unfolding of Floride's love for Amadour, coupled with her unsuccessful efforts to hide its progress from herself, her mother and from him. Since all of the various characters seek to convey the impression of conformity between being and being seen, dissimulation is one of the prime sources of tension within and between them. Amadour hides his intentions behind words, whereas Floride struggles to maintain self-possession through silence: 'Mais, voyant sa mere pleurer très fort, laissa aller quelques larmes pour luy tenir compaignye, afin que, par trop faindre, sa faincte ne fust descouverte' (p. 68) ('But seeing her mother weeping bitterly, she shed a few tears with her, lest her secret be discovered by being too well disguised', pp. 136–37). 'Mais, craignant que la joye qu'elle avoit de le veoir luy fist changer de visaige … se tint à une fenestre, pour le veoir venir de loing. Et, si tost qu'elle l'advisa, descendit par ung escallier tant obscur que nul ne pouvoit congnoistre si elle changeoit de couleur' (p. 70) ('But she was afraid lest the joy she felt at seeing him again should show in her face … she stood at a window to watch his arrival from afar. Immediately he came into sight she went down by way of a staircase, which was dark enough to prevent anybody seeing whether her cheeks changed colour', p. 138).

Dialogue has a similarly conflictual and disjunctive effect. Thus when Amadour breaks his silence and confides in Floride, hoping thereby to increase the degree of intimacy between them, his eloquence merely succeeds in arousing her suspicion: 'J'ay si grand paour que, soubz vos honnestes propos, il y ayt quelque malice cachée pour decepvoir l'ingnorance joincte à ma jeunesse, que je suis en grande perplexité de vous respondre' (p. 64) ('I am rather afraid that there is some evil intent hidden away underneath all these fine words, and that you're trying to beguile me because I'm young and innocent. It makes me very uncertain as to how I should reply to you', pp. 131–32).

In the third place, writing here is applied to the strict presentation of situation. The picturesque and the particular are limited or eliminated. The fact that there is little or no physical description, either of people or places, is a clear indication of Marguerite's intention to privilege relationships. Relative pronouns and the conjunction 'que' are the most significant grammatical features. This is not an uncommon phenomenon in sixteenth century prose, but it is especially relevant in a story where no relationship is straightforward or transparent.[10] In a word, the tenth *nouvelle* is 'true' in its writing; it is a product of text in that the story it tells is both reflected in and consubstantial with the texture of its writing.

In the fourth place, there are a number of pivotal events, intended to promote the release and revelation of emotions, arousing joy or deception: Floride's marriage with the Duc de Cardonne; Amadour's decision to marry Avanturade, to court Poline, to bare his heart to Floride; his repeated departures for the battlefield and subsequent returns; his long imprisonment; Avanturade's death; the two rape scenes. These critical events are turning points in the story in that each marks the irruption of a textual nucleus with which subsequent narration will have to contend.

Finally, another element determining the promotion and progress of text is the qualification of degrees of love. Thus the incipient desire of Floride for Amadour is depicted as 'quelque chose plus qu'elle n'avoit acoustumé' (p. 65) ('At these words Florida was filled with delight beyond bounds. Deep within her heart she began to feel stirrings that she had never felt before', p. 133), something gradually and inwardly experienced rather than outwardly manifested or expressed. Her growing attraction becomes more demanding once jealousy enters the picture: 'Et commencea l'amour, poulcée de son contraire, à monstrer sa très grande force' (p. 66) ('Love, having been thwarted, was aroused now, and began to demonstrate its power', p. 134). All of these semantic unfoldings are also textual unfoldings, that is, the coming together of contrary strands, forming as well as configuring a tangled and intolerable situation.

While the text seems clear in its denunciation of an equivocal relationship, the narrator's point of view remains ambiguous. The narrative voice presents two distinct ideologies, which imply different interpretations of the story according as one reads it from Amadour's or Floride's standpoint. Thus, she has words of praise for both Floride and Amadour and intimates that victory here is also a kind of defeat. Moreover, without questioning the truth or the facts of Parlamente's story, the *devisants* are quick to take issue with her conclusion that Floride was tried to the limits of her endurance or that she put up a virtuous resistance in the face of it all. Their debate revolves around the meaning of virtue as it relates to a number of courtly concepts, 'honneur', 'parfaict amour', 'debvoir', 'maistresse', 'serviteur', all of which are defended according to the gender of the speaker. Thus the word 'virtue', which, as etymology tells us, means virility, manly courage, is a quality in which Amadour is found lacking by the male *devisants*. For Floride and the female *devisants*, the word has the acquired meaning of chastity, integrity and self-respect. Although Amadour is as audacious in love as on the battlefield, his virtue, thwarted by Floride's virtue, results in conflict and catastrophe: 'Et pour en venir à l'intention de mon compte, je vous diray que sa trop grande hardiesse fut esprouvée par la mort' (p. 82) ('Indeed, to bring my story to its conclusion, this bravery, going beyond all bounds, was demonstrated at the last in death', p. 151). For Parlamente, both Amadour and Floride remain 'virtuous', each in his or her own way. Thus she enjoins the ladies 'en prenant exemple de la vertu de Floride, diminuer ung peu de sa cruauté, et ne croire poinct tant de bien aux hommes, qu'il ne faille, par la congnoissance du contraire, à eulx donner cruelle mort et à vous une triste vie' (p. 83) ('I hope you will take Florida's example to heart, but at the same time I would beg you to be less harsh, and not to have so much faith in men that you end up being disappointed when you learn the truth, drive them to a horrible death and give yourselves a miserable life', p.152).

If neither is to blame, what then is the lesson of the story? Since there is no general agreement among the *devisants*, are we to conclude that there is none, that Marguerite means to amuse but not to instruct? Or does she expect us to be better readers than they are and realise that the fault lies elsewhere, not in the respective virtues of her protagonists but, rather, in their fatal confrontation? Taken separately, their stories are related to one another, but asymptotically, in that both Floride and Amadour are victims, less of unreciprocated desire, than of its impossible fulfilment. Their stories intersect nevertheless, and it is the story of their intersecting which is the subject of the tenth *nouvelle* and which the text, through its convolutions, describes as constrained and improper.

In re-reading the tenth *nouvelle*, I have concentrated on those elements and structures of writing susceptible of indicating Marguerite's intentions and our understanding of them, despite her absence and the conflicting interventions of the various *devisants*. The *devisants* are as 'true' as the stories they tell, formed in the image of the readers of the day, self-centred, worldly, without transcendent or uniform expectations. Their inability to agree implies criticism of their criticism. Moreover, the status of their commentary is analogous to that of a gloss, and the revalorisation of the text to the detriment of the gloss is one of the principal achievements of Renaissance writing. Whereas re-writing for the *devisants* is an acceptable form of reading, for Marguerite, it is wrong reading. Right reading is reading according to the text, and the text writes right, as the story of Floride and Amadour shows, in tangled lines. While the *devisants* deconstruct the text, we are expected to reconstruct it, returning to the story itself to re-evaluate the significance of its foldings and unfoldings. The texture of the text is indeed a trap, designed to involve us in its problems and pleasures, drawing us effortlessly and resolutely into a web of converging and opposing lines of development, resisting immediate resolution rather than deferring it indefinitely. Authority, abrogated by the author and relegated to the *devisants*, is transferred peremptorily to the reader. Caught between objectivity and subjectivity, interpretation is informed finally by a reciprocal logic founded on the primacy of writing itself. The text, which relates the story, may write our reading, but it is the text of the text, that is, the writing which shapes the story, which reveals its direction and meaning.

# Notes

1 For the French text, see Marguerite de Navarre, *L'Heptaméron*, ed. Michel François, Paris, Garnier Frères, 1964, p. 400. The English translation is by P. A. Chilton, *The Heptameron*, Harmondsworth, Penguin Books, 1984, p. 512. Further references will be to these editions.

2 'Et si je vous en nommois une, bien aymante, bien requise, pressée et importunée, et toutesfois femme de bien, victorieuse de son cueur, de son corps, d'amour et de son amy, advoueriez-vous que la chose veritable seroit possible?' (p. 54) ('And

just suppose … that I were able to name a lady who had been truly in love, who had been desired, pursued and wooed, and yet remained an honest woman, victorious over the feelings of her heart, victorious over her body, victorious over her love and victorious over her would-be-lover? Would you admit that such a thing were possible?', p. 120).

3 '… car mon histoire est si belle et si veritable, qu'il me tarde que vous ne la sachiez comme moy. Et, combien que je ne l'aye veue, si m'a-elle esté racomptée par ung de mes plus grands et entiers amys, à la louange de l'homme du monde qu'il avoit le plus aymé' (p. 54) ('It's such a true, such a lovely story, that I'm anxious for you to hear it without more ado. I was not an eye-witness to the facts, but they were recounted to me by a very close friend of mine, a man who was devoted to the hero of the story and wished to sing his praises', pp. 120–21).

4 Patricia Cholakian, *Rape and Writing in the 'Heptaméron' of Marguerite de Navarre*, Carbondale and Edwardsville, Southern Illinois University Press, 1991, p. 96.

5 Cholakian reads Amadour's character as sinister and his story as the history of the formation of a rapist: 'From the beginning, Amadour is depicted as a maker of devious plots' (p. 89). Or 'Meanwhile, the wily Amadour has wormed his way more and more into the countess's confidence' (p. 91).

6 'Couverture' means both 'garment' and 'the art of covering with a garment', or, to cite Cotgrave's translation, both 'apparell, rayment, attire' and 'an arraying, cloathing, cladding, attiring'. See Randle Cotgrave, *A Dictionarie of the French and English Tongues*, Columbia, University of South Carolina Press, 1950.

7 The word 'froidement' in the sixteenth century, according to the Robert *Dictionnaire historique de la langue française*, 'n'est plus en usage au sens concret; il s'emploie au figuré avec le sens de "avec calme"'.

8 Remembering perhaps Briçonnet's instruction in a letter dated 26 February 1522: 'et ne doibt le chrestien plus vivre que vie spirituelle, laquelle ne congnoisse raison, par ce qu'elle luy est contraire' (Guillaume Briçonnet, Marguerite d'Angoulême, *Correspondance (1521–1524). Années 1521–1522*, édition du texte et annotations par Christine Martineau et Michel Veissière, avec le concours de Henry Heller, Geneva, Droz, 1975, vol. 1, p. 172).

9 'Ramené à la formule la plus simple, l'*Heptaméron* peut être considéré comme une suite d'histoires relatant la lutte entre les passions et la raison' (Henri Vernay, *Les divers sens du mot 'raison'. Autour de l'oeuvre de Marguerite d'Angoulême reine de Navarre (1492–1549)*, Heidelberg, Carl Winter, 1962, p. 123).

10 'La relative apparaît donc comme un élément important de la structure narrative de l'*Heptaméron*, c'est notamment par elle que les différents thèmes s'enchaînent et que le récit progresse, par étapes, vers sa fin' (Eliane Kotler, 'Syntaxe et narration: Le rôle des relatives dans les passages narratifs de l'*Heptaméron*', *Colloque Marguerite de Navarre 15–16 février 1992*, Université de Nice-Sophia Antipolis, Faculté des Lettres, Arts et Sciences humaines, 1992, p. 89). See also Alexandre Lorian, whose statistics show that, out of 21 authors considered, only Marguerite and Monluc exceed the norm: *Tendances stylistiques dans la prose narrative française au XVIe siècle*, Paris, Klincksieck, 1973, p. 246.

CHAPTER 6

# Fetishism and Storytelling in *Nouvelle* 57 of Marguerite de Navarre's *Heptaméron*

*Nancy M. Frelick*

According to Jacques Lacan, fetishism is a fundamental example of the dynamics of desire.[1] It illustrates both the illusory nature of the object of desire – which, in the case of the fetishist, has been displaced from the original object of desire (the other) as a result of his frustration – and the way in which the subject attempts to (re)constitute himself through his relation with the fetishised object. As we shall see, the fifty-seventh *Nouvelle* of Marguerite de Navarre's *Heptaméron* is a particularly striking literary illustration of the dynamic described by Lacan.

Some may argue that a Lacanian approach to a work written during the Renaissance is shamefully anachronistic. Indeed, how can any modern reader pretend to escape that problem? We are all products of our times and bound to our subjectivity. The best strategy might be to abandon the chimeric ideal of objectivity and put our subjectivity to good use. Subjectivity is, paradoxically, universal. Similarly, certain aspects of the human condition are timeless. Such is the case with desire, which is at the heart of all human endeavours. It is a fundamental structuring principle of thought and expression. Language itself therefore bears the mark of unconscious desires. Indeed, for Lacan, the unconscious is structured like a language. The discourse of the Other, of the unconscious, invades all utterances, whether spoken or written, undermining the illusory mastery of conscious thought and expression. Meaning, which is never as straightforward as we might wish, is therefore revealed not only through the signified(s) to which the signifiers are presumed to point, but also via the play of signifiers in the text.

Of course, it must be stated right from the start that it is dangerous to use psychoanalytic theories literally in literary criticism. Most terms, such as the phallus, are metaphors, and the concepts attached to them function by analogy. As Lacan reminds us, Freud uses the mother's missing phallus to illustrate his theories of the fetish, but he warns us not to interpret the Austrian psychoanalyst's words literally; this does not designate a real phallus that does or does not exist. It is, rather, a symbolic object, insofar as it represents and functions in terms of its absence. For Lacan, who is heavily indebted to French structuralists, everything in the economy of exchange is always both presence and absence (Lacan (1994), p. 152). In order to illustrate the symbolic nature of the phallus, Lacan points out that it is generally men who are fetishists, though in reality they are not the ones with the missing phallus (Lacan (1994) p. 154). Through this symbolic object, a structural cycle of imaginary threats can have a real, physical impact – known to us as the *castration complex*. Yet, for Lacan, its symbolic dimension is by far the most important one. It organises all human interaction and is referred to, as the *law of the signifier* or the *Non/Nom du père* in Lacanian terminology. When Lacan speaks of the phallus, it is as a metaphor for the laws of the realm of the Symbolic. Throughout his work, he stresses that what he describes are structural relationships. These structural relations are universal in that they govern all human affairs – whether it be on the level of individual behaviour or in the realm of artistic expression – and because they are all organised according to the logic of the signifier.

In the fifty-seventh *Nouvelle* of the *Heptaméron*, the Sieur de Montmorency meets an Englishman with an elaborately decorated lady's glove pinned to his shirt as a love-token or plaster over his heart. When the Englishman tells his story, it becomes clear that he prefers the trophy to the lady, the fetish to the woman. The lady, who remains conspicuously absent, is only a pre-text to storytelling. The English gentleman (*millort*) tells his tale to Montmorency because he notices the Frenchman's gaze returning to the glove and because, as the narrator, Parlamente, tells us, the Englishman believes the story to be to his credit: 'il estimoit le compte estre bien fort à sa louange' (François, pp. 353–54) ('thinking that the story (…) could only redound to his praise').[2] He tells it to be praised: 'si j'ay bien faict, vous m'en louerez, ou sinon, vous excuserez l'amour qui commande à tous honnestes cueurs' (François, p. 354) ('I know you will applaud me if I have acted rightly. If not, you will, I know, excuse me for submitting to Love, who holds sway over every noble heart'). Clearly, the gentleman wishes to be seen as the very model of courtliness.

Marguerite is no doubt criticising the idolisation of women as antifeminist. As Paula Sommers puts it, she 'subjects the courtly tradition and its fetishizing of gloves to severe criticism'.[3] From the perspective of the Englishman, the glove

> is supposed to identify him as a *parfait amant* and confer a kind of heroism that derives from amatory verse and fiction [...]. This perspective naturally leads him to anticipate Montmorency's approval, but the latter has no respect for the refinements of *honnête amour*. For him the glove represents absence, rejection and defeat. This limp, empty thing encrusted with jewels like some kind of profane reliquary is the very opposite of the phallic vigor with which he identifies. (Sommers (1993), pp. 133–34)

*Nouvelle* 57 can be read as a commentary on texts that use synecdoches and part-objects to portray the beloved – this was common practice in poetry, especially in the *blasons*. The decorated glove may also be reminiscent of texts, such as Marie de France's *L'Aüstic*, where objects that come to symbolise love or the beloved are turned into sacred relics representing the religion of love. At the end of *L'Aüstic*, for example, the bejewelled box containing the bird that represented love seems more valuable to the lover than the lady, and though it is cherished as a holy relic, it contains only the dead symbol of a past love. Such intertexts serve to emphasise the way in which the appearance of love (the trophy or reliquary) is generally preferred to actual love (the lady). In such texts, courtly love is presented as a sterile, idolatrous practice, fetishistic in the sense that objects or tokens representing love become more important than loving and indeed replace the object of love. The narcissistic lover is not interested in the identity of the other – the lady – only in the construction of his own identity, which is mediated by the courtly religion of love and its paraphernalia.

Even though the English lord speaks of his love for the lady, what he feels can more properly be described as an imaginary desire. For Lacan, what is often called love is directed at something lacking in the object – what is desired is never in the object itself but beyond (*au-delà*). Desire is always associated with lack, with absence. Unlike a need, desire is always impossible to satisfy because it has no specific object; its object (or *objet a* in Lacanian terminology) exists only as an idea, a phantasm in the imagination of the lover. As Peter Brooks explains,

> For Lacan, the unconscious is 'the discourse of the Other', which means *inter alia*, that the individual's desire is always structured for him or her by that

impersonal Other that defines the individual's ego, at the mirror stage, as alienated, that is as the product of others' gazes and perspectives. In Lacan's conception, the demand for love is always absolute, a demand for recognition that never can be fulfilled, based on infantile scenarios of original lack. Desire, born in the discrepancy or lack between need and demand, is thus not desire for this or that, but desire tout court, driven by radical unsatisfaction, for which any given object is a stand-in, an 'imaginary' and hence deceptive simulacrum. What a lover desires is the 'desirer in the other', that the lover be 'called to as desirable' by the person chosen as the object of desire.[4]

It is the image or idea he has created of the lady and of his role with respect to her that the lover desires, not the lady herself. That is why the lady mentioned in *Nouvelle 57* is devoid of any distinguishing features. She has no name, no specific identity. As an imaginary object, she is replaceable; she need only represent a type. Indeed, she has been replaced, 'metonymized' (to use Brooks' term), reduced to a part-object incarnated by the synecdoche of the glove. Although the lady herself is not described, the glove is described in minute detail. Moreover, the glove is, according to Brooks' terminology, an 'improper synecdoche' in that it does not truly represent the lady but rather the lover's desire, which is complicated by the need to be seen, by the need to be perceived as having value in the economy of desire (which, in this case, also partakes of the courtly and market economies). This is why the focus is always on the Englishman, rather than on the lady. It also explains the gentleman's narcissism and exhibitionism: he must be the object of the gaze and the glove he bears is ultimately a synecdoche of his desire to become an object of desire.

Clearly, his is an instance of 'triangular desire', as described by René Girard in *Mensonge romantique et vérité romanesque*.[5] The Englishman is fashioning himself after the courtly paradigm, which serves as the mediator of his desire, much in the same way as Don Quixote emulates the model of chivalry portrayed in *Amadis of Gaul* (see Girard (1961), pp. 11–13). It is not so much the lady herself that the lord desires, but the place occupied by the ideal he imitates. He must therefore set himself up as the model to be emulated. This is why the visual field is so important to the Englishman. He wants to be seen by others; it is the gaze of the other that validates his desire and is supposed to turn him into an object of desire (in the sense that others are supposed to desire what he 'has'). As Brooks puts it, 'Desire is always desire of the other, and of the other's desire; there is no such thing as simple, unmediated, unproblematic desire on the part of the subject' (Brooks (1993), pp. 273–74).

Possession affects being; the identity of the English lord is predicated on it. For him, *avoir* is confused with *être*. Having and being are conflated since seeking to possess or to be the object of desire determines the lover's identity. Possession of the glove is instrumental to the construction of the Englishman's persona in visual and symbolic terms, through the gaze of the other and through storytelling. The lord's desire for the part-object rather than the lady herself is also related to his role as storyteller. The glove is a pre-text to re-creating, rewriting the story of love. It is the sign of a story begging to be told (it is a kind of advertisement for a love-story), yet it also tells a story itself in visual terms, and, as we shall see, ultimately serves as an invitation to reflect on the very nature of storytelling. Juliana Schiesari (discussing Tasso) describes the phenomenon in terms that suit the Englishman well: 'he engenders a fetishized model of the body that both points to the subject's rejection of the female body [...] and to his desire to replace it with a preferred body, the body of the text, of disembodied words [...]'.[6]

His lack of a true object of love also reminds us of the way in which the Englishman, as a storyteller, seeks to avoid reaching the end of his story, which would mean, in Brooks' terms, 'the death of desiring, the silence of the text' (Brooks (1993), p. 20). By having no specific object or final goal to his desire, the Englishman makes sure he never reaches the end of his storytelling; instead, he can endlessly repeat his tale in the hopes of becoming an object of desire himself and creating a discursive mirror in which he can admire himself. The irony is, of course, that this mirror has its dangers; as he loses himself in his narcissistic relation to the illusory mirror/text, he ignores the fact that what he sees is an inverted world. Thus, although he perceives the glove as a prize to be admired, the glove appears empty to others, for it serves as a symptom, a metaphor, of the impossibility of his desire.

The glove is a complex symbol. It is important to note that it is taken by force from the lady. Normally a symbol of fealty, of loyalty by a vassal to his lord, a glove must be freely given in order to have meaning as a token of love and devotion. The lady's glove, taken violently and through trickery, is therefore a sign of the violation of the codes of courtliness and chivalry. In addition, the glove also represents the hand metonymically. It is what is given in marriage. Here, the violation of that institution is also implied, as the hand is not given but withdrawn, leaving behind only a lifeless shell to remind observers of its absence. Moreover, as a sexual symbol, this empty glove evokes impotence. Removed from the hand that wore it and alone, away from its mate, the glove also becomes a symbol of disunity, reminding us that the lover must forever remain alone with his lonely glove. All the embellishments in the world cannot hide the fact that the glove must remain a sign of his unsuccessful bid to possess the other. Indeed, far from adding to his prestige as a lover, the decoration of the glove only serves to emphasise his failure. As Marcel Tetel suggests, 'Precious stones [...] automatically convey a notion of falseness in Marguerite's aesthetics; they reflect a negative condition, the very opposite of their intrinsic beauty [...]. Precious stones represent form rather than substance, a bitter and artificial substitute for love'.[7] The decoration of the glove represents not only the rejection of the lady as is and the construction of an idealised persona that no longer has anything to do with the woman herself, but also the embellishment and transformation of the story. Indeed, the decoration of the empty glove mirrors the Englishman's narcissism and storytelling: it points to the emptiness and sterility of his kind of love and to the fact that no matter how much he embellishes his tale, his words must remain empty. They bespeak only the absence or lack he is so desperately trying to cover up. As Sommers explains,

> Montmorency [whose perspective serves as a guide for the reader] views the glove as a sign of emptiness, but emptiness or absence in this case involves more than a failure to achieve sexual conquest. Gone, along with the hand that serves as substitute for the lady's body, is the idealistic society that accepted the values of pure, courtly love. Gone are the principle of a truly selfless devotion and the possibility of Neoplatonic transcendence. By bandaging his heart in public the Englishman effectively inscribes himself as a victim of narcissism and self-dramatization. The wearing of the glove becomes a form of performance art that recalls the written performances of Petrarchan or courtly poets. Jeweled glove and ornamental discourse are both sign systems that exalt the lover and reify an absent lady. Within the context of the 57th novella, they signify, not a profound or sincere passion, but the triumph of form over substance, the emptying of traditions by those who fail to appreciate the subtle truths these conventions once conveyed. (Sommers (1993), pp. 134–35)

The glove is supposed to be a trophy but becomes a symbol of loss, of failure, of lack. As the story suggests, it is a plaster or bandage that covers a wound, a loss, and thus also serves to reveal it. It is like the fetish described by psychoanalysts: a sign of lack, of symbolic castration, that functions as a 'substitute for what is not there' (Brooks (1993), p. 102). It symbolises a desire that cannot be fulfilled. In order to illustrate the imaginary projection fetishism implies, Lacan uses metaphors related to the veil, the curtain, or projection screen (Lacan (1994), pp. 155–58). For Lacan the very function of this screen is absence. Its presence signals absence or lack, for it is on this screen that absence is projected, imag(in)ed. Like any signifier, it stands in for what is missing. While seeming to promise something beyond itself, it is clear that there is nothing behind the curtain. In other words, what is desired is absent. The fetish stands in for that absence; it takes the place of lack. The fetish is thus both an image of the desired object and of lack – of what is lacking beyond the object.

Lacan stresses that there is a fundamental ambiguity and ambivalence in the subject's relation to the fetish. The illusion is sustained and cherished as such (illusion is more precious to the subject than reality), yet at the same time it is maintained in a precarious equilibrium, a delicate balance that is always in danger of collapsing, capable of vanishing with the rise or fall of the metaphorical curtain (Lacan (1994), p. 156). However, while the illusion is sustained, it gives the subject a feeling of power or mastery he could not have with the desired other. There is great satisfaction to be had from an inert object that is fully at the mercy of the subject. Through the fetish, the subject attempts to take back the power he lost in his frustrating encounter with the other.

The fetish is a symbol, a metaphor, a sign, a symptom. Lacan and Granoff remind us that Freud's statement – a 'fetish has to be deciphered like a symptom or a message' – stresses the fact that its most important function lies in the Symbolic realm: 'From the beginning, such an approach places the problem explicitly in the realm of the search for meaning rather than in that of vague analogies in the visual field'.[8] That is why it can be replaced by another symbolic object. One symbolic object that can stand in for the fetish is speech. The role of speech is essential in all this, because the power of the other to refuse a request indefinitely makes the other all-powerful. Moreover, it is through speech (and through the fetish) that the subject tries to reclaim mastery over the other. Both symbolic objects give the subject the illusion of control so that he comes to believe he can do with them as he pleases. Yet, his symbolic acts cannot fully succeed: the symbolic game is both deceptive and disappointing (*décevant*) (Lacan (1994), p. 183). The subject can never control the Symbolic. His desire is (for the) impossible. Symbolic law has to do with prohibition and is often referred to as *l'interdit* by Lacan, pointing both to the impossibility of ever satisfying desire and also to the lack of control the subject exerts over his speech, or over any symbolic act, since the Other (the unconscious) always slips through, between the lines (*l'inter-dit*).

In *Nouvelle* 57, it is clear that the English lord has little control over his symbolic acts. Speech fails him – it does not help him attain what he desires from the lady – so he perpetually sets himself up through speech to repeat the experience with others. This can be likened to the Freudian notion of repetition compulsion, wherein the subject repeats a painful experience in an attempt to master it by taking over its authorship.[9] He is under the illusion that if he can successfully recount it, if he can integrate it into an acceptable narrative, the subject can find integration and wholeness.

The question of speech, central to the act of narration itself, is important to the story right from the start. Parlamente is inspired to recount *Nouvelle* 57 after Simontault states that some reasonable men desire only speech and do not require the lady's euphemistic *mercy*: 'il y en a de si raisonnables, qu'ilz ne demandent rien que la parolle' (François, p. 353) ('some men are so reasonable that they ask nothing more than the word'). What Simontault sees as praiseworthy is put into question as the reader asks whether it is so much better for a man to tell the story of his love for a lady than to desire *mercy*, since being an object of gossip can be as devastating to her reputation as action. As Ann Rosalind Jones points out, the ideal woman 'was distinguished by what she did not do, or, equally important, by what men did not do to her; she was unseen, unheard, untouched, unknown – at the same time that she was obsessively observed'.[10]

This issue arises out of Simontault and Parlamente's discussion (after *Nouvelle* 56) of Alain Chartier's *Belle Dame sans mercy* and of the ambiguity of the word *mercy*, which is linked to the values of Christian love or *caritas*, characterised by compassion and charity on the one hand, and on the other, with granting the physical favours desired of the lady by the long-suffering concupiscent lover:

> Je sçay, dist Parlamente, combien de foys vous vous plaingnez des dames; et toutesfoys, nous vous voyons si joyeulx et en bon poinct, qu'il n'est pas à croyre que vous avez eu tous les maulx que vous dictes. Mais *la Belle Dame sans mercy* respond qu'*il siet bien que l'on le die, pour en tirer quelque confort.* – Vous alleguez ung notable docteur, dist Simontault, qui non seullement est facheux, mais le faict estre toutes celles qui ont leu et suivy sa doctrine. – Si est sa doctrine, dist Parlamente, autant proffitable aux jeunes dames, que nulle que je sçache. – S'il estoit ainsy, dist Simontault, que les dames fussent sans mercy, nous pourrions bien faire reposer nos chevaulx et faire rouller noz

harnoys jusques à la premiere guerre, et ne faire que penser du mesnaige. Et, je vous prie, dictes-moy si c'est chose honneste à une dame d'avoir le nom d'estre sans pitié, sans charité, sans amour et sans mercy? – Sans charité et amour, dist Parlamente, ne faut-il pas qu'elles soient; mais ce mot de *mercy* sonne si mal entre les femmes qu'elles n'en peuvent user sans offenser leur honneur; car proprement mercy est accorder la grace que l'on demande, et l'on sçait bien celle que les hommes desirent. (François, pp. 352–53)

'I know that you're always bemoaning the treatment you receive from ladies,' said Parlamente, 'yet you always look so fit and cheerful, it's hard to believe you've suffered as much as you say. But then, according to the *Belle Dame sans Mercy*, it is well to say it's so, for such comfort as you may gain.'
'The celebrated doctor you are quoting,' said Simontaut, 'is not only disagreeable in himself, but causes the ladies who follow his doctrine to be disagreeable also.'
'Nevertheless,' she replied, 'his doctrine is of greater value to young ladies than any other I know.'
'If it were the case,' he went on, 'that all ladies were "sans mercy", we might as well put our horses to grass and let our armour go rusty till the next war comes along, and think about nothing but domestic affairs. Is it, I ask you, to any lady's good name to be known for being without pity, without charity, without love, in fact "sans mercy"?'
'Charity and love,' replied Parlamente, 'she should not be without. But this word "mercy" has an unpleasant ring among women. They can't use it without offending their honour, because *mercy* really means granting the favour that one is asked. And one well knows what favours men desire'.

The quote from the *Belle Dame sans mercy* cited by Parlamente is also about speech, emphasising the comfort that can be gained from speaking of one's suffering.[11] Thus, Parlamente (whose very name conflates speech and love) points to the positive side of speech, leaving any conclusions about its negative aspects for the reader to deduce from the tale and from its ensuing discussion (see the question of truth or lies in the frame). No doubt, Parlamente's comment is also a message to Simontault, who sees himself as her *serviteur*, indicating that speech is the only comfort he may find for his unrequited love, and reminding him that the expression of suffering need not besmirch a lady's reputation nor need it result in antifeminist statements.

Speech is fraught with danger. As we can see in *Nouvelle 57*, speech, directed at the lady, can result in a loss of favour. The *millort* states that initially he did not speak to the lady about his love for seven years:

pour ce que mon cueur eut plus de hardiesse de s'adresser en ung bon lieu, que ma bouche n'eut de parler, je demoray sept ans sans luy en oser faire semblant, craignant que, si elle s'en apparcevoit, je perdrois le moien que j'avois de souvent la frequenter, dont j'avois plus de paour que de ma mort. (François, p. 354) my heart was bolder in choosing the object of its love than was my tongue in declaring it, and for seven years I did not dare give the slightest hint of it, for fear that if she perceived my love, I should lose such opportunities as I then had of being in her company – a possibility that was more dreadful to me than death itself.

By speaking of his love, the Englishman does indeed lose the privilege of addressing the lady. Yet his emphasis on the seven years of silence is ironic because all he has done since he dared speak to her is talk about his love to others, either verbally or visually (by wearing the glove). It is as if the expression of desire, repressed for so long, cannot stop repeating itself, insisting to the point where it becomes more important than the object of desire itself. As with the fetish, speech manifests the return of the repressed as it gives voice to the repetition of the traumatic event.

On another level, it is also interesting to note the way in which the speech of the Englishman betrays his true desires. The use of the expression 'faire semblant' when he speaks of revealing his love to the lady subtly undermines the sincerity of his love right from the beginning of the story. 'Faire semblant' means 'to pretend' or 'make a pretence of'. The use of these words suggests a form of what Lacan terms the discourse of the Other, the expression of the unconscious through language (a kind of Freudian slip). The truth will not be suppressed; it must come out, if indirectly. If we take things one step further, might we not also see these words as a reference to 'Faulx Semblant' in Chartier's *Belle Dame sans mercy*, a reminder that the personified 'False Pretence' often uses courtly language in order to take advantage of ladies?

> Faulx Semblant fait l'umble et le doulx
> Pour prendre dames en aguet,
> Et pour ce chascune de nous
> Y doit bien l'escute et le guet. (ll. 749–52)[12]

> False Pretence acts humble and sweet / In order to deceive ladies, / So each one of us / Must be watchful and vigilant.

The English lord is deceptive. When he does speak to the lady, it is in a roundabout way destined to trick her into putting her gloved hand over his heart:

> Mais, ung jour, estant dedans ung pré, la regardant, me print ung si grand batement de cueur, que je perdis toute couleur et contenance, dont elle s'apperceut très bien, et en demandant que j'avois, je luy dictz que c'estoit une douleur de cueur importable. Et elle, qui pensoit que ce fut de maladie d'autre sorte que d'amour, me monstra pitié de moy; qui me feit luy suplier vouloir mectre la main sur mon cueur pour veoir comme il debatoit: ce qu'elle feit plus par

charité que par autre amityé; et quant je luy tins la main dessus mon cueur, laquelle estoit gantée, il se print à debatre et tormenter si fort, qu'elle sentyt que je disois verité. Et, à l'heure, luy serray la main contre mon esthomac, en luy disant: «Helas, ma dame, recepvez le cueur qui veult rompre mon esthomac pour saillir en la main de celle dont j'espere grace, vie et misericorde; lequel me contrainct maintenant de vous declairer l'amour que tant long temps ay cellée, car luy ne moy ne sommes maistres de ce puissant dieu.» Quant elle entendit ce propos que luy tenois, le trouva fort estrange. Elle voulut retirer sa main; je la tins si ferme que le gant demeura en la place de sa cruelle main. (François, p. 354)

But one day, in a meadow, as I was gazing upon her, I was overcome by such a violent fluttering of the heart that I quite lost my colour and my composure. I collapsed. She noticed, and asked me what the matter was. I replied that I was sick at heart. Unbearably. She, not realizing that I was sick for love, expressed her concern for me. This made me beg and beseech her to place her hand upon my heart, so that she might know how fast it was beating. This she did, more out of kindness than affection. As I held her gloved hand upon my heart, it began to race and jump, and she saw that I had spoken the truth. Then, pressing her hand to my side, I said, 'Alas! Madame, take this heart which strives to break my sides, so that it may leap into the hand of her from whom I hope for mercy, for pardon and for life. It is the heart that constrains me now to declare the love which for so long I have kept hidden, for neither my heart nor I are masters of this powerful god.' Taken aback by these words, she tried to withdraw her hand. But I held it tight, and as she pulled away her cruel hand, her glove remained.

The lady's reaction is understandable. Nevertheless, the Englishman attributes cruelty to her through the synecdoche of her hand, stressing the adversarial nature of his kind of love, wherein the woman is a *belle dame sans mercy*.

We recall Parlamente's warning that *mercy* only gets women into trouble when she answers Simontault's question in the discussion before the tale (pp. 352–53, cited above) and the Lady's caution in Chartier's text:

Pitié doit estre raisonnable
Et a nul desavantageuse,
Aux besoingneux tresprouffitable
Et aux piteux non domageuse.
Se dame est a autruy piteuse
Pour estre a soy mesmes crüelle,
Sa pitié devient despiteuse
Et son amour hayne mortelle. (ll. 665-72)[13]

Pity must be reasonable / And disadvantageous to none, / Profitable to the needy / And not damaging to the charitable. / If a lady is piteous to others / In order to be cruel to herself, / Her pity becomes harmful, / And her love mortal hatred.

*Nouvelle* 57 exemplifies these warnings, for as the Englishman explains, the lady in the tale puts her hand on the heart of her admirer more out of charitable feeling than out of any other kind of friendship: 'plus par charité que par autre amityé' (p. 354). The appeal to her charity is a trap into which she falls unwittingly and her kindness can bring her no good for it offers the English gentleman the opportunity to turn her into a story of conquest, even if it is in this case a failed conquest. In this adversarial model, the woman represents at once a kind of territory to be possessed and the very obstacle to its possession (a *topos* beautifully and tragically illustrated in *Nouvelle* 10, the story of Floride and Amadour). Indeed, the Englishman attributes a territorial value to the glove, a metonymy of the lady, by comparing its worth to that of the kingdom of England:

> Et, pource que jamais je n'avois eu ny ay eu depuis plus grande privaulté d'elle, j'ai attaché ce gand comme l'emplastre la plus propre que je puis donner à mon cueur, et l'ay aorné de toutes les plus riches bagues que j'avois, combien que les richesses viennent du gand que je ne donnerois pour le royaulme d'Angleterre, car je n'ay bien en ce monde que j'estime tant, que le sentyr sur mon esthomac. (François, pp. 354–55)

> And because I had never before been so close to her – nor have I since – I affixed this glove as a sticking plaster, the most fitting I could find, to my wounded heart! I have adorned it with the richest rings in my possession, though the riches I receive from the glove itself I would not exchange for the crown of England. There is nothing in the world more precious to me than to feel it as it presses against my side.

He will not give up the territory he has conquered for anything. The wealth of jewels with which it is adorned further complicates the glove's symbolic value. Not only does the adversarial nature of the relationship turn the glove into a symbol that represents the spoils of war, but its adornment also confers upon it a commercial value, alluded to in its initial description ('dessus les joinctures des doigs y avoit force diamans, rubiz, aymerauldes et perles, tant que ce gand estoit estimé à ung grand argent'; 'It was fastened with gold hooks, and the fingers were covered with diamonds, rubies, emeralds, and pearls. The value of that glove was thought to be very high'), and emphasised by the economy of exchange to which the lord refers. Ironically, the more the exchange value of the glove is stressed, the less value it obtains as a symbol of love. The emphasis on exchange reminds us that the lord has already all too eagerly accepted a substitute for his love in the form of the glove.

From the gentleman's perspective, perhaps this is another attempt to reappropriate the power lost to the lady in his unsuccessful bid for love by reincorporating the desired woman into the cycle of exchange to which she belongs according to the symbolic laws of the patriarchal system. The reference to the lady's cruelty is more than just an antifeminist statement. The lady is cruel from the lord's perspective because she has the power to refuse him the gift of *mercy* he seeks (Lacan (1994), p. 185). As such, she dominates the system of exchange, the symbolic system of requests, gifts and refusals.[14] He feels impotent before the beloved because his request has been frustrated and he blames her for the power he feels he has lost, attributing special powers to her. Ultimately, one can say that he has suffered a kind of symbolic castration, so that from his point of view, the lady comes to be seen as possessing the symbolic phallus and the control over the realm of signifiers that it entails. Her *mercy* therefore becomes more than physical gratification; it acquires metaphysical properties as he projects onto her the ability to grant him power as an object of desire, an identity that could make him transcend his situation in the metonymic chain of desire and help him acquire meaning by becoming more than just an *effet de signifiant* for another signifier.[15]

The Englishman's frustrating encounter with the lady is analogous to the primordial trauma that occurs when the subject first encounters the prohibitive laws of the Symbolic. For Lacan, this follows the 'mirror stage',[16] when the subject first senses his alienation from the Real and becomes aware of lack. According to Lacanian theory, people are alienated from the Real by their entry into the realms of the Imaginary and the Symbolic. Although the Imaginary, the Symbolic, and the Real co-exist in reality,[17] they are perceived as falling apart when individuals first enter the Imaginary order. This is when they become aware of themselves, when they first perceive the image of their bodies as separate from those of others. Entry into the Symbolic order occurs when they learn to use signs or language. 'Language is symbolic behavior *par excellence*' (Lacan and Granoff (1956), p. 272). These three realms co-exist, yet the Symbolic can be said to be dominant because our lives are ordered by symbols. The successive entries into the Imaginary and Symbolic are experienced as successive stages of alienation from the Real, from oneness with the universe. The entry into the Imaginary is alienating because human beings come to see themselves as separate entities from the rest of the world. The entrance into the Symbolic is a further alienation because things are now perceived not only via disparate images, but also through symbols. It is at this stage that desire and lack become problematic. As the subject becomes aware of lack and seeks to satisfy his desire for oneness, he encounters the prohibitive laws of the Symbolic that make the satisfaction of desire impossible. As we saw earlier, the Symbolic realm is associated with rules. It is ordered through symbols or names (*le Nom-du-Père* or the Name of the Father) and laws (*le Non-du-Père*, the No of the Father). These are associated with the prohibitive role of the father: the *Nom/Non du Père*. In the Symbolic order, which is organised according to the metonymic law of the signifier, the satisfaction of desire is eternally deferred. There is no end to desire, just as there is no end to the symbolic chain; signifiers can only ever refer to other signifiers and therefore never lead to any ultimate signification.

As we have seen, the fetish is a visual sign, a metaphor, a symptom of constitutive lack that functions both on the level of the Imaginary, in the realm of images and on the metonymic plane, or in what Lacan names the Symbolic. Since it marks the place of a wound, of the repression of a traumatic experience, the fetish becomes the signifier that *insists*, that repeats itself in the subject's efforts to rewrite the story of love. Thus, even though the English lord tells his tale in order to be admired, his storytelling, like the glove, becomes a sign of his failure.

In order to illustrate the relationship between fetishism and the metonymic or symbolic chain, Lacan takes his metaphor of the fetish as an image projected on a screen further, explaining that it can be compared to a memory-screen that has stopped at a particular image. Like the still frame of a movie frozen in time, it is the sign, the marker of the interruption of a story; the moment where it stops is fixed, suggesting both a break in the film and its continuation beyond that point. There is a stoppage in the metonymic chain of the narrative. Yet, just as the diachronic chain can be presumed to go on, the rest of the story must be there, beyond. Its absent continuation is now veiled, what comes after, repressed (Lacan (1994), pp. 157–58). What Lacan speaks of here is the chain of the Symbolic. Yet this phenomenon also partakes of the Imaginary. The fetish is at once an image of displaced desire and a signifier, a marker that indicates the point where the story is interrupted, which is both where repression has occurred and where the subject has constituted a beyond.

The relationship to the object of love thus also participates in both the Imaginary and the Symbolic. The transference of love to the desire for the illusory object occurs on the metaphorical plane, in the Imaginary, whereas the constitution of the object as an Object capable of granting power to the subject is not metaphorical but metonymic, and has to do with the Symbolic order (Lacan (1994), p. 158). Of course, these realms are intertwined since 'the imaginary is decipherable only if it is rendered into symbols' (Lacan and Granoff (1956), p. 269). In *Nouvelle* 57 of the *Heptaméron*, the metaphoric dimension is revealed largely in visual terms, on the level of images, whereas the metonymic is evoked through the field of verbal expression, in terms related to speech and storytelling. Thus one can say that issues related to vision and to narration in the text of *Nouvelle* 57 are emblematic of the realms of the Imaginary and Symbolic in Lacan.

The glove on the gentleman's breast in *Nouvelle* 57 suggests a series of displacements, not only from other to *objet a*, from the lady to the fetish, but from inside to outside (as if he were wearing his heart on his sleeve), from concealment to overt display, from gaze to speech, from Imaginary (phantasm) to Symbolic (expression). These displacements are part of an attempt to regain mastery over the traumatic event. As we have seen, the substitution of the fetish and of speech for the lady show the ways in which the English lord endeavours to take back the power he feels he has lost through the Imaginary and the Symbolic. The subject tries to recount the traumatic experience in a desperate attempt to find wholeness and to gain some sense of power or control over his overwhelming experience. Of course, this project is impossible. These substitutions cannot ultimately succeed in giving him the power he desires. Words and fetishes are themselves only signifiers and cannot grant meaning or wholeness. Besides, one can never go back.

As we can see in *Nouvelle* 57, instead of leading to mastery, the continual repetition of his traumatic encounter only multiplies the signs of the nobleman's failure. He is like the 'fetishist who accumulates signs of loss, in order to both affirm and deny the fact of castration, to make a gain out of loss itself' (Schiesari (1992), p. 48). Both the fetish and the act of storytelling come to symbolise the English lord's abject failure not only to obtain the lady's affections, but also to become an object of desire and admiration himself. Paradoxically, he continually 'sets everything up so that the object of his desire becomes the signifier of this impossibility'.[18] The satisfaction of his desire must be forever deferred – a fact that is subtly suggested by the series of critical gazes embedded in a narrative, which, far from being transparent, is complicated by optical layers reminiscent of the play of mirrors in a game of infinite regress. If the Englishman is subject to what Irigaray terms 'phallic gaze', he is in turn the object of Montmorency's critical gaze, whose perspective mediates that of the reader, but not before it is subtly scrutinised by the feminine point of view implicated in Parlamente's narration and in Marguerite's authorial voice.

Perhaps Marguerite's text can also serve as a commentary on the nature of reading, which may lead to another kind of fetishism, with its own set of pleasures and dangers. Literature is, after all, a play of illusion in which we are happily deceived. The danger is that we may, like the fetishist, try to cover up the gaps in the text at the level of the signifier and 'set up the signified in its own right as firm, self-consistent and solid – to treat meaning as a truth which is given rather than constructed, standing thus as a kind of fetish'.[19]

# Notes

1 Jacques Lacan, *La relation d'objet, Le Séminaire, livre IV (1956-57)*, ed. Jacques-Alain Miller, Paris, Seuil, 1994, p. 165.

2 All quotations are from *L'Heptaméron*, ed. M. François, Paris, Garnier, 1991; all English translations are from *The Heptameron*, trans. P. A. Chilton, Harmondsworth, Penguin, 1984.

3 Paula Sommers, 'The Hand, the Glove, the Finger and the Heart: Comic Infidelity and Substitution in the *Heptaméron*', in *Heroic Virtue, Comic Infidelity: Reassessing Marguerite de Navarre's 'Heptaméron'*, ed. Dora E. Polachek, Amherst, Mass., Hestia, 1993, p. 133.

4 Peter Brooks, *Body Work: Objects of Desire in Modern Narrative*, Cambridge, Mass., Harvard University Press, 1993, p. 269.

5 René Girard, *Mensonge romantique et vérité romanesque*, Paris, Grasset, 1961.

6 Juliana Schiesari, *The Gendering of Melancholia: Feminism, Psychoanalysis and the Symbolics of Loss in Renaissance Literature*, Ithaca, Cornell University Press, 1992, p. 229.

7 Marcel Tetel, *Marguerite de Navarre's 'Heptaméron': Themes, Language and Structure*, Durham, NC, Duke University Press, 1973, p. 69.

8 Jacques Lacan and Wladimir Granoff, 'Fetishism: The Symbolic, the Imaginary and the Real', in *Perversions: Psychodynamics and Therapy*, ed. Sandor Lorand and Michael Balint, New York, Random House, 1956, pp. 265–76.

9 Jane Gallop, *Reading Lacan*, Ithaca, Cornell University Press, 1985, p. 169.

10 Ann Rosalind Jones, 'Surprising Fame: Renaissance Gender Ideologies and

Women's Lyric', in *The Poetics of Gender*, ed. Nancy K. Miller, New York, Columbia University Press, 1986, pp. 74–95; p. 79.

11 The lines cited by Marguerite are those of the Lady in the poem (ll. 267–68). The complete stanza (XXXIV) reads as follows:

> Si gracïeuse maladie
> Ne met gaires de gens a mort,
> Mais il siet bien que l'on le die
> Pour plus tost actraire confort.
> Tel se plaint et garmente fort
> Qui n'a pas les plus aspres deulx,
> Et s'amours greve tant, au fort
> Mieulx en vault un dolent que deux. (ll. 265–72)

> 'Such a gracious illness / Rarely kills people, / But it is often said to, / So that one may get comfort. / One who suffers not the bitterest torment / Complains and laments greatly / And grieves his love so much that after all / It is better there be one victim rather than two'.

All quotations are from *The Poetical Works of Alain Chartier*, ed. J. C. Laidlaw, Cambridge, Cambridge University Press, 1974. The translations are mine.

12 The Lady also speaks about Faulx Semblant in lines 361–68 of *La Belle Dame sans Mercy*.

13 It is interesting to note that the same passage from *La Belle Dame sans mercy* is also referred to in the frame of *Nouvelle* 12. In both cases it is Parlamente who speaks of Chartier's work and both times it is to criticise the notion of young men using love-sickness to attract the attention of the ladies. In each case mention of Chartier's poem gives rise to a story told by Parlamente. In *Nouvelle* 13 the notions of silence and speech and deception are also central.

14 For Lacan, frustration is a result of the refusal of the gift, insofar as the gift is a symbol of love: 'la frustration [...] n'est pensable que comme le refus de don, en tant que le don est symbole de l'amour' (Lacan (1994), p. 181).

15 Jacques Lacan, *Le transfert. Le Séminaire, livre VIII (1960–61)*, ed. Jacques-Alain Miller, Paris, Seuil, 1991, p. 208.

16 In real life, this is supposed to occur when children are between 6 and 18 months of age.

17 In Lacanian theory, the Real is not equated with what we normally call *reality*. On the contrary, for Lacan the Real is the inaccessible realm of the gods, and contact with the Real is profoundly disturbing. Such contact has been variously interpreted as religious experience, an encounter with the supernatural or even a psychotic episode, depending on the interpreter's context.

18 Jacques Lacan, 'Desire and the Interpretation of Desire in *Hamlet*', trans. James Hulbert, in 'Literature and Psychoanalysis. The Question of Reading: Otherwise', *Yale French Studies*, vol. 55–56, 1977, pp. 11–52.

19 Anthony Easthope, *Poetry and Phantasy*, Cambridge, Cambridge University Press, 1989, p. 97.

CHAPTER 7

# Creative Choreography: Intertextual Dancing in Ronsard's *Sonnets pour Hélène*: II, 30

*Malcolm Quainton*

One of the initial difficulties facing the twentieth-century reader of French Renaissance poetic texts in general (and amatory utterances in particular) is that s/he must divest her/himself of anachronistic (post-Romantic?) hermeneutic models which mechanistically equate sincerity and lived experience with originality, inspiration and creative excellence. It is often a challenging and painful process (for both teacher and student alike!) not only to have such comforting assumptions subverted, but also to have to contend, firstly, with such notions as (creative) imitation, rhetorical writing strategies, conventions and received *topoi*, and, secondly, to learn to trace the distinctive nature and the value of a poem to the ways in which received norms are personalised, rejuvenated and transcended by technical craftsmanship, by subtle deviations and patterns of emphasis and foregrounding, and by other complex and allusive processes of intertextual adaptation.[1]

It is perhaps only natural, therefore, that a surface reading of the much-admired dance *blason*[2] from Ronsard's *Sonnets pour Hélène* should first of all seek to anchor the text in the poet's autobiography and personal witness, before acknowledging the manner in which this (apparent) lived experience interfaces ambiguously with, and is mediated through, classical reminiscence[3] and variations of familiar Petrarchist stylistics (antithesis, hyperbole, synecdoche) and *concetti* – the *innamoramento* (the first meeting) and the effect on the lover-poet of the woman's artistic accomplishments (here dancing, but, often, her singing or playing musical instruments), the omnipotence of love, the power of the eyes and the divinity of the woman:[4]

> Le soir qu'Amour vous fist en la salle descendre
> Pour danser d'artifice un beau ballet d'Amour,
> Vos yeux, bien qu'il fust nuict, ramenerent le jour,

Tant ils sceurent d'esclairs par la place respandre.    4
   Le ballet fut divin, qui se souloit reprendre,
Se rompre, se refaire, & tour dessus retour
Se mesler, s'escarter, se tourner à l'entour,
Contre-imitant le cours du fleuve de Meandre.    8
   Ores il estoit rond, ores long, or' estroit,
Or' en poincte, en triangle, en la façon qu'on voit
L'escadron de la Grüe evitant la froidure.
   Je faux, tu ne dansois, mais ton pied voletoit    12
Sur le haut de la terre: aussi ton corps s'estoit
Transformé pour ce soir en divine nature.[5]

On the evening when Love drew you down into the ballroom / To dance with such exquisite art a beautiful ballet of Love, / Although it was night your eyes restored the day, / So abundant were the beams of light they flashed across the room. / The ballet was divine: time after time it restarted, / Separated, reformed, and, turning and re-turning, / Merged, parted, circled round and round, / Imitating the course of the river Maeander. / Now it was circular, now long, now narrow, / Now coming to a point, forming a triangle, like when you see / A flight of Cranes migrating from the cold. / No, I am mistaken, you were not dancing; rather your feet were flying / Above the surface of the ground: and your body was / Transformed for that evening into a divine essence.

Beyond these surface levels of reception (the interface between lived experience and the adaptation of Petrarchist conventions), Ronsard is preoccupied here less with love and personal witness, and more – as elsewhere throughout his entire poetic corpus – with patterns and processes of change, with disorder and order, diversity and unity,[6] and with those rhetorical strategies and techniques of *enargeia*[7] which capture and fix mobility as a privileged moment of heightened reality beyond time and space.

The evocation of movement, flux and transformation is achieved by the frequent and emphatic use of lexical, stylistic, rhythmical and phonological devices (the sheer abundance of these items collectively enable one to talk of the writing strategy of overdetermination and redundancy in respect of this text).[8] On the semantic and thematic level, movement and transformation are rendered by the copious use of active verbs of motion (some fifteen in total), by lexical items of metamorphosis and changing shape (ll. 3–4, 8, 9–10, 12–14), by ever-shifting locations and spatial items (ll. 5–8 in particular, but see also 'en la salle', 'par la place', 'evitant la froidure', 'Sur le haut de la terre'), and by the fluidity of time itself and the restless interchange of verb tenses (use of infinitives, past historic, imperfect, present and pluperfect tenses). The transformation of time (ll. 3–4) and space (ll. 5–13) into an eternalised (atemporal) privileged moment has a parallel in several changes of *status* within the poem – from the physical to the divine, from being passively acted upon ('Amour vous fist … descendre') to being active agent, from location in time and space to flight and momentary apotheosis.[9] The full importance of this pattern of changes and of the distance travelled in the sonnet can be measured by contrasting lines 1 and 13–14, and by giving full value to the poem's two images of the river Maeander and the migratory Cranes, for these foreground respectively the fluctuating nature of spatial/geographical and temporal/seasonal ('evitant la froidure') phenomena. At the same time the subversion of the status of reality and identity as fixed concepts has a counterpart in the movement in the text from 'vous' (ll. 1–3) to 'tu' (ll. 12–13), as well as in the temporary inability of human senses (here, sight: l. 12) to distinguish between external phenomena (both of these features appear frequently throughout the cycle and have already become familiar to the reader from earlier sonnets).[10]

Significant also in the painting of movement in the sonnet is the presence of a number of rhetorical tropes – simile and metaphor (ll. 8, 10–11, 12–13), *correctio* (a moment of re-formulation or the modification of a statement or of first impressions, here caused by the deceptive nature of sight and its inability to decode signs clearly: l. 12), hyperbole (ll. 3–4, 13–14), synecdoche (part of the body for the whole person: ll. 3–4, 12), an accumulation of antithetical features (ll. 3, 5–7, 9–10, 12, 13–14). Such rhetorical processes, however, are not arbitrary or superfluous: rather they support sense, for by replacing and re-presenting one thing by another, all tropes involve a mental process of displacement and transference, and this act of cognitive exchange mimes stylistically the idea of the change and ambiguity of status located in the sonnet.

Something similar can be seen in the manner in which appearance and reality are confused and things are transformed into something else by the fluidity of rhythmical, phonological and graphological effects. The rhythmical agility of the sonnet is rendered, firstly, by the repetition of infinitive structures (ll. 1–2, 4, 5–7), arranged in the second quatrain in two ternary patterns of reflexive (-*RE* and -*ER*) verbs to suggest the self-energising nature of the ballet; secondly, by the accumulation of lexical items ('ores'/'or"; 'en': ll. 9–10); thirdly, by the syllabic deviations and disturbances within the alexandrine lines, and the multiplicity of *enjambements* and shadow pauses (ll. 1–2, 3, 6–7, 9–11, 12–14).

Phonologically, the status and identity of sound systems is rendered shifting and fragile by a process of interchangeability and cross-patterning. This complex and subtle process is best illustrated by the manner in which the phoneme [R] dominates the sonnet as a phonic marker (note that this consonant is heard in all the rhymes of the octet and in three of the rhyming words of the sestet). However, at the same time the phoneme [R] receives its variety (and fragility) of status by the way it is transformed by a changing scheme of supporting vowel sounds – [uR] of the 'B' rhymes and internally in lines 1, 2, 6, 7, 8; [ɔR] in lines 9–10, 13–14; [(w)aR] in lines 1, 2, 4, 7, 14; [ɛR] in lines 3, 4, 6, 13 and in the sixteenth-century pronunciation of -ER infinitives; [yR] internally in lines 4 and 13 and in the 'D' rhymes (note the way in which the rhyme of line 14 [tyR] returns us to the rhymes of lines 6–7 [tuR] which are in turn echoed internally in the same lines). The fluctuating nature of this patterning is seen in a particularly heightened and dense manner in lines 13–14 in the following sequence: [syR], [tɛR], [kɔR], [...fɔRme], [puR], [swaR], [...tyR].

Finally, certain other phonological and graphological features parallel the ambiguous and mobile status of reality, and, by drawing attention to the fluidity and interchangeability of language as a sign system, emphasise its arbitrary nature. The ease with which one word is converted into another, and meaning and identity are subverted, can be best illustrated by the presence of a series of deceptive cognates, by homophones ('sceurent'/'sur': ll. 4, 13), *polyptota* ('fist'/ 'artifice': ll. 1–2; 'tour'/'retour'/'tourner'/'entour': ll. 6–7), *paronomasia* or *allusio* – a rhetorical figure whereby the meaning of words is tenuously separated by the slight alteration of a single phoneme ('rond'/'long'; 'estoit'/'estroit'; 'cours'/'corps'; 'fist'/'fust'/'fut'/'faux': ll. 9; 8, 13; 1, 3, 5, 12), or of several phonemes ('salle'/'ballet'; 'respandre'/'reprendre'; 'imitant'/'evitant': ll. 1–2, 4–5, 8, 11). The same processes of verbal conversion and of the displacement of identity are present in the visual reproduction of words ('ores' is repeated visually in '*or*' *estroit*' in line 9), by the subtle interplay between voiced and unvoiced sounds (b/p; v/f), and by a momentary confusion in which the mind proposes one word instead of another because of linguistic and grammatical interference ('beau ballet'/'beau [belle]').

Simultaneously, and paradoxically (until one is familiar with Ronsard's aesthetic notion of *libre contrainte*,[11] an idea to which I will return shortly), many of the *same* stylistic and formal features recently noted establish networks and resonances across the sonnet and provide it with its structural order and coherence. In addition to the firmness and stability which results from various forms of repetition (binary, ternary, accumulation) – antithetical patterns, infinitives, 'ores'/'or"; 'en' (echoed in lines 10 – 'entour' – and 14), – we should note the structural unity afforded the sonnet by lexical, phonological and graphological parallelisms, and by the diverse processes of circularity and enclosure which provide links between the closing tercet and the opening quatrain ('le soir'/'ce soir'; 'danser'/'dansois'; 'pour'/'pour'; 'vous'/'tu'; 'voz yeux'/'ton corps'; the antithesis between descent/flight, reality/apotheosis; phonic echoes in 'faux'/'haut'/'aussi'/ 'beau' [o]; in 'terre'/'esclairs'/'ramenerent'/'danser' [ƐR]; in 'nature'/ 'sceurent' [yR]; in the alliterative [s/d/t] pattern of lines 1–2 ,5–7, and 13–14).[12]

It is clear, from what has already been suggested, that the dance refers to something beyond itself; to, on the most obvious level, Ronsard's life-long obsession with exploring the thematic and stylistic implications of the concept of *discordia concors*, the tension between freedom and constraint, the fragmentary and the coherent. Indeed familiarity with poetry in general, and with Ronsard's poetry in particular, leads one to the conclusion that this text – like many poetic utterances – says one thing and *means* something else, and what that 'something else' is depends to a large extent on our literary competence and our individual reading response.[13] The dynamics of the reading process as described by Iser and Fish[14] are such that the receiver is an active participant in, and co-producer of, the work and its meaning, for s/he decodes a complex sign system (at once linguistic and graphological) by actualising the areas of a text which are implied and potential rather than written and formulated. Meaning is not inscribed in the work (be it an individual utterance or a macro-text) as something objective, fixed and determinate, but rather as a process of personal discovery and experience, an individual negotiation with the text whereby the reader extrapolates from its promptings and clues, and fills in the gaps and silences, its indeterminate areas, by her/his linguistic and literary competence. Moreover, since no single utterance exists in isolation (especially not within a sonnet cycle) an important part of this process of extrapolation and 'gap-filling', and of our ability to penetrate the surface layers of a text and suggest deep-structure readings, relates to our competence as receivers to create contexts and to discover links and allusive patterns

of intertextuality[15] and self-quotation which resonate within the utterance itself, within the collection, within other collections written or
published at the same time and, indeed, within the entire corpus of the
poet's work.

There is external evidence both elsewhere in Ronsard's work and
within the *Sonnets pour Hélène* itself to authorise a 'symbolic' interpretation of the dance sonnet and to propose alternative meanings
concealed under surface levels. Firstly, there are Ronsard's frequent
theoretical pronouncements concerning the fact that one of the functions of divinely-inspired poetry is to 'feindre & cacher' ('feign and
hide') deeper truths under a mantle or veil of poetic fictions, fables
and literal levels of language.[16] More importantly, a number of poems
in the *Sonnets pour Hélène* reveal an interest in semiotic readings and
in the decoding of sign systems, both verbal (including the etymology
and significance of proper names) and non-verbal,[17] and throughout
the collection Ronsard declares a preference for symbolic truths and
effects rather than for the external reality of the signified:

> Oranges & Citrons sont symboles d'Amour:
> Ce sont signes muets[...]

> Oranges and lemons are symbols of Love: / They are silent signs.[18]

In this respect the dance is no different from other non-verbal 'signes
muets' within the sonnet sequence, whose silent eloquence has to be
decoded – agate (I, 31), letters (II, 28 and 29), a myrtle and laurel
crown (II, 39), a gesture of the hand (I, 9) and pomegranates (*AD*, 49).

What then does the dance signify? What concealed 'truth' does the
sonnet yield? I would suggest that the dance is yet another sign of
Ronsard's self-reflexive preoccupations with poetics and with reading
and writing strategies – an interpretation valorised by the sonnet itself,
by its immediate context (sonnets 28 and 29) and by allusive intra-tex-
tual references across the collection. Firstly, the sonnet itself suggests
a parallel with the writing act – the lexicon ('artifice', 'contre-imitant')
provokes such an association, and the movement from reality to
heightened reality, from physical location, the body and descent to
flight, divinity and apotheosis, reminds us of the role of imagination
and inspiration in the creative and mimetic process. Similarly the reference to the river Maeander (l. 8) has suggestive links with Apollo
Musagetes, god of music and poetry, with the beautiful song of the
dying swans ('cygnes') which frequent the river, and with Ronsard's
interest in signs and in the word-play surrounding the homophone

'cygne'/'signe' which is found elsewhere in the sonnet cycle and in several later texts of Ronsard.[19] Moreover, this sonnet and the lexical item 'artifice' recall an earlier sonnet of the collection (II, 4) in which dancing is described as being synonymous with theatrical falsehood and feigning:

> Tandis que vous dansez & ballez à vostre aise,
> Et masquez vostre face ainsi que vostre coeur
> [.....]
> Le Carnaval vous plaist: [...]

Whilst you take the floor and dance as you please, / And mask your face as well as your heart / [...] You enjoy the Carnaval.

This parallel between dancing and deception in turn reminds one of those frequent occasions elsewhere in the *Sonnets pour Hélène* (and indeed throughout the entire corpus of Ronsard's work) in which he associates the art of poetry with lying, and raises questions of fictionality and counterfeiting as attributes of mythic texts and as necessary features of imaginative invention and 'truthful' mimetic expression.[20]

More evidence for such a reading of sonnet 30 is found throughout the collection where auto-referential matters of literary and linguistic importance are amongst Ronsard's central concerns, and where our attention is repeatedly drawn to the cycle's self-reflexivity (to a discussion of the function and nature of poetry) and to its status as poetic artifact.[21] Indeed, whilst the arrangement of the sonnets into two books raises (largely unfulfilled) expectations concerning a developmental or chronological disposition, it is perhaps not without significance that the preponderance of self-reflexive references are found in Book 2 as if the collection increasingly comments on its own mimetic function and its own poetic discourse. Finally, and more precisely, the two poems preceding the dance sonnet (II, 28 and 29) focus directly and overtly on aspects of writing and reading, on the persuasive and emotional effects of the written word, on the silent witness of facial and written signs, and by doing so contextualise and prepare us for a self-reflexive reading of the dance sonnet.

However, sonnet 30 is not only about poetics and writing strategies – about reality and the transforming processes of mimetic representation, about Ronsard's life-long adherence to the creative principle of *libre contrainte*, with its simultaneous balance of diversity and unity, disorder and order. It is also a commentary on, and a paradigm for, our reception of the entire sonnet cycle in the way that it mimes the ever-moving and ambiguous experience of our reading and interpretive processes, and illustrates 'the more extreme consequences of the dialogue between integration and fragmentation' which characterises Ronsard's writing according to Terence Cave.[22] In a recent essay on 'Ronsard's *Sonnets pour Hélène* and the alternative Helen myth'[23] I have argued that the simultaneous presence of two apparently irreconcilable versions of the Helen myth and of two different Hélènes within the French sequence has significant implications for the status of the text and for our interpretation of it. With more than one referent for the word 'Hélène', and with the themes of duplication and deception creating epistemological and ontological confusion by subverting the status of reality and identity as stable and definitive concepts, an interpretation of the collection as a record of lived experience and as autobiography is further discredited, and we are encouraged instead to adopt readings which respect the ambiguities and 'le caractère factice' of the sequence.[24] The *Sonnets pour Hélène* is a composite and heterogeneous collection, characterised by internal inconsistencies and surprises, ruptures and discontinuities: it sets up expectations which it denies, coherences which it disrupts, in a reading response which continually demands mental adjustments, revisions and displacements from the receiver as s/he seeks to extract a configurative meaning. Our experience of the French collection, with its emphasis on the provisional and the ever-changing , is in continual movement and tension, and, like the dance, it constantly constructs and deconstructs itself, fragments and reforms, loses shape and identity whilst retaining organisation, form and unity within diversity. As Cave has written about Ronsard's poetry in general, 'the process of writing constantly (and at times expressly) postpones completion, exploring instead the pleasures of repetition and fragmentation. [...] The text and its reader are caught up in a pursuit of integration which, if not fruitless, is none the less bound to be frustrated'.[25]

Further patterns of intertextuality, self-quoting and specularity reveal the ways in which Ronsard re-works this dance sonnet from the Hélène collection after the manner of a palimpsest in other contemporary and subsequent poems,[26] and he does so in a way which illustrates yet another aspect of his writing practices. The first of these palimpsests occurs in sonnet 21 from *Les Amours Diverses* of 1578, which was to find its definitive place in Book I (sonnet 19) of the *Sonnets pour Hélène* in the 1584 and 1587 collective editions. Here Ronsard's continuing interest in semiotics (in the 'marque d'amitié' and the 'vrais signes d'amour' – the 'mark of friendship' and the 'true signs of love') and his refashioning of similar lexical and stylistic practices from the Helen dance sonnet (including the accumulation of antithetically organised infinitives, many of them reflexive verbs) are employed to evoke the fluctuating and contradictory emotional states of love. Here too priority is given to effects as signifiers rather than to signifieds:

> Tant de fois s'appointer, tant de fois se fascher,
> Tant de fois rompre ensemble, & puis se renouër,
> Tantost blasmer Amour, & tantost le louër,
> Tant de fois se fuyr, tant de fois se chercher,
>   Tant de fois se monstrer, tant de fois se cacher,
> Tantost se mettre au joug, tantost le secouër,
> Advouër sa promesse, & la desadvouër,
>   Sont signes que l'Amour de pres nous vient toucher. (XVII, 305)

So many reconciliations, so many quarrels, / So many separations, and then reunions; / Now denouncing Love and now praising him, / So many times avoiding each other, so many times seeking one another, / So many times revealing oneself, so many times concealing oneself, / Now submitting to the yoke, now shaking it off, / Giving one's promise and retracting it; / These are signs that Love touches us deeply.

A much closer re-writing, and a conflation, of both this sonnet from *Les Amours Diverses* and the dance sonnet from the Helen cycle appear in a *Cartel* of 1584 (XVIII, 110–11) which describes an equestrian ballet in identical terms of movement and control, diversity and unity. In this *Cartel*, too lengthy to quote in entirety here, Ronsard adds a social and political dimension (ll. 27–36) to his aesthetic statement of *libre contrainte*, whilst retaining from the 1578 Helen sonnet similar tropes of displacement and transformation (the similes concerning the river Maeander and the migratory flight of the cranes re-appear: ll. 1–4, 25–26). Present too in this later text are those now-familiar rhetorical, lexical, rhythmical and phonological processes designed simultaneously to evoke freedom and control, and to create ambiguity by subverting identity and the status of reality ('Contrefaisant la guerre au semblant d'une paix'). These processes include the antithetical patterning of infinitives, the repetition of binary (often contrastive) lexical items (ll. 19–21), the fluidity of alexandrines dislocated by a diversity of internal caesura breaks, the restless movement of verb tenses and the wide temporal perspective (heightened by the use of frequent mythological and 'historical' references: ll. 5–14), the presence of anaphora (the word 'tantost' at the same time marks the moments of change and gives the text structural and rhythmical stability):

> Tantost vous les voirrez à courbettes danser,
> Tantost se reculer, s'approcher, s'avancer,
> S'escarter, s'esloigner, se serrer, se rejoindre
> D'une pointe allongée, & tantost d'une moindre,
> Contrefaisant la guerre au semblant d'une paix,
> Croizez, entrelassez de droit & de biais,
> Tantost en forme ronde, & tantost en carrée [...].[27]

> Now you will see them dancing in curvets, / Now retreating, advancing, pushing forward, / Separating, moving away, coming together, closing ranks / To form a point, now tapering, now broader-angled, / Simulating war under the guise of peace, / Criss-crossing, intersecting at right angles or diagonally, / Now in a circular figure, and now in a square one.

In the preceding lines from this *Cartel* Ronsard had already quoted and re-visited an early ode 'Au Seigneur de Carnavalet' of 1550, and he had done so in order to develop the controlling art of horsemanship as a metaphor for the principle of *libre contrainte* in both its aesthetic and moral dimensions. Between these lines from the *Cartel* quoted below and sections of the 1550 ode there are a number of shared features – a reminiscence from Pindar (*Olympian*, XIII, 63–73), a reference to a mythological detail concerning Pallas Athene, many common lexical echoes – and these are sufficiently insistent to suggest a conscious re-writing of the earlier text after the manner of a palimpsest:

> Pallas qui les conduit, a de sa propre main
> Façonné leurs chevaux, & leur donna le frein,
> Mais plustost un esprit, qui sagement les guide
> Par art, obeissant à la loy de la bride.

> Pallas who leads them, has with her own hand / Trained their horses, and given them the bit, / But [it is] rather a mind, which wisely guides them / By art, obeying the law of the bridle.[28]

Similarly a passage from the *Hymne du treschrestien roy de France Henry II. de ce nom* of 1555 (VIII, 11–12, 113–42) draws a parallel between horsemanship and the art of kingship, and here too many lexical and stylistic items prefigure the *Cartel* of 1584 where reference is also made to Henri's statecraft in the context of the equestrian ballet.[29]

The force which has directed our commentary of the dance *blason* and which has informed our theoretical and methodological models, has been largely centrifugal in nature in that it has involved diverse processes of intertextuality, contextualisation and amplification. In a sonnet interested *ostensibly* in love, personal witness and lived experience, deeper and wider levels of reading revealed preoccupations with patterns and strategies of displacement and transference, and with the thematic and stylistic implications of a *discordia concors* (diversity and unity, order and disorder, the fragmentary and the coherent). In turn, these preoccupations were found to be a sign of Ronsard's self-reflexive interests, of the way in which his poetry not only openly or allusively discusses its creative functions and its own writing processes, but also illustrates by example and statement its concern with the principle of *libre contrainte*, with signs and 'symbolic' effects, with the subversion and imaginative transformation of reality, and with mimetic re-presentation. At the same time this sonnet can be seen as iconic, as a paradigm for our reception of the entire cycle, in the manner in which it parallels the ever-shifting and ambiguous experience of our own reading and interpretive processes as we attempt to grapple with a collection in which the status of reality, identity and meaning as stable and definitive concepts is alternately constructed and deconstructed, questioned and subverted. Such a reading was seen to rely upon our literary and linguistic competence as receivers to decode allusive signs within the sonnet itself and to create ever-widening contexts, associations and patterns of intertextuality (within the cycle itself, within other contemporary collections, and across the wider corpus of Ronsard's *oeuvre*). A particularly interesting and heightened example of intertextuality is that of self-quotation and self-imitation, and the way in which Ronsard re-fashions his dance sonnet from the Helen sequence in contemporary and later texts after the manner of a palimpsest, reveals yet another aspect of his creative processes of *inventio* and *elocutio* – an aspect which is all the more significant because the sonnets of 1578 and, more especially, the *Cartel* of 1584 are in turn contaminated by re-writings of passages from an ode of 1550 and a *hymne* of 1555.

*For Tara*

# Notes

1 Some of these questions are discussed and illustrated with reference to Ronsard's amatory verse in my article 'The Love Poetry of Pierre de Ronsard:

Convention and Beyond', *Durham University Journal*, vol. LXXX, 2, June 1988, pp. 193–99. An explanation of some of the terminology used throughout this essay can be found in G. Leech, *A Linguistic Guide to English Poetry*, London and New York, Longman, 1969. For a definition of the rhetorical devices, see L. Sonnino, *A Handbook to Sixteenth-Century Rhetoric*, London, Routledge and Kegan Paul, 1968.

2 For the *blason* in sixteenth-century poetry, see D. Wilson, 'Le blason' in *Lumières de la Pléiade* (neuvième stage international d'études humanistes, Tours, 1965), Paris, Vrin, 1966, pp. 97–112; *Descriptive Poetry in France from Blason to Baroque*, Manchester, Manchester University Press, 1967; A. Saunders, *The Sixteenth-Century 'Blason Poétique'*, Bern, Peter Lang, 1981. The *blason* in praise of the woman's body has become the focus of much feminist critical attention: see in this present volume, the essay (and a fuller bibliography on this Renaissance genre) by Ann Jones, pp. 85–106.

3 The image of the migratory birds is found in Homer (*Iliad*, II, 459ff.; III, 2) and Virgil (*Aeneid*, VI, 310; VII, 33; X, 264; *Georgics*, I, 383). See W. B. Cornelia, *The Classical Sources of the Nature References in Ronsard's Poetry*, New York, Columbia University Press, 1934, p. 150.

4 On Petrarchism, its history, transmission, and thematic and stylistic features, see J. Vianey, *Le pétrarquisme en France au XVIe siècle*, Montpellier, Coulet, 1909 (reprint: Geneva, Slatkine, 1969); H. Weber, *La création poétique au XVIe siècle en France*, 2 vols, Paris, Nizet, 1956, chapters IV & V; L. Forster, *The Icy Fire: Five Studies in European Petrarchism*, Cambridge, Cambridge University Press, 1969; S. Minta, *Love Poetry in Sixteenth-Century France*, Manchester, Manchester University Press, 1977; *Petrarch and Petrarchism: The English and French Traditions*, Manchester, Manchester University Press, 1980.

5 My text and numbering of the *Sonnets pour Hélène* (by book and sonnet) follow that of the 1578 edition reproduced in *Ronsard. Oeuvres complètes*, 20 vols, ed. P. Laumonier; revised and completed by I. Silver and R. Lebègue (Société des Textes Français Modernes), Paris, Hachette; then Droz, then Didier, 1914–75. The *Sonnets pour Hélène* is published in vol. XVII (1959). Also included in this present study are those sonnets from *Les Amours Diverses* (1578) which Ronsard places in the *Sonnets pour Hélène* in the 1584 or 1587 editions. These sonnets are referred to by the initials *AD* and sonnet number. References to other works of Ronsard are to the Laumonier edition. On this dance sonnet, see G. Castor, 'Petrarchism and the Quest for Beauty in the *Amours* of Cassandre and the *Sonets pour Helene*', in *Ronsard the Poet*, ed. T. Cave, London, Methuen, 1973, pp. 114–15; J. Dhouailly, 'Explication d'un texte de Ronsard: "Le sonnet du Bal"', *Information Littéraire*, vol. 36, 1984, pp. 38–41; O. Pot, *Inspiration et mélancolie: L'épistémologie poétique dans les 'Amours' de Ronsard*, Geneva, Droz, 1990, pp. 402–406; J. Fallon, *Voice and Vision in Ronsard's 'Les Sonnets pour Hélène'*, New York, Peter Lang, 1993, pp. 67–69.

6 On this feature of Ronsard's poetry, see I. D. McFarlane, 'Aspects of Ronsard's poetic vision', in *Ronsard the Poet*, pp. 13–78; M. Quainton, *Ronsard's Ordered Chaos: Visions of Flux and Stability in the Poetry of Pierre de Ronsard*, Manchester, Manchester University Press, 1980.

7 On the rhetorical process of *enargeia*, see T. Cave, '*Enargeia*: Erasmus and the rhetoric of presence in the sixteenth century', in *The French Renaissance Mind: Studies presented to W. G. Moore*, ed. B. C. Bowen, *L'Esprit Créateur*, vol. 16, 1976,

pp. 5–19; P. Galand-Hallyn, *Le reflet des fleurs: Description et métalangage poétique d'Homère à la Renaissance*, Geneva, Droz, 1994.

8 On the notions of overdetermination and redundancy, see respectively M. Riffaterre, *Semiotics of Poetry*, Bloomington, Indiana University Press, 1978; and L. Norman, 'Risk and Redundancy', *Publications of the Modern Language Association*, vol. 90, 1975, pp. 285–91.

9 For a discussion of the temporal limits imposed on Hélène's divine transformation and the ambivalence created by 'pour ce soir' ('for this evening', l. 14), see Castor, p. 115.

10 For the restless movement between 'vous' and 'tu' as mode of address in the collection, see for example I, 1–3; 32–35. On this aspect, see *Ronsard. Sonnets pour Hélène*, ed. M. Smith (Textes Littéraires Français), Geneva, Droz, 1970, p. 32, n. 14. This is the only example in the collection where the shift from 'vous' to 'tu' occurs within a single sonnet: as such it could be said to pattern the move from the human to the divine ('tu' being used in the elevated style when addressing the Divinity). On the deceptive nature of sight ('voir'/'decevoir') or of initial judgements and perceptions based on sight, see I, 16; II, 30 (12-14); 35 (13); 36; *AD*, 29; 38; 49; 50. The rhetorical trope *correctio* is often used in such contexts to evoke a mental re-positioning or re-definition prompted by incorrect first sense impressions.

11 On Ronsard's notion of *libre contrainte*, see M. Quainton (1980), Index, 'aesthetic considerations', p. 237; 'Ronsard et la *libre contrainte*', in *Ordre et Désordre dans la civilisation de la Renaissance*, Université de Saint-Etienne, 1996, pp. 271–84.

12 For circularity as a closural device and as a feature of structural coherence in Ronsard's love poetry, see M. Quainton, 'Mythological Reference, Circularity and Closure in Ronsard's *Amours de Cassandre*', in *Ronsard in Cambridge. Proceedings of the Cambridge Ronsard Colloquium, 10–12 April 1985*, ed. P. Ford and G. Jondorf, Cambridge, 1986, pp. 67–80; 'Le cercle et les différentes formes de structure cyclique et close dans les *Amours de Cassandre* (1552–1553)', in *Etudes Ronsardiennes II. Ronsard en son IVe centenaire*. Actes du colloque international Pierre de Ronsard (Paris-Tours, septembre 1985), publiés par Y. Bellenger, J. Céard, D. Ménager, M. Simonin, Geneva, Droz, 1989, pp. 53–61. In addition to those multiple aspects of circularity noted above (including the phonic patterning around the phoneme [R] and supporting vowel sounds), see also the role played by the lexical parallelism 'divin'/'divine' (ll. 5, 14) and by several graphological and phonological phenomena – capitalisation (ll. 1, 2, 8, 11), the visual and phonic network 'estoit'/'voletoit'/'voit'/ 'estroit'/'estoit'/'souloit' (ll. 13, 12, 10, 9, 5) and the way that the feminine rhymes of the sonnet (ll. 1, 4, 5, 8, 11, 14) all end in -RE with supporting dental sounds [d/t].

13 'The art work [...] says something other than the mere thing itself is, *allo agoreuei*. The work makes public something other than itself; it manifests something other; it is an allegory [...] a symbol' (Martin Heidegger, *Poetry, Language, Thought*. Translations and Introduction by A. Hofstadter, New York, Harper & Row, 1971, pp. 19–20). On the notion of literary competence, see J. Culler, *Stucturalist Poetics: Structuralism, Linguistics and the Study of Literature*, London, Routledge and Kegan Paul, 1975, pp. 113–30.

14 See W. Iser, *The Implied Reader: Patterns of Communication in Prose Fiction from Bunyan to Beckett*, Baltimore, Johns Hopkins University Press, 1974; *The Act of Reading: A Theory of Aesthetic Response*, Baltimore, Johns Hopkins University Press,

1978; S. Fish, 'Literature in the Reader: Affective Stylistics' and 'Interpreting the *Variorum*', in *Reader-Response Criticism: From Formalism to Post-Structuralism*, ed. J. P. Tompkins, Baltimore and London, Johns Hopkins University Press, 1980, pp. 70–100, 164–84.

15 On intertextuality and allusion in Ronsard's verse, see G. Mathieu-Castellani, 'Intertextualité et allusion: Le régime allusif chez Ronsard', *Littérature*, vol. 55, 1984, pp. 24–36. On intertextuality, and for full bibliographies on the subject, see *Intertextuality: Theories and Practices*, ed. M. Worton and J. Still, Manchester, Manchester University Press, 1990.

16 Ronsard, ed. Laumonier, XII, 50, 77–82; 71–72, 71–80; XIV, 4–5, 15–31; 196–97, 83–104; XVIII, 96–97, 1–16. On this question, see H. Weber (1956), I, pp. 132–38; I. Silver, 'Ronsard's Theory of Allegory: The Antimony between Myth and Truth', *Kentucky Romance Quarterly*, vol. XVIII, 1971, pp. 363–407; M. Smith, 'The Hidden Meaning of Ronsard's *Hymne de l'Hyver*', in *French Renaissance Studies in Honor of Isidore Silver*, ed. by F. Brown, *Kentucky Romance Quarterly*, vol. XXI, 1974, Supplement no. 2, pp. 85–97.

17 See, for example, I, 3; 9; 26; 31; 33; II, 6; 9; 26; 28; 29; 39; 49; *AD*, 21; 49.

18 I, 26. See also, II, 28; *AD*, 49 (12–14). Cf. O. Pot (1990), pp. 321–22, 323, 337, 335 ('L'effet symbolique compte impérativement plus que la réalité du phénomène': 'The symbolic effect counts necessarily more than the reality of the phenomenon').

19 For the word-play 'cygne'/'signe', see *Sonnets pour Hélène*, I, 9; II, 39; and XVIII, 180, s. VI, 3–7; and Pot, pp. 329–32. For the myth linking swans to the river Maeander, see VIII, 79, 134–36; XVII, 81, 376–77. On the wider question of the role played by swans in the poetic theory of the Pléiade, see R. J. Clements, *Critical Theory and Practice of the Pléiade*, Cambridge, Harvard University Press, 1942, pp. 155–63.

20 For this idea in the Hélène cycle, see in particular I, 33; II, 9. On the relationship between poetry and falsehood/truth in the work of Ronsard and the Pléiade, see G. Castor, *Pléiade Poetics: A Study in Sixteenth-Century Thought and Terminology*, Cambridge, Cambridge University Press, 1964, pp. 114–25. On this question in classical writings, see Plato, *Phaedo*, 61B; *Republic*, X, 597E ff.; Aristotle, *Metaphysics*, i, 2; Plutarch, *Moralia*, 15C–16F, 346F–348D. For the history and transmission of this idea, see E. R. Curtius, *European Literature and the Latin Middle Ages*, translated by W. R. Trask (Bollingen Series XXXVI), Princeton University Press, 1973, pp. 206 n.; 217 ff.; 235; 397; 454 n.; 459; L. Pratt, *Lying and Poetry from Homer to Pindar: Falsehood and Deception in Archaic Greek Poetics*, Ann Arbor, University of Michigan Press, 1993.

21 See, for example, the association of love, imagination and inspiration (II, 46; 52; *AD*, 25); Hélène as archetype of perfection and the difficulty of the artist to recognize and represent the Ideal Beauty (II, 11; 36); the priority of imagination over sight (considered deceptive) and the evocation of diverse imagined visions and patterns of replication and specularity (II, 15; 23; 26); the power of the written word as mediator of emotion and as substitute for an inarticulate Ronsard (II, 29); the relationship between art and imitation, beauty and nature, imagination and invention [I, 4 (3); 27 (1–3 var.); II, 32 (9–11)]; a definition of the mimetic role of poetry [I, 57 (13–14)]; the immortality conferred by Ronsard on others and, more significantly, on himself (II, 2; 37; 39; 49); Ronsard's election as poet and his surrogate role as Homer

(I, 7; II, 16; XVIII, 312, s. 61); the link between the creative act, re-presentation and memory (I, 20; II, 48); references to other poets (II, 16; 33); the medicinal, magical enchantment of love poetry as drug or pharmakon [I, 5; II, 16; AD, 26; see Homer, *Odyssey*, IV, 230; Gorgias, *A Defence of Helen* (see *Ancient Literary Criticism: The Principal Texts in New Translations*, ed. D. A. Russell and M. Winterbottom, Oxford, Oxford University Press, 1972, pp. 6–8); Plutarch, *Moralia*, 15C]; the power of names, their etymology and anagrammatical possibilities, and the relationship between words and things (I, 3; II, 6; 9; 26; 49); language and art(ifice) (I, 33; II, 9); the decoding of 'signes muets' ('Le silence parlant vaut un mauvais langage': 'Eloquent silence is worth poorly expressed language', II, 29) and an interest in interpreting verbal and non-verbal sign systems, with the associated word play on 'signe'/'cygne' (I, 9; 26; 31; II, 39; AD, 21). Other self-reflexive features of the French sequence are more oblique but no less significant: they include a lexicon of art and visual representation, of aesthetics and poetics [I, 27 (1-3 var.); 42 (7, 13); 55; II, 43 (4); AD, 18 (7–8)] as well as the allusive re-reading of certain texts (including II, 30) and certain rhetorical tropes, in order to cast light on the manner in which they can be said to parallel the processes of reading and writing (see, for example, the way in which the beauty of Hélène as a composite construct of copious divine qualities and virtues has associations with the 'diversity in unity' principle of aesthetics, with the rhetorical figure of *exemplum* [II, 18; 38 (9–11)] and with the imitative process of *contaminatio*. See also on this aspect, J. Fallon (1993).

22 T. Cave, *The Cornucopian Text: Problems of Writing in the French Renaissance*, Oxford, Clarendon Press, 1979, p. 224.

23 In *(Ré)Interprétations: Etudes sur le seizième siècle*, ed. J. O'Brien, *Michigan Romance Studies*, vol. XV, 1995, pp. 77–112.

24 On the sonnet cycle as 'un recueil factice' ('a contrived collection'), see especially *Ronsard: Sonnets pour Hélène*, ed. M. Smith, pp. 17–22, 26. In addition to the references given by Smith, p. 32 n. 14, see also the inconsistencies between Platonic and anti-Platonic statements and between Ronsard's shifting priorities in the body versus soul/mind debate (I, 20; 41; 42; 45; II, 44); between the way in which love alternately robs him of language (I, 2) and renders him articulate (II, 46); between the emphasis on his freedom and volition in love (I, 1) and the fact that he was 'destiné par sentence des cieux' ('predestined by heavenly decree') to love Hélène (I, 22); and between the differing versions of the *innamoramento* [I, 12 (10–11); 22 (5–8); 37 (1–2); II, 27 (12–14); 52].

25 Cave (1979), p. 223.

26 On the notion of the palimpsest as a writing strategy, see G. Genette, *Palimpsestes: La littérature au second degré*, Paris, Seuil, 1982. For Ronsard and palimpsests, see A. Tournon, 'Palimpsestes, échos, reflets: Le dédoublement dans la poétique de Ronsard'; and M. Huchon, 'Le palimpseste de l'*Abbrégé de l'Art Poétique françois*', in *Aspects de la poétique ronsardienne*, actes du Colloque de Caen, décembre 1985, publiés sous la direction de Philippe de Lajarte, Université de Caen, 1989, pp. 27–40, 113–28.

27 Ronsard contaminates his borrowings from II, 30 of the Hélène collection with certain details from AD, 21 – the anaphoric structure of 'tantost' and the war and peace image [cf. AD, 21 (14); line 5 of the extract of the 1584 *Cartel* quoted above; and the *Sonnets pour Hélène*, II, 28 (4)].

28 *Cartel*, lines 11–14. Cf. I, 92–96, 45–104. For the common vocabulary, see 'Au Seigneur de Carnavalet', ll. 47 ('ta main'), 48 ('façonner la jeunesse'), 50 ('ton art'), 51 ('l'esprit'), 52, 68 ('frain'), 53, 60 ('Pallas'), 60 ('guide'), 65, 71, 88, 98 ('chevaus/cheval'), 101 ('obeissant à tes lois'), 102 ('conduite'). In the 1555–87 editions of this ode another common lexical item is found (l. 98, 'main sage'). For the moral dimension, see Laumonier, I, 93, n. 1.

29 The common lexical items include 'cheval', 'tourner', 'façonner', 'bride', 'ronde', 'frein', 'serrer', 'courber', whilst syntactical repetition ('soit que ... soit que', 'tantost ... tantost') and the use of infinitive structures appear in both texts.

# CHAPTER 8

# An Overshadowed Valediction: Ronsard's Dedicatory Epistle to Villeroy

*Thomas Greene*

The epistle placed by Ronsard at the head of his *Amours Diverses* in the 1584 edition of his *Oeuvres* opens as a valedictory farewell to poetry, to love, and more broadly to the active life at court the poet had spasmodically pursued throughout most of his mature career. But the *tone* of this valediction, as it emerges in the opening thirty lines, is not easy to categorise, mingling as it does regret, self-satisfaction, foreboding, resignation, fatalism, and pride. The note of personal apprehension, specifically the fear of advancing age, illness, and death, is sounded in the very first line, which evokes a future of a winter racked with bodily storms. But this private tempest will merge, as the poem continues, with the public tempests of past and future that have nearly undone the body politic of the French nation, riven as it has been for twenty years by savage religious conflict. It is against that prospect that the poet counts his fifty-six years, an age considered more advanced by his era than ours, seeming to abjure the composition of poetry in line 3 (although he is of course occupied in writing a longish poem) and to abjure sexual pursuits (although his text prefaces a collection of 'Amours'). Taking leave of '[le] plus beau de mes jours' ('the best days of my life': l.4),[1] he knows that any hope of inner serenity is likely to be undermined by the tormented nation about him, sinking ever deeper into anarchy.

Yet there is an astonishing composure in the retrospective view of his life which, he writes, has tasted all the pleasures. The phrasing here is elegant: the speaker has *tasted* as a connoisseur the range of pleasures, but, with discrimination guided by reason, has only admitted some to his friendship:

Je les ay tous goustez, et me les suis permis
Autant que la raison me les rendoit amis.

I have tasted them all, and allowed myself / As many of them as reason made welcome as friends: ll. 7–8.

This is a ripe and judicious epicureanism that makes companions of self-indulgences but assigns to each that measure of intimacy appropriate to the speaker's role and dress upon the stage of life. This is a kind of retrospection that avoids both hypocrisy and confession to maintain quietly a reflective pride. But some part of the composure, as will shortly appear, stems from a melancholy resignation to chance and fate that qualifies the poet's view of human affairs (ll. 17–22). The dramatic complexity of tone that emerges from the opening of this epistle, playing off as it does tragedy against serenity, is in itself an admirable creative achievement.

But the complexity of the dramatic temper in this opening raises questions about what kind of a poem it is introducing. In view of the competing personal, public, poetic, moral, and metaphysical motives thrusting across each other, it is not clear after this where the epistle can go, what sort of resolution it might be expected to reach, what semblance of unity it could patch together, what status a poetic text could claim which begins by renouncing poetry (l. 3). What in fact is the status of language itself as the speaker walks away, satiated, from the community bound together by language?

Je m'en vais soul du monde ainsi qu'un convié
S'en va soul du banquet de quelque marié.

I am departing from the world, satiated, like a guest / Departing, satiated, from a wedding feast: ll. 23–24.

The festive exchange of the wedding banquet lies behind the departing guest who leaves alone, in a passage where the repeated signifier 'soul' ('surfeited') drifts toward its phonetic neighbour 'seul' ('solitary').[2] What is that figure, no longer a member of the party, able to say in a public statement?

It is true that the poetic genre Ronsard adopted here left space for plenty of digressions and ramifications. His use of a poetic tradition his contemporaries would have associated with the *Epistulae* of Horace was nothing if not flexible. Ronsard made relatively little use of it until he was well into his thirties, but in the latter stage of his career he returned frequently to poems of middle length written in rhymed couplets and a middle style, addressed to a friend or patron and introducing more or less extended praise of the dedicatee into random reflections on experience and 'philosophy'. Although the term *Epître* is not found in this poem's title, it needs to be grouped with counterparts that appear scattered in many of the divisions that make up the successive editions of his *Oeuvres*: 'Elégies', 'Poèmes', 'Discours des miseres de ce temps', even a few of the 'Hymnes'. (Most of these verse epistles also lack the appropriate term 'Epître' in their titles). If one sets aside the love sonnet, which Ronsard continued to compose throughout his long career, one can discern a tendency to move away from the strophic structure of the ode, which ranged from middle to high style and which was the dominant genre of his early period, to versions of discursive epistolary experiments in couplets (*rimes plates*), seldom abandoning the middle style. Within the loose generic expectations of this later poetry, a good deal of thematic inconsistency was allowed. Thus the questions that I have suggested are posed in the opening of the epistle to Villeroy might conceivably have been elided in the systematic rambling of the chosen form, mainly committed only to compliments addressed to a dedicatee who was commonly powerful and wealthy. This category eminently fitted this dedicatee, Nicolas de Neufville, seigneur de Villeroy, Secretary of Finance under Henri III, who had received Ronsard on several occasions at his *château* in Conflans, situated not far from Paris. One way to read this poem in fact would be to consider it as essentially a bread-and-butter letter written as repayment for hospitality received, introduced by a few irrelevant personal remarks. Ronsard might even be said to encourage this view by describing his poem toward its close as a repayment for Villeroy's generosity (ll. 144–48). But such a reading would be misleading and reductive. What is most interesting in the epistle is the interplay between its apparently rambling fluidity and its continuous underlying subject, which is time.

This subject is introduced dramatically by the first word of the poem: 'Ja' ('déjà' – 'already'). This 'Ja', which undergoes anaphoric repetition at the opening of the next line, will emerge as full of fore-boding; it suggests a passage of time which is out of control and whose recognition requires courage. The grim premonition of a bleak future in line 1 shifts to a present in lines 2–4 that demands certain perma-nent renunciations, and then in line 5 to a retrospective past that will continue, with reflective digressions, through line 30.

The return of a more extended use of anaphora in lines 11–17 organises a passage whose modulations invite attention:

J'ay veu lever le jour, j'ay veu coucher le soir,
J'ay veu greller, tonner, esclairer et pluvoir,      12
J'ay veu peuples et Rois, et depuis vingt annees
J'ay veu presque la France au bout de ses journees,
J'ay veu guerres, debats, tantost tréves et paix,
Tantost accords promis, redefais et refais,      16
Puis defais et refais.

I have seen the day break, I have seen the night fall, / I have seen hail, thunder, lightning, and rain, / I have seen nations and Kings, and for the past twenty years / I have seen France almost at the end of her days, / I have seen wars, disputes, now times of truce and peace, / Now pacts promised, broken again and made again, / Then broken and made again: ll. 11–17.

Here the first line of the series evokes a rhythmic regularity of time that apparently stipulates a rhythmic alternation of light and dark in human experience. The poet who has watched and experienced these alternations seems to refer to them with seasoned detachment. But the following line evokes natural phenomena somewhat less regular, where some measure of good is evoked by the verb 'esclairer', but where the hail, thunder, lightning and rain predominate. This transitional line then leads to a passage which drops the metaphoric use of nature, regular and irregular, to describe twenty years of historical conflict that altogether lacks rhythm and predictability.

Ronsard is writing in or around the year 1580, if one is to take literally the reference to his age in the second line, so that the twenty years mentioned in line 13 embrace the hideous confusion, violence, and suffering of the civil strife he perceives to have begun with the Huguenot conspiracy of Amboise in 1560. These years were marked by outbreaks of religious warfare lasting typically a year or two, each outbreak ending with an armistice that would inevitably be violated by one side or the other and thus collapse with the fresh renewal of fighting. Here the key adverb has shifted from 'Ja' to 'tantost', from a threatening linearity to a sinister alternation of faked agreements and savage betrayals. As events swing out of control from one 'tantost' to the next, they could only be said to parody the regularity of 'jour' and 'soir' that opens the passage. The language that refers to this dismal history imitates its eccentricity: after 'tantost tréves & paix' (l. 15), the reader would expect something like 'tantost guerres' ('now wars'), but Ronsard disorientates us by writing '… tantost accords promis', so that the *promise* of peace turns out to be the antonym of peace. The brilliant series of past participles that follows is also slightly disorientating, since the reader might expect 'redefais' to follow rather than to precede 'defais' (ll. 16–17). The echoing syllable *fais* repeated four times suggests in its context a crazy pattern of senseless circularities no one can master, and thus prepares the meditation on the power of chance 'to bind the hands', 'enchesne(r) les mains' (l. 20) of men and women.

From this fatalistic perspective time becomes a jolting succession of lurches, during which an individual like the speaker can hope at best to find some measure of personal dignity. At lines 25–30 he is reaching again for a rhythmic regularity in nature, but one that here will balance his approaching death with the advent of a replacement who will take the poet's place according to the law of nature (l. 29). Thus the available conceptions of time in this rich introductory section amount to two, either the contingent staggering of history or the natural recurrences that lead to night and death. What is missing is any hope for temporal continuity spanning the cycles of the day, the year, and the human life-span. What is also missing is any basis for the composition of poetry, including the poem one is in the process of reading. A linear version of time compels the aging writer to abandon poetry and love simultaneously (l. 3), as though creative impotence accompanied sexual impotence. But the contingent version of time as the product of chance binds the hands, and we are given no reason to exclude from this binding the hand that guides a pen. In the double crisis of the poet's bodily deterioration and the nation's fated exhaustion-unto-death, no vitality seems available for poetry. This very text risks appearing as an anomaly.

The next verse paragraph however (ll. 31–44) offers an alternative version of time by recalling an event occurring during the preceding century which was transformative and irreversible – the discovery of America, and with it, the discovery of the southern hemisphere. There is no need to examine Ronsard's historiography here too scrupulously; what matters is the shift away from the experience of history in pure passivity to a history which human resolution ('Des hommes dont les coeurs à la peine constans': 'men with hearts steadfast in the face of hardship', l. 40) can on occasion dominate. After the ravages of Time the destroyer in the introductory section, with its boundaries and bindings, this opening toward immense physical geography comes as a kind of solace; the entry into the southern Atlantic ('L'autre Neptune inconneu de nos voiles': 'that other domain of Neptune unknown to our ships', l. 41) acquires a portentous and grandiose aura, and the constellated southern cross ('son pole marqué de quatre grand estoiles': 'its pole marked by four huge stars', l. 42) introduces an emblem of mysterious cosmic hope. This fresh vision of a geophysical marvel signals the possibility of a prodigious novelty that the future cannot undo. It also offers a fresh role to the poet, who adopts the attributes Virgil assigned to 'Fama', 'fame', 'la Renommee', in the *Aeneid* (IV, 173–88), in order now to trumpet a momentous human achievement.

This abrupt swerve away from the sombre resignation and political despair of the first section, which is also a swerve away from silence toward the privilege of poetic annunciation, derives from no foreseeable development in the poem's thematic materials. It has no internal logic and barely any visible connection with what precedes it. In the unfolding of the poem, it has to be seen as an arbitrary and unmotivated volte-face. But to the knowledgeable reader of Ronsard, this kind of swerve is a familiar phenomenon, and it is particularly common in the loosely structured epistle or discourse typified by this poem. It is in fact a characteristic Ronsardian gesture. His poems of middle length like this one seem to move by dynamic impulses that follow no predictable pattern and are organised by serial charges of verbal energy, energy that will sometimes visibly flag as the impulse spends itself, to be succeeded possibly by another impulse, possibly in a different direction. Or one might more sensitively speak of a *flow* of this poet's imaginative language, a flow like a river's moving more or less rapidly according to its bent, a flow that winds according to its own inner compulsions and even circles back on itself following its own whimsical will. It is this sense of flow in the on-going succession of sinuous couplets that produces the impression of organicity in Ronsard's strongest poetry. And the sense of flow also stems from the reader's ignorance about the ultimate destination of the text. Precisely because it swerves and winds so unforeseeably, the ultimate destination of the meandering movement remains a mystery up to the end.

As though to reassert its propensity to swerve, the poem now abruptly moves away from geographic discovery to introduce the figure of the dedicatee Villeroy in the four couplets that follow. From this point on, despite occasional digressions, he will occupy the epistle's central focus, and if the text offers any new element of hope, any affirmation to balance political and military turmoil, such positive factors will be connected with the king's Secretary of Finance. If the paean to geographic discovery presented that activity as the sole source of human honour on earth, the sole reason 'que l'honneur de ce siecle aux Astres ne s'en-volle' ('why the honour of this century does not fly up to the stars', l. 37), now the source of honour and virtue will become Villeroy. And if exploration was seen to retain honour here below somewhat precariously, in view of the rest of the historical record, so the turn now to Villeroy is scarcely more reassuring, as his 'ame noble et divine' ('noble and divine soul') is represented to be alone in maintaining those virtues elsewhere repudiated. The emergence of Villeroy returns us from a heroic past to a present that is a monstrous mother of vices, that inundates men and women with a pitiless and impetuous wave of misfortunes. Again the balance of virtue against destruction is narrowly precarious. The composition of poetry, which only a few lines above had found an object of celebration, now seems condemned to the role of complaint, a role lightened only by the obligation to praise one allegedly noble soul. Praising in such an age might almost become a burden, and in fact the tribute to Villeroy in lines 45–47 gives way in lines 48–52 to lament, becomes inundated by the aggressivity of evil whose measure one's ancestors could never have imagined. The pressure of complaint on compliment is reflected in the syntactic breakdown in these lines 45–52, lacking as they do a main verb. The tragic absence of moral, social, and political continuity could be said to be mirrored in the absence of grammatical continuity. The poet, whose imminent departure was to find a replacement at the table of life, may prove luckier than the virtuous man Villeroy, whose successor at this point has not appeared.

A word is called for here concerning the presence of flattery in so much of Ronsard's verse. It is true that the socio-economic facts of his existence encouraged poetry of compliment; it is true that few court poets could survive without extolling the wealthy and powerful; it is true that early modern poetry abounds in the epideictic art of praise, and not only in France. Having recognised that, it must be said that Ronsard practised this art systematically and assiduously, and where he did, the modern reader is inclined on the whole to find his poetic verve halting and his imagination thin. Since he expected to be regarded as a major poet and was so regarded by his contemporaries, it could be said that the relative emptiness of his pages of flattery should weigh the more heavily against him. But to leave the matter there would oversimplify it. The reader suspicious of the poet's mendicity needs to weigh, in any given case, the organic function of the suspect passages in the text as a whole. The reader, that is, needs to listen to a given passage in order to judge its structural contribution to the complete poem, if indeed there is any case to be made for a contribution. We cannot know, in most instances, to what degree the dedicatee deserved the praise; it is after all conceivable that he or she may in fact have merited some. But we can try to judge, without a priori prejudice, whether a given passage is so flat and so irrelevant as to justify its immediate dismissal, or whether, on the contrary, it *earns* its place by the authentic energy of its language and the density of its links with its context. The epistle to Villeroy seems to this reader to pass this test more successfully than most of its counterparts. The very frankness in offering itself as recompense for generosity (ll. 133–48) disarms in some degree our suspicion of a vulgar motive.

What is notable and surprising in the long tribute now to be paid to Villeroy is its emergence from the darkest intuition yet of the meaning of time. The first brief tribute, as we have already noted, was immediately cut off by a lament for the disastrous present (ll. 42–52), and before returning to Villeroy, the flow of verse turns to a nightmare still more hellish, to that apocalyptic future which all the auguries appear to predict (ll. 53–68). The sky is haunted by a comet; a single year has seen two eclipses; two kings of France have died in their youth;[3] the plague has been gathering its grisly harvest. Soothsayers who can read the stars predict that in four years chaos will come again; the carnivorous peasantry will rise against the nobility; all human life will finally be wiped out. The predictions of the late mountebank astrologer Nostradamus, which Ronsard like so many contemporaries took seriously, could be interpreted to forecast this ultimate catastrophe. It did not require in those years an exceptionally credulous fancy to read into the moral and political breakdown of past and present a harbinger of this millennial total ruin in the future, when appetite, the universal wolf, as Shakespeare's Ulysses has it, 'must make perforce an universal prey, / And last eat up himself'.[4] Nostradamus' delphic forecast as interpreted here by Ronsard would bring to an end all temporal continuity, would cancel time itself.

It is against this zero-future that Ronsard chooses to turn finally to his extended commendation of Villeroy. Against the ghastly non-future he has just evoked, Villeroy appears as the one figure of enduring substance. Whatever he was in his historical existence, the poem needs him here as a *functional* presence of human decency, and his encomium begins by presenting him as the negation of negation, as an absence in this 'siecle de boue' ('age of filth', l. 69) of that absence of moral distinction now destroying France. The clemency of Fortune has brought him into being as an adversary of adversarial evil:

> Entre les vanitez la paresse et le vice,
> Et les seditions qui n'ont soin de justice,
> Entre les nouveautez, entre les courtizans,
> De fraude et de mensonge impudens artizans,
> Entre le cry du peuple et ses plaintes funebres ...

> Amid the vanities, the sloth and vice, / And the seditions which pay no heed to justice, / Amid the changes, amid the courtiers, / Brazen fabricators of fraud and deceit, / Amid the cries of the people and their funereal laments ... : ll. 73–77.

Against all this and more the poem needs a structural counterweight, the theoretical possibility of uncorrupted virtue, to which it assigns a name, Villeroy, a name presumably as acceptable to the modern reader as any other. The reappearance here of that rhetorical figure of anaphora, which lent its force to the opening of the poem, signals the intensity we are to recognise in the confrontation of social pathology and personal integrity.

Fully to grasp the implications of this confrontation, implications poetic as well as moral, one has to step back from this particular text to recall the beliefs and intuitions that counted for the most in Ronsard's imaginative and religious life. Although he described himself as a Christian and had taken minor orders in the church, one has to take seriously the admission (in one of his anti-Huguenot polemics, of all places) that without the Christian revelation, he would instinctively have been a pagan devotee of sun and moon, Ceres and Bacchus, fauns and nymphs and the Earth itself.[5] What Ronsard believed in most spontaneously and profoundly was a divine cosmic energy which accounted for the movements of celestial bodies, for the dynamism of nature, for the force of sexual desire, and for the magical power of poetry. All of these realms were animated for him by the same immanent divinity:

> Dieu est par tout, par tout se mesle Dieu,
> Commencement, la fin et le milieu
> De ce qui vit, et dont l'ame est enclose
> Par tout, et tient en vigueur toute chose,
> Comme nostre ame infuse dans nos corps.

> God is in everything, everything is imbued with God, / The beginning, the end and the middle / Of all that lives, whose soul is enclosed / In everything, and who keeps everything in being, / Like our soul which is infused in our bodies: *Le Chat*, ll. 1–5: ed. cit., II, 699.

This belief in a pantheistic energy enlivening the physical and poetic universes explains the recurrence in his work of the Muses, of Eros as Neoplatonic creator, of fauns, naiads, and dryads. These figures embody a faith in the divinity of the universe, of earthly nature, and of the inspired word. At the end of his career, as the world about him seemed to collapse into chaos and as poetry flowed less spontaneously from his pen, the drama takes the shape of a loss of faith in the immanent divinity that once had, for him, inhabited his writing and the world alike. The dynamism that had once guaranteed the vital order of word and cosmos threatens to yield to a crazy, lethal travesty. Thus the vision of present turmoil and future apocalypse carries not only social, political, and metaphysical dangers but also the risk of poetic sterility. The 'tempeste' of the first line in this epistle appears to refer primarily to the throes of age, illness, and death, but in view of what follows, it has to be read as that cosmic disorder that will just as effectively cut the speaker off from poetic inspiration. With no principle of harmonious continuity available any longer, the poetic word loses its indwelling life.

The encomium of Villeroy which occupies most of the latter half of the epistle has to be understood in the terms of this crisis. Villeroy is a man who holds out against the taint of the century, against the era of mud, as he serves his king faithfully while never succumbing to the anti-democratic snobbery of other grandees. Villeroy is said to spend his life on his royal service, 'tant la vertu active eschauffe ton courage' ('so strongly does your ardent virtue fire your courage', l. 98), and in this line one glimpses a kind of remnant of cosmic energy still animating the labour of one good man. As the encomium continues, however, it begins to focus more firmly on one quality embodied by that man, his capacity as survivor and continuer. We hear early on (ll. 88–92) of Villeroy as a counterpart to Ulysses. In the long episode that closes the encomium (ll. 111–32), we hear of a visit Ronsard will make to the underworld of spirits to bring up to date three virtuous men who had been close to Villeroy during their lives. The message he will carry will stress in particular Villeroy as the sustainer of their qualities: 'Je leur diray comment tu ensuis leurs vertus' ('I will tell them how you follow in the path of their virtues', l. 120), nor will he forget to mention the epitaphs Villeroy has had engraved on their tombs:

> ... a fin que la memoire
> De ces trois demydieux à jamais fust notoire,

Et que le temps subtil à couler et passer,
Par siecles infinis ne la peust effacer.

… so that the memory / Of these three demi-gods would be forever renowned, / And that time which slips and slides swiftly by, / Throughout endless ages would fail to efface it: ll. 125–28.

These epitaphs engraved in three languages constitute more than anecdotal detail; they represent one human response to instability and mutability. But so does the very life of Villeroy in its relation to his older friends, and in the last glimpse we have of them during this projected visit of the poet, they are dancing with joy that their living associate maintains their values, *continues* their careers.

Ces trois nobles esprits oyans telle nouvelle,
Danceront un Pean dessus l'herbe nouvelle,
Et en frappant des mains feront un joyeux bruit
Dequoy sans fourvoyer, Villeroy les ensuit.

These three noble spirits hearing such news, / Will dance a paean upon the fresh grass, / And clapping their hands will make a joyful sound / Because without going astray, Villeroy is following in their steps: ll. 129–32.

It is in this verb 'ensuit' that the direct encomium of Villeroy culminates, not by accident. It represents an affirmation that human virtue can persist despite the unpromising context of values and events.

The encomium has necessarily led us away from the personal drama of the poet, which can now return in a different atmosphere. What receives stress at this juncture is his poverty—most visibly his inability to repay Villeroy what he owes in return for his benefactor's largesse, but more broadly the poverty of life and verve that lead him to an almost suicidal depression.

Presque à regret je vy, et à regret je voy
Les rayons du Soleil s'estendre dessus moy.
Pource je porte en l'ame une amere tristesse,
Dequoy mon pied s'avance aux fauxbourgs de vieillesse.

I almost regret being alive, and I regret seeing / The rays of the sun stretch forth above me. / This is why I carry in my soul a bitter sadness, / Because my steps take me over the threshold of old age: ll. 139–42.

As the poem flows back toward the figure of its creator, it appears to reformulate the pathos of its opening in starker terms. The reader must be prepared for a continued flow in that direction, since the poem to this point has found no convincing image of its own life and continuity. The flow away from Villeroy, whose own powers of continuing have been underscored, towards the emptiness of the poet's purse and of his creative potency, tends to separate further the one who survives a tempest from one who succumbs. This dismal contrast of the patron and poet does however modulate into a somewhat more hopeful hypothesis: perhaps the patron will permit the poet to open his coffer and present him with the present poem and the pen that wrote it out, the pen that is capable of prolonging the patron's praise to posterity (ll. 145–48). Here is a gift that belies abject poverty, and here is another stay against oblivion. With this turn the poem redirects its flow for the last time and begins to move toward its luminous conclusion.

'Reçoy donc mon present, s'il te plaist …' ('Please accept therefore my gift …') writes the poet, equating implicitly the dignity and worth of his poetic language with the worldly largesse he has received. The hopeful hypothetical vignette in which the coffer is opened and the precious gift transferred restores a measure of confidence. The last vision of the future we meet is an extension of the poetic gift to celebrate the wider subject of Villeroy's estate at Conflans, and in these final lines the distinction of the future poetry is indistinguishable from the nobility of the site. This present poem will remain in Villeroy's 'belle maison de Conflans' ('beautiful house at Conflans', l. 150) only as an earnest of a longer unwritten poem; will remain until:

> … Apollon m'eschauffe le courage
> De chanter tes jardins, ton clos, et ton bocage,
> Ton bel air, ta riviere et les champs d'alentour
> Qui sont toute l'année eschauffez d'un beau jour,
> Ta forest d'orangers, dont la perruque verte
> De cheveux eternels en tout temps est couverte,
> Et tousjours son fruit d'or de ses fueilles defend,
> Comme une mere fait de ses bras son enfant.

> … Apollo inspires my heart / To sing of your gardens, your orchard, and your woodland, / Your pure air, your river and the surrounding fields / Which are all year round warmed by fine weather, / Your grove of orange trees, whose green head / Is covered in all weathers with eternal tresses, / And forever protects its golden fruit with its leaves, / As a mother protects her child with her arms: ll. 153–60.

Who could have foreseen that this poem streaked with violence would end in delight? The meandering flow of the couplets seems to reach almost by accident this miraculous apparition of the orange grove, this bizarre and redemptive epiphany of stability which draws both upon civilised husbandry and natural plenty. For the strictly logical needs of prose statement, these lines are irrelevant, but for the underlying dialectic of order and destruction, preservative time and ruinous time, they offer a brilliant and whimsical close. The quaint caprice of the 'perruque verte' fails to weaken the affirmation of the 'cheveux eternels' (ll. 157–58), and the maternal protection of the fruit by the leaves provides a gesture of human protectiveness the text needed and can now rest upon.

Here among other things is an image of human, natural and poetic felicity. These lines, lest we forget, are promising the poem Ronsard has yet to write, but which of course he *is* now writing. The lines through which the oranges are visible are part of that poem; they are poetic oranges and supply their life, their gaiety, and their continuity into the indefinite future as the most hopeful tokens of poetic endurance. The tribute to the estate at Conflans and its oranges makes no attempt to mitigate the savagery surrounding it, but brings into being a plausible oasis of continuing felicity.

In the last four lines, the boundary already blurred between culture and nature breaks down as the 'livre', which is to say this poem, takes its place in Villeroy's personal library, bringing with it a scent like that of orange trees. The poem can aspire again to organic life. One is allowed to hope that both the books and the trees will survive the darkening storm, although we have no reason to think it will abate. The power of the estate's resistance has not yet been fully tested. We are left with a certain delicacy in this limited nuance of hope, a delicacy that forms the most telling critique of the vulgar violence beyond it. The role of poetry seems to emerge from the text as a whole as the custody of beleaguered values and the precise registering of moral feeling on the eve of their probable disappearance.

# Notes

1 All quotations from Ronsard are taken from his *Oeuvres complètes*, ed. J. Céard, D. Ménager, and M. Simonin, 2 vols (Paris, Gallimard, Bibliothèque de la Pléiade, 1993). The poem under study can be found in volume I, pp. 439–43. Line references appear in parentheses after the English translation of each quotation.

2 Ronsard was doubtless remembering here, as his editors have pointed out, Lucretius, *De rerum natura*, III, 935–39:

> Nam si grata fuit tibi vita anteacta priorique
> et non omnia pertusum congesta quasi in vas

commoda perfluxere atque ingrata interiere:
cur non ut plenus vitae conviva recedis
aequo animoque capis securam, stulte, quietem?

If the life you have lived till now has been a pleasant thing – if all its blessings have not leaked away like water poured into a cracked pot and run to waste, unrelished – why then, you silly creature, do you not retire as a guest who has had his fill of life and take your care-free rest with a quiet mind? (trans. R.E. Latham).

To compare this passage with Ronsard's version is to be struck with the complications of moral attitude imposed on it by the French version. Ronsard's speaker has tasted the pleasures of life with discrimination rather than having assumed their uniform desirability, and no counterpart exists in his future to the Lucretian 'securam … quietem'.

3 François II died in 1560 at the age of 16, Charles IX in 1574 at the age of 24.
4 *Troilus and Cressida*, I, 3, 123–24.
5 *Remonstrance au peuple de France*, ll. 57–84 (II, 1021–22).

# CHAPTER 9

# 'De l'amitié' (*Essais* 1.28): 'Luy' and 'Moy'

*Ann Moss*

*Contemporary Readings* is an ambivalent subtitle for a book of essays, and this reading of an essay by Montaigne is suitably ambivalent. It is a 'contemporary reading' in the sense that it will try to indicate reading routes that would have been familiar to Montaigne's contemporaries. But no modern reader is Montaigne's contemporary in that sense. If only because of the strangeness of Montaigne's language, a 'contemporary reading', in the sense of 'modern reading', starts necessarily from an awareness of the historical distance which separates us from his contemporary readers. The original readers of the *Essais* were invited to pick their way through them by reading signs different from those we are used to. 'Different' but not unintelligble. The purpose of the present essay on 'De l'amitié' is to make those signs legible, and so to constitute a dialogue between past and present 'contemporaries'.

The reason why 'De l'amitié' seems an appropriate stage for such a dialogue is because in it we can hear Montaigne's own dialogue with the dead. His dead friend belongs to an irrecoverable past, more at one now with those who spoke the dead languages of admired Antiquity than with Montaigne's contemporary present. 'De l'amitié' attempts to put in place a complex set of dialogues over that space of time. In the attempt Montaigne both finds his own singular voice and constructs a cultural modernity from contemporary strategies of discourse. It is those strategies, recognisable to his contemporaries but not always to us, that my essay aims to uncover, bringing us nearer perhaps to the process of writing as it was then. Even so, modern readers can do no more than attune their ears to long defunct patterns of speech. We still find ourselves listening from an unbridgeable

distance, a distance as unbridgeable as that which Montaigne ultimately saw between himself and his own dead past, and between himself and the Antiquity in whose image he had been formed. Yet it was
precisely by reading that distance from the perspective of his present
that Montaigne found himself and spoke so forcibly to his contemporaries. It is also by adopting the language of their contemporaries that
modern readers may find themselves enabled to read signs pointing
towards other productive forms of dialogue with the past. This contemporary reading will seek to make the past speak, but it will also
hint at how the present may respond with a richness of insight derived
from the dialogic model exploited by Bakhtin and from theories of
personal development like those of Lacan, for whom chains of
signifying speech invent continuously the writer's and the reader's
common place. However, it is by way of an archaic sense of the
commonplace that we shall initiate our dialogue with Montaigne.

Montaigne's essay on friendship with its ensuing (non)chapter,
placed so pivotally in the central space of his first book, has always
drawn attention.[1] Most modern studies have read the essay as a
constituent part of a whole, whether that whole be the evolutionary
pattern of Montaigne's thinking, his process of production diachron-
ically perceived, or the design of the work overall. Each 'chapter' does
indeed contribute to a holistic reading of the *Essais*. But for Montaigne's contemporaries, there was another, now obsolete meaning of
the word 'chapter' or 'chapitre'. They would be conditioned by their
schoolboy training to read the word more literally, as the heading
(*caput*) for a collection of quotations assembled to illustrate a particular topic in a commonplace-book. Montaigne's readers who had
studied ancient texts, even at the most elementary level, at schools run
according to principles of Humanist pedagogy, would have been
trained to compile notebooks of quotations from what they read.
Almost all the titles to Montaigne's chapters, be they single abstract
concepts or sententious statements proposed for debate, would have
been perfectly recognisable to his contemporary readers as potential
*capita* or *tituli* heading up sections of a commonplace-book, and
under them they would expect to find an abundance of extracts, 'flowers' gathered from a diversity of prior texts. Cross-references there
might well be from one section to another, but perusers of commonplace-books (and by Montaigne's time this universal aid to classroom
composition had proliferated in print) would tend to read discretely,
evaluating the riches collected within each separate container labelled

by its *titulus*. They would be alert to relationships of similarity and difference between the more or less fortuitously assembled array of quotations, and trained to deploy them for the rhetorical amplification of newly invented discourse and to regroup them strategically for specific targets according to dialectical procedures. The 'Montaigne' of the following pages will be primarily a compiler, critic and manager of commonplaces on the topic 'friendship', and we his modern, but perhaps not too 'insuffisans lecteurs' ('incompetent readers').[2]

The exordium to the essay on friendship insinuates many of the commonplaces which will orchestrate the later amplifications of its theme, not least by constructing a space for an overlapping series of dialogues.[3] The first of these dialogues sets the essay's author in relationship with 'un peintre que j'ay' ('a painter I have'), a curiously ambivalent relationship in which the writer seems both to own the painter, 'mon peintre' ('my painter'), and to 'follow' or 'imitate' him, 'l'ensuivre'. The act of writing is here construed as imitation, imitation of a cultural artefact which is at one and the same time part of the writer's domestic interior and out of his reach. The painting at the centre of the artist's work, 'riche, poly et formé selon l'art' ('rich, polished, and fashioned according to the rules of the art'), is a product of the 'suffisance' ('competence') of its creator. Measuring his own abilities against that achievement, Montaigne, the imitator, locates his own 'suffisance' in what appeared to be the margins of the more perfect work, in the grotesque designs of its surround, 'corps monstrueux, rappiecez de divers membres, sans certaine figure, n'ayants ordre, suite ny proportion que fortuité' ('monstrous bodies, piece-meal assemblies of a variety of limbs, without clear-cut shape, without order, continuity, or proportion, except it be by chance').[4]

This dialogue of art-forms has many threads, of which we can only disentangle some. Firstly, there is the parley between the perfectly contrived picture which Montaigne has, but cannot reproduce, and the grotesques with which he associates his own writing in the *Essais*. Both are varieties of imitation. One represents mimetic replication, for it must be assumed that the central 'tableau' is essentially either an imitation of nature or an imitation of a prior painting. The language used to describe the other form of composition available for Montaigne to imitate is reminiscent of the way discourse was generated by the commonplace-book method, pieced together from discontinuous fragments of dismembered texts more or less fortuitously assembled under diverse heads. Within the first few lines of the exordium it is this second type of imitation which is moved to the centre, in a chiasmus which juxtaposes painterly and writerly grotesques and relegates the 'tableau élabouré ... formé selon l'art' ('the picture elaborated and fashioned according to the rules of the art') to the outer perimeters. It is in this central space, as it is constructed by the writer, not the perfect painter, and at the point where Montaigne recognises the futility of his initial imitative gesture, that he both appropriates fragmentation and speaks in the first person: 'je vay bien ... je demeure court ... ma suffisance' ('I get along ... I stop short ... my competence'). The modern reader may, at this initial moment of the essay, already hear in Montaigne's words that tension between, on the one hand, mirror-image construction and, on the other, disintegration apprehended as 'corps morcelé' ('body dismembered') which Lacan locates early in the formation of the 'je'.[5]

However, at the surface of the text, there is another adjacent and more interfering dialogue. This is the dialogue between Montaigne's two languages, French and Latin. His French inscribes his grotesques. Latin is and is not his. The line from Horace inserted here is an alien import, an unassimilated quotation fragment from the start of the *Ars poetica*, where coherence and unity, 'simplex et unum', the characteristics of 'un tableau ... formé selon l'art' ('a picture fashioned according to the rules of the art'), are commended to the detriment of 'peintures fantasques' ('fantastic paintings') where lovely ladies end in fishes' tails. But, paradoxically, by means of the quotation selected, Latin is made to represent the aesthetic of the various and the discontinuous, which Montaigne has claimed for himself. As we pursue analogies with writing procedures generated by commonplace-books, we must bear in mind that the *disiecta membra* in the disjointed sections of commonplace-books did indeed still have a Latin voice. In the dialogue between French and Latin, Montaigne allows no easy division of roles; in him the present and the ancient past are viscerally entwined.

But how does the exordium lead us into the commonplace of the title, friendship? The rest of Montaigne's introduction insinuates his friend La Boétie into the dialogue he has already started. The painter's perfect picture is replaced (or seems to be going to be replaced) by La Boétie's book, *De la Servitude volontaire*, but whereas the imagined picture was firmly 'located', 'log[é]', La Boétie's verbal composition is a very mobile thing. It has no certain title. It 'escaped' accidentally; it 'runs' from hand to hand. Its place, as we discover at the end, is at best in the margins, at the beginning and the end of the essay, never firmly in the middle. It was indeed a work of the author's youth, written 'par maniere d'essay' ('a trial-piece'), more like Montaigne's own grotesques than the promised 'tableau', a product of the common-place-book method of La Boétie's schooling, 'subjet vulgaire et tracassé en mille endroits des livres' ('a very ordinary theme, chewed over in a thousand places in books').[6] Moreover, its reception by its contemporaries is uncertain and out of control. Its initial effect on Montaigne as sympathetic reader is described in terms of movement, 'acheminant ainsi cette amitié' ('thus setting in motion this friend-ship'); its later history delivers it to a hostile Other, and allies it with restlessness and change within the state. As is well known, it never finds its place within the *Essais*; like La Boétie's other writings, it is destined to slip away 'ailleurs' ('elsewhere').

What, then, of La Boétie's image remains stable enough to focus the essay? The book that La Boétie did not write would have had that solidity:

> si ... il eut pris un tel desseing que le mien, de mettre par escrit ses fantasies, nous verrions plusieurs choses rares et qui nous approcheroient bien pres de l'honneur de l'antiquité (p. 219).

> If he had conceived a plan like mine, putting down in writing whatever came into his imagination, we would now see several choice things which would bring us very close to what we honour in Antiquity.

The dialogue continues from the earlier lines of the essay. If La Boétie had played Montaigne's part, the grotesques, the 'peintures fan-tasques', would have had a substitute: a 'tableau ... formé selon l'art', nearer to the ideal described by Horace. Would it have been a more perfect picture, an image of Montaigne and La Boétie perfectly at one in the process of conception and execution, a better mirror for writing? Such perfection, substituted for Montaigne's 'corps mon-strueux', would deny Montaigne the 'suffisance' he has already iden-tified as his. Yet the lure of that perfection begins to dominate a dialogue which soon ends by freezing out of the temporal flux that unique and once and only friendship 'si entière et parfaite que certainement il ne s'en lit guiere de pareilles, et, entre nos hommes, il ne s'en voit aucune trace en usage' ('so entire and perfect that it is certain that few such are to be found in books, and in the practice of our contemporaries no trace at all of any such is visible', pp. 219–20). The preceding dialogic process has indeed already situated the image of La Boétie firmly in a particular cultural context, which is not the present time. La Boétie is not to be identified with the 'maniere d'essay' ('trial-piece'), the mobile script which escaped into an uncertain future, but with the 'honneur de l'antiquité' ('what we honour in Antiquity'), both its style of writing and its moral style: 'il avoit son esprit moulé au patron d'autres siecles que ceux-cy' ('he had a mind moulded to the model of eras other than this', p. 232). The only 1595 addition in the exordium is careful to insert at the centre of a sentence, between references to La Boétie's elusive, diverse, fragmentary literary remains, the reminder that Montaigne was 'héritier de sa bibliothèque' ('made heir to his library'), a library, no doubt, of books which fixed in print the model of 'eras other than this'.

It is indeed into a library of texts that we enter as we move from the exordium into the main body of the essay. The discourse on friendship is grounded on a series of references to Greek and Latin authorities, and the final additions made to the essay stress that this is so by putting names to quotations and by inserting new ones. In the latest state of the essay, the concept of friendship with which we start is freighted intertextually with allusions to ancient culture, primarily to ancient moral thought in the recall of Aristotle's *Nicomachean Ethics*, secondarily to ancient social structures implied in the 'quatre especes anciennes' ('four species of friendship known to Antiquity', p. 220). Montaigne's quotation from the first chapter of Book VIII of the *Ethics* and his summary of the distinction Aristotle draws in chapters three and four between the most noble form of friendship and inferior friendships based solely on utility and pleasure, establish a much clearer basis for any future dialogue between past and present than was apparent in earlier versions of the essay, where the distinction is slipped in later (p. 224) and is not culturally contextualised. Montaigne's latest thinking situates friendship unequivocally and from the beginning within the environment of ancient moral philosophy, where it is considered 'a kind of virtue, or implying virtue', as Aristotle says in the first sentence of Book VIII. It is not just friendship which is at issue, but the whole moral ideal of ancient philosophy, in which perfect friendship was inseparable from goodness: 'friendship in the truest sense is friendship between good men'.[7] And the friendship between Montaigne and La Boétie was formed in the image of that high ideal, that 'souveraine et maistresse amitié' ('that sovereign and supreme friendship') distinct from 'amitiez ordinaires et coustumières' ('common and ordinary friendships', p. 226).[8]

The analysis of friendship into distinct social types with which the latest edition proceeds, 'ces quatre especes anciennes,' ('those four species known to Antiquity') produces an alienating effect which is longer to take hold in the original essay, where we wait for the 'shocking' quotations from ancient writers on family relationships to trigger the distancing (p. 220). The analysis imputed to Antiquity does not fit snugly with modern social structures. 'Amitié hospitaliere' ('guest-friendship'), though well known to students of the ancient world, is an institution without equivalent in modern society and without a place in Montaigne's essay. The connection of ancient culture with the alien is crucial, and we shall return to it, but it does seem as if it was the later Montaigne, reading himself, who saw how crucial it was. The writing Montaigne of the essay's earliest version was perhaps more engaged with problems of how to use his reading of others to amplify his topic.

Writing, for writers who had learnt their skills in composition from Humanist schoolmasters, could broadly take one of two forms: close imitation or topical invention. We have witnessed a dialogue between them represented pictorially on the inner walls of Montaigne's house. Of the two, it is topical invention fed by commonplace-book method, 'rappiec[é]' ('assembled piece-meal') from the 'divers membres' ('variety of parts') collected under commonplace-heads, which Montaigne chose in the first instance, in order to fill out his subject with a proliferation of grotesques, rather than to elaborate it within the stricter confines of mimetic art. His choice of procedure is clearer if we follow the original plan of the essay, and note if and when interference from the final state of the text reinforces or counters what seems to be the original design.[9]

The most obvious sign of commonplace-book composition is an abundance of the forms of enunciation which were generally collected under appropriate subject-heads: short extracts from poets; prose definitions; *sententiae*; apophthegmata; similitudes; *exempla*, and so on.[10] Montaigne's essay is obviously replete with 'fleurs estrangeres' ('imported flowers') of this sort, culled in a diversity of Greek and Latin fields. On a closer look, some will be seen to have been taken ready picked. At least six of the quoted 'famous sayings' or apophthegmata, are taken from a collection assembled from Greek and Latin authors by Erasmus, his *Apophthegmatum sive scite dictorum libri sex*, first published in 1531. In the last additions he made to the essay, inserting extra apophthegmata and specifying the ascription of one already there, Montaigne went out of his way to signal this source, thereby contextualising the essay more explicitly within the culture of quotation-collections.[11]

However, Montaigne's collected fragments, as he was to say elsewhere for a slightly different purpose, are not just for display, arrayed as 'exemple', 'authorité' and 'ornement' ('example', 'authority', and 'ornament'), but for 'l'usage que j'en tire' ('the use I make of them').[12] Let us return to the 'quatre especes anciennes'. This seems to mark the start of a development of the theme by way of division. I have already suggested that this added diversion towards the social patterning of ancient society is a lure, a mirror-moment which proves vain and inconsequential. But it also functions as a reinforcement to the argumentative procedure already inscribed, rather more faintly, in the earliest version of the essay. That version hinged on a division of the general concept, 'societé', into three species of human relationship operating in the private sphere, that is to say, falling within the overall classification 'economic', rather than 'political'. These species were: family relationships (further subdivided as relationships between father and son, brother and brother); 'conjugal' relationships (subdivided as amatory, marital, and homosexual); and relationships based on mutual advantage (pp. 221–24). The Latin word *amicitia* in humanistic usage was susceptible of the same range of application as the French 'societé'. Montaigne's later addition of a definition of friendship (p. 220) to the head of this argument from *genus* to *species* makes it clearer that the *genus* 'societé' is indeed 'amitié' in its widest sense; and it is also clearer that its *species*, now named, are to be both enumerated and also examined critically to see whether they 'conviennent', that is to say, 'agree' with Aristotle's ideal friendship of 'those who are good, and similar in their goodness'.

Now, although it would take more time to demonstrate this, the type of ratiocinative discourse which Montaigne here sets in train is the topic-based, dialectical argumentation for which commonplace-books supplied the material and with which they were closely allied at the more advanced stages of the northern Humanists' pedagogic programme.[13] The theme is drawn through places of proof which will establish its parts, its compatibilities and incompatibilities, causes and effects, similarities and differences, and other features plausibly demonstrated by standard inferential procedures. These 'places of argument' derive from ancient dialectic and rhetoric, but employed as the basic procedure for generating discourse, they produce rather different textual concatenations than compositions closely imitating particular classical models. Topical method tends to proliferation and subdivision. It uses the 'proof' of 'authority', in the form of quotations, generously, but also constructively, incorporating quotation into ratiocinative discourse to substantiate argument, to set up comparisons and negations, to engender debate. It allows room, as did the commonplace-book which resourced it, for the continual addition of further subdivisions and 'pièces rapportées' ('gathered material'). It implies, and thereby constructs, not a competent imitator, but an author who manages his text and intervenes in it to judge what does and does not carry conviction.

Montaigne contrasts friendship with other forms of domestic social relationship by putting suggested subdivisions of the genus 'friendship' through compatibilities and incompatibilities, thereby refining his definition of his theme. Later in the essay he amplifies a general proposition about friendship (that friends have all in common), by a division (union of wills, communality of goods) and then by apposite *exempla* retold from Cicero and Lucian (pp. 225–29). Here again, a type of locution collected in commonplace-books is employed as a dialectical operator. The *exempla* further argument, functioning both as validators of propositions and as propagators of debate. Montaigne's grotesques may be not quite as fortuitously or aimlessly contrived as he would have us believe. However, they are a different kind of composition from the mimetic art of his painter, as Montaigne implied in his exordium. The early versions of the essay let the matter rest there. In the latest version, contrasting styles of composition articulate a dialogue into which the older Montaigne wrote the crisis of his narration of himself.

Quotations and paraphrases of classical texts are not just the 'divers membres' ('variety of limbs') which go to build a new body of discourse. They bring with them a history. They have referents in a past culture, which may be occulted in present use, but which may also be recovered to provide the other voice in a dialogue across time and across cultures. We have already heard this in the added 'quatre especes anciennes' ('the four species known to Antiquity'). It can be heard again, a little more insistently, at the end of the passage on marital friendship. Montaigne himself is prepared to envisage conditions in which women could be true friends with men, but of such friendship there is no example to cite, 'et par le commun consentement des escholes anciennes en est rejetté' ('and by the common consent of the

Ancient schools of philosophy the female sex is excluded from friendship', pp. 222–23). For Montaigne change is possible beyond the discourse of the past, but the world of the Ancients is immovably fixed,
frozen out of temporal evolution. The phrase just cited makes the
point very deliberately. It is an addition from the last revision, and was
itself revised several times in the Bordeaux copy before Montaigne
decided to specify 'escholes anciennes', in preference to his first
thought, 'philosophie' in general.

By stages we come to the longest and most significant of the inser-
tions made in the latest version. Homosexual love, that alien 'licence
Grecque' ('licence of the Greeks'), is 'justement abhorrée par nos
moeurs' ('rightly abhorrent to our standards of behaviour'). But not
to the 'moeurs' of classical Antiquity. Montaigne's latest thinking on
the subject amplifies his initial lapidary statement considerably, but to
do so he does not employ contemporary commonplace-dialectical
method. He reaches back to ancient texts in order to restore in their
words, 'de [leur] part' ('taking their point of view'), a 'peinture' ('a
painting') of a foreign, culturally institutionalised practice which
belongs in the past (pp. 223–24). His 'painting' takes the form of a
synopsis from the orations of Phaedrus and Pausanias in Plato's *Symposium*, phrased as reported speech and framed by quotations from
consecutive paragraphs of Cicero's *Tusculan Disputations*, setting this
'tableau' apart from the surrounding 'grotesques'. At the closing of
this window on the ancient world, Cicero, in the *De amicitia*, is made
to enunciate a judgement between true friendship and ancient homosexual love, a judgement 'plus equitable et plus equable' ('more equitable and more fair') than Montaigne's own initial 'description',
because the ancient world is allowed to judge its own culture on its
own terms and in its own language.

Bilingual, bicultural, imaginatively conversant with an alien and
unrepeatable past, Montaigne has in his rereading and rewriting of
the essay made explicit a dialogic substructure which was much
weaker in the first version, dialogue between the past and present, the
fixed and the mobile, the mimetic and the more freely generative.
And, with respect to La Boétie, the text of that dialogue is repeated.
The perfect friendship had from the beginning been located in an
almost irrecoverable space: 'il ne s'en lit guiere de pareilles... il ne s'en
voit aucune trace en usage' ('few such are to be found in books...
no trace of it is visible in practice', pp. 219–20). It had been contextualised in ancient moral philosophy, and later in the essay that

contextualisation is to be reinforced by apophthegmata from Aristotle and by *exempla* from antiquity's major writers on friendship, Cicero and Lucian.

Yet, in the first version of the essay, no language seems adequate to express the experience itself. We read repeatedly that 'cela ne se peut exprimer' ('it cannot be expressed', p. 224), that 'les discours mesmes que l'antiquité nous a laissé sur ce subject, me semblent lâches au pris du sentiment que j'en ay' ('to me even the thoughts Antiquity has left us on the subject seem weak compared to the feeling I have about it', p. 230). And among his contemporary readers, Montaigne little expects to encounter a 'bon juge' ('good judge'), a 'juge equitable' ('equitable judge') of this very private experience, 'untried' ('essayé') by them, and 'eslongneé du commun usage' ('far removed from common practice', p. 230). Did the rewriting Montaigne, rereading this passage when he added his 'more equitable' depiction of the alien homosexual culture of the ancients 'selon leur usage' ('according to their practice') apply to it this same notion that only the 'essaying', in this case verbal 'essaying', of experience 'eslongnée du commun usage' can produce an equitable judgement of it? Certainly, the texture and composition of his 'essay' on homosexuality locates it in a past which cannot be recalled except in language borrowed from the past.

In the dialogue of Montaigne's friendship with La Boétie, the last revision of the essay produced a parallel script. Montaigne finally, latterly, did put at the centre of his essay a 'tableau', a tiny painting of a particular moment in that friendship to which he otherwise refers in the abstract terms appropriate to 'effects inimaginables à qui n'en a gousté' ('effects which cannot be imagined by anyone who has not had a taste of them', p. 229). But the speaker adequate to that moment is not Montaigne. It is La Boétie, in Latin, in verse:

> il escrivit une Satyre Latine excellente, qui est publiée, par laquelle il excuse et explique la precipitation de notre intelligence, si promptement parvenue à sa perfection (p. 225).[14]

> he wrote an excellent satire in Latin, which has been published, in which he defends and explains the swift onset of our mutual understanding, which so suddenly reached its perfection.

In the bilingual consciousness of Montaigne, La Boétie belongs to the fixed forms of Latin poetry, Montaigne to the sinuous movement of French prose. In the bicultural split, La Boétie and perfect friendship are for ever locked away in a closed world of ancient moral virtues, 'moulé au patron d'autres siecles que ceux-cy' ('moulded to the model of eras other than this').

Montaigne, finally hazarding a portrait at the centre of his essay, sensed that the only proper language for the memorial of his dead friend was the dead language of dead poets. Yet, on each side of the inserted 'tableau' and its absent Latin explanation, the grotesques are given an added turn. By the end, Montaigne knew that survival outside and beyond the narcissistic ideal of a perfect and ineffable union of souls depended on finding words in French, in plainest prose, 'en respondant: Par ce que c'estoit luy; parce que c'estoit moy' ('replying: because it was him; because it was me', p. 224). These words, despite their careful reciprocity, tear apart the perfect whole. Montaigne does exactly the same in the 'grotesque' commentary on the other side of the picture of the formation of that union. Where the earlier version speaks only of 'je ne sçay quelle quinte essence … qui, ayant saisi toute ma volonté, l'amena se plonger et se perdre dans la sienne' ('I know not what quintessence [of mingled considerations], which, having seized my whole will, brought it to immerse itself and lose itself in his'), the later text draws back from this plunge of the self towards its image in the Narcissus-pool, adding reciprocally: 'qui, ayant saisi toute sa volonté, l'amena se plonger et se perdre en la mienne, d'une faim, d'une concurrence pareille' ('which, having seized his whole will, brought it to immerse itself and lose itself in mine, with like hunger, with like rivalry', p. 225). Gesturing desperately towards the obliteration of self and other in a seamless union, the text, 'corps monstrueux' ('that monstrous body'), merely reflects a double, and its inalienable scissure. The survivor is a grotesque: 'il me semble n'estre plus qu'à demy' ('I feel I am now only a half', p. 231).

However, despite the pain, the previous Montaigne obscurely, and the later Montaigne with a firmer hold on the dialogue he had earlier anticipated, recover and recuperate this grotesque. Perfect friendship, ancient culture, dead friend, dead language, all the order of 'mirror-images, identifications and reciprocities', so carefully associated in the text with an order of verbal composition based on imitation, are framed off, frozen, fixed.[15] In a bitter irony, the products of La Boétie's modelling of himself on consecrated images of style and culture, his praise of republican virtue, his Petrarchan sonnets, his Latin satire, have all been dissipated, vanished 'ailleurs' ('elsewhere'). But the

grotesque survivor survives and grows. He has his parallel and finds
his own voice in a style which is based on the fragmentary, discontinuous, disjointed, contradictory, open-ended paradigm of the commonplace-book. In following the twists and turns of that style, and in
finding there the places on which to link chains of thought, he begins
to construct himself.[16]

The commonplace-book method of composition, as I have
described it, is not, of course, a definitive account of the writing-pro-
cedure of the mature Montaigne. Nevertheless, in the essay on friendship, it is possible to discern Montaigne, particularly the later
Montaigne, himself discerning a certain parting of the ways which
was a painful birth for both man and writer. It was not surprising that
man and writer essayed themselves first by way of a method of production which they would have known from adolescence. Afterwards,
and even here, Montaigne can be seen increasingly appropriating and
making his own whatever parts of commonplace-book method were
still cast too fixedly in the mould of an alien discourse. *Exempla*,
apophthegmata, *sententiae*, quotations became forms of self-expression: 'je ne dis les autres, sinon pour d'autant plus me dire' ('I only
speak with the voice of others, the better to speak myself').[17] In the
essay on friendship, the *exemplum* of the self already outvoices all
other *exempla*.

The use of commonplace-books formed other habits of mind as
well, less consciously, but perhaps the more deeply. Even a modern
reader of commonplace-books, totally unschooled in their use, finds
herself slipping into a mode of attention which was as much recommended by their promoters as concentration on the members of a
single head. Inevitably, given the disjunctions, you browse through the
quotations, picking up here and there similarities of wording inter-
larded with differences of intent, making loops back and forth across
the dividing lines of the containing heads. Start such a treasure-trail
in a Montaigne essay, particularly one of the more complex, later
ones, and the pleasure of reading will be plenteously gratified.[18] 'De
l'amitié', also, even in its earliest version, has its rewards. The dialectic of this essay's argument seems, after the first half, to have sidelined
fathers, sons, mothers, daughters, brothers, male and female lovers.
But the tenuous links which still hold them in play, repeated words,
*exempla*, and, above all, the poetry of Virgil, Horace, and Catullus,
loop them back (pp. 230–31). It is no accident that the same poem
by Catullus is quoted at the beginning and the end of the essay,

reminding us, if we care to listen, that these quotations have another context: Virgil's Aeneas making the memorial of his father; Horace sharing Virgil's tears for his male friend; and, in the last lines Montaigne quotes before his original insertion of texts by La Boétie, Catullus (LXV) weeping for his dead, silent brother like the nightingale singing for a dismembered boy. It is not irrelevant that Catullus LXV originally introduced a now lost text transposed from an admired and imitated past culture. The more mature Montaigne will play these games more seriously, and by no means with quotations only, inviting the shifting attention of the reader to follow both the linear dialectical development of his argumentation and the intricate weave of his verbal web. Or, in the polyphony metaphor used by Lacan, whose sense of language as Symbolic Order has its origins in a given literary language which itself has a history:

> Nulle chaîne signifiante en effet qui ne soutienne comme appendu à la ponctuation de chacune de ses unités tout ce qui s'articule de contextes attestés, à la verticale, si l'on peut dire, de ce point.[19]

> There is indeed no signifying chain which does not have hanging, as it were, at the cadence between each of its units all that can be articulated from all contexts that can be adduced, vertically suspended at that point.

Bereft of its mirror-image and its ideals of consistency, sameness, oneness, and self-replication, confronted with the potential threat of total dismemberment, how indeed is the subject to be constituted? Our near contemporary, Lacan, would reply: by language as such a chain of signifiers, 'in a manner always disjoined and intermittent':

> Ce que cette structure de la chaîne signifiante découvre, c'est la possibilité que j'ai, justement dans la mesure où sa langue m'est commune avec d'autres sujets ... de m'en servir pour signifier *tout autre chose* que ce qu'elle dit. Fonction plus digne d'être soulignée dans la parole que celle de déguiser la pensée (le plus souvent indéfinissable) du sujet: à savoir celle d'indiquer la place de ce sujet dans la recherche du vrai.[20]

> What this structure of the signifying chain uncovers, is the possibility I have, precisely to the extent that I inhabit its verbal universe in common with others ... to use it to signify things quite other than what it says. This function of language is more worth emphasising than that of disguising the thought of the subject (which is more or less indefinable); what this function does is to point to the place of this subject in the search for truth.

Montaigne's contemporaries looked to their commonplace-books in order to assemble themselves from scattered parts of dead men's speech collected in ordered places. Montaigne's chains of grotesques, 'disjoined and intermittent', 'n'ayants ordre, suite ny proportion', form a verbal universe in which the present can confer with voices from the past, in order to articulate the matter of his book, which is himself.

# Notes

1 There is a brief review of previous literature in P. Henry, *Montaigne in Dialogue: Censorship and Creative Writing, Architecture and Friendship, the Self and the Other*, Stanford French and Italian Studies, 57, Saratoga, ANMA libri, 1987, pp. 73–100; to be supplemented by, among others, A. Wilden, '"Par divers moyens on arrive à pareille fin": A Reading of Montaigne', *Modern Language Notes*, vol. 83, 1968, pp. 577–97; G-A. Pérouse, 'La lettre sur la mort de La Boétie et la première conception des *Essais*', in *Montaigne et les 'Essais' 1580–1980*, ed. P. Michel, Paris and Geneva, Champion-Slatkine, 1983, pp. 65–76; F. Rigolot, *Les Métamorphoses de Montaigne*, Paris, Presses Universitaires de France, 1988, pp. 61–78; P. Desan, 'The Book, the Friend, the Woman: Montaigne's Circular Exchanges', in *Contending Kingdoms: Historical, Psychological, and Feminist Approaches to the Literature of Sixteenth-Century England and France*, ed. M-R. Logan and P. L. Rudnytsky, Detroit, Wayne State University Press, 1991, pp. 225–62.

2 Taking into account the commonplace-book aspect of the *Essais* (not, of course, the only reading choice available) has one happy side-effect in that it seems to me to give an historical grounding to the 'philological' method employed in such an illuminating manner by Jules Brody: see his latest *Nouvelles lectures de Montaigne*, Paris, Champion, 1994. Montaigne obliquely signals the commonplace-book methodology underlying the *Essais*: 'je m'en vay, escorniflant par cy par là des livres les sentences qui me plaisent, non pour les garder, car je n'ay point de gardoires (i.e. he claims that he does not preassemble his quotations in manuscript commonplace-books, though he certainly used the recommended system of marking his printed texts), mais pour les transporter en cettuy-cy' ('my way of going about things is to scrounge from books *sententiae* which please me, not to put them into store, for I have no storage-places, but to transport them into this book'); moreover, he is at one with contemporary promoters of the method in insisting that quotation is for idiosyncratic use, not mere display (*Essais*, ed. A. Thibaudet, Paris, Gallimard, 1950, pp. 167, 1186; all subsequent references are to this edition).

3 The 'insinuating' exordium would have been well known to Montaigne and his humanist readers, see Cicero, *De inventione*, I, xv, 20: 'exordium in duas partes dividitur, principium et insinuationem ... insinuatio est oratio quadam dissimulatione et circumitione obscure subiens auditoris animum' ('the exordium is divided into two species, introduction and insinuation ... insinuation is a mode of address which by dissimulation and indirection unobtrusively steals into the mind of the listener').

4 The essay 'De l'amitié' is pp. 218–32 of the edition cited; the exordium is the first paragraph of that edition, pp. 218–20.

5 See J. Lacan, 'Le stade du miroir comme formateur de la fonction du Je', in *Ecrits I*, Paris, Seuil, 1996, pp. 89–97.

6 The other 'margin', at the end of the essay, forms a separate paragraph in the original, beginning 'Parce que j'ay trouvé …' (pp. 231–32).

7 Aristotle, *Nicomachean Ethics*, trans. by J. A. K. Thomson, revised by H. Tredennick, Harmondsworth, Penguin, 1976, p. 267. The other most familiar ancient treatise on friendship, the *De amicitia* of Cicero, from which Montaigne draws directly later in the essay, connects friendship to virtue in exactly the same way: 'sed hac primum sentio, nisi in bonis amicitiam esse non posse' ('but this is my first thought on the subject: there can be no friendship except the friendship of good men', v, 18).

8 La Boétie was indeed 'moulé au patron d'autres siecles que ceux-cy' ('moulded on the model of eras other than this'). In the letter recounting the death of La Boétie which Montaigne published in 1570, Montaigne has La Boétie say, just before he makes Montaigne 'successeur de ma Bibliotheque et de mes livres' ('inheritor of my library and my books'): 'Mon frere … que j'avois choisy parmy tant d'hommes, pour renouveller avec vous ceste vertueuse et sincere amitié, de laquelle l'usage est par les vices dès si long temps esloigné d'entre nous, qu'il n'en reste que quelques vieilles traces en la memoire de l'antiquité' ('My brother … whom I had chosen from among so many men, in order to revive with you that virtuous and sincere mode of friendship, the practice of which vice has banished from among us so long ago that all that remains of it are old traces remembered in Antiquity': *Oeuvres complètes de Michel de Montaigne*, ed. A. Armaingaud, 12 vols, Paris, Louis Conard, 1924–1941, vol. XI, 1939, pp. 174–75). La Boétie's definition of friendship in *De la Servitude volontaire* (ibid., p. 153) is a digest of sentiments to be found in Aristotle and Cicero. For some sense of the transmission of the ancient ideal of friendship and of the static, distanced image it had, see B. Weller, 'The Rhetoric of Friendship in Montaigne's *Essais*', *New Literary History*, vol. 9, 1978, pp. 503–23.

9 That does not mean to say that there are not also signposts in the essay towards a more 'Ciceronian' process of composition, developing the material through the standard six parts of rhetorical *dispositio*: see E. M. Duval, 'Rhetorical Composition and "Open Form" in Montaigne's Early *Essais*', *Bibliothèque d'Humanisme et Renaissance*, vol. 43, 1981, pp. 269–87; the two methods of exposition are in dialogue, but I would argue that the method of grotesques is made to overwrite the more closely imitative model of six-part *dispositio*.

10 Examples of tidily arranged commonplace-books which assembled quotations according to these different types of locution are the *Anthologia* (1598) and the *Polyanthea nova* (1604) of Joseph Lang; although they were produced a generation after Montaigne, they are compiled from earlier commonplace-books very widely known and used in previous decades, and they are relatively common in present-day libraries.

11 An even closer look suggests that Montaigne began to use Erasmus' *Apophthegmata* in conjunction with this essay at the time of the 1588 revision. One of the very few additions made at the time ascribes a particular saying to Chilo (p. 226), as does Erasmus, whereas the same saying is attributed to Bias by Cicero in the *De amicitia*, which is one of Montaigne's acknowledged sources in 1580. Montaigne does appear to have read the *Apophthegmata* consecutively, as Erasmus intended. It is clear

that he has not simply had recourse to the index: not all his quotations can be found by just looking up 'amicus'.

12 *Consideration sur Ciceron*, 1.40, p. 289.

13 For commonplace-books, and the rhetoric and dialectic associated with them, see A. Moss, *Printed Commonplace-Books and the Structuring of Renaissance Thought*, Oxford, Clarendon Press, 1996. A book which gives some idea of commonplace-book method and is relatively easy to find is the *Theatrum vitae humanae* of Theodor Zwinger, whom Montaigne met at Basle on his Grand Tour. The *Theatrum* was published first at Basle in 1565 and many times afterwards with ever more and more additions; the entry for *amicitia* demonstrates divisions and subdivisions of the genus (the primary divisions are *amicitia politica*, *amicitia oeconomica*), and then provides an abundance of *exempla*, mostly with ascriptions, under the various heads of the subdivisions. For parallels between *exempla* collected by Montaigne and *exempla* assembled by 'celui qui a fait le *Theatrum*', see F. Garavini, 'Montaigne et le *Theatrum Vitae Humanae*', in *Montaigne et l'Europe*, ed. C.-G. Dubois, Mont-de-Marsan, Editions InterUniversitaires, 1992, pp. 31–45.

14 Note that La Boétie 'explique' ('explains') the formation of the friendship, ascribed originally by Montaigne to 'ne sçay quelle force divine et fatale' ('I know not what divine force of destiny'); but 'divine' is changed in the final version to 'inexplicable', contrasting more forcefully with La Boétie's Latin representation of the event.

15 Cf. Lacan, 'Le stade du miroir'; M. Bowie, *Lacan*, London, Fontana Press, 1991, p. 92.

16 It is, I am sure, not unimportant that Montaigne, who clearly had Cicero's *De amicitia* very much in mind as he wrote and revised this essay, should deliberately have chosen not to imitate the moving memorial to his dead friend with which Laelius begins and ends his disquisition on friendship. This refusal of the model would repay more attention.

17 1.26, p. 179.

18 For example, in the 'philological' reading promoted by Jules Brody, see his latest *Nouvelles lectures de Montaigne*.

19 Lacan, 'L'instance de la lettre dans l'inconscient', *Ecrits I*, p. 261; very interesting from our point of view is Lacan's enthusiasm for Erasmus' *copia*, cf. Bowie, *Lacan*, pp. 113–17.

20 Lacan, ibid., p. 262; Bowie, *Lacan*, pp. 65–68, 92–93.

# CHAPTER 10

# Montaigne's Death Sentences: Narrative and Subjectivity in 'De la diversion' (*Essais* 3.4)

*Lawrence D. Kritzman*

Montaigne's 'De la diversion' (3.4) dramatises and exemplifies the manner in which the human subject turns itself away from the anxiety produced by the fear of death. The essential question underlying this essay is how to talk about death or rather how to avoid it. If diversion is an issue in this text, it is ultimately the result of the essayist's inability to become consubstantial with the object of the writing act itself: death. 'Nous pensons toujours ailleurs' (p. 834) ('Our thoughts are always elsewhere', p. 939), proclaims the essayist.[1] According to Montaigne's own formulation, the human subject is always already the victim of the radical discontinuity of the self; the kinetic energy generated by the mind renders it other to itself by displacing the subject from the *locus* where in principle it should be. As the essayist puts it in 'Du repentir'(3.2), depicting the writing of the essays: 'C'est un contrerolle de divers et muables accidens et d'imaginations irresoluës et, quand il y eschet, contraires: soit que je sois autre moy-mesme, soit que je saisisse les subjects par autres circonstances et considerations' (p. 805). ('This is a register of varied and changing occurrences, of ideas which are unresolved and, when need be, contradictory, either because I myself have become different or because I grasp hold of different attributes or aspects of my subjects', p. 908).

Montaigne's 'De la diversion' enacts the scene that his essay depicts, the vain movement of diversion, by mirroring the theoretical strategy that is the subject of his writing. By essaying the idea of diversion through a variety of examples of the mind's remarkable ability to redirect its own thoughts, the text becomes the symptom of the very malady that it claims to diagnose: displacement and diversion. In essence, the performance of the essay becomes the object that it designates by becoming the example of that which it writes. Through the displacement of the subject of diversion, the writerly subject displaces itself in a series of fragments that emblematises the subject's failure to become whole.

Montaigne's narrative thus produces a text not just about diversion per se, but one in which a theory of the self emerges as the rhetorical effect of the subject's quest to come to terms with the idea of death. As such, it can be described as the interminable story of the difficulty of uttering the name 'death'. Conscious of its mortality, the human subject, as described by Montaigne, can only relieve itself through a discursive ex-centricity that leaves in its wake a lack or void that is the result of its ontological emptiness. Accordingly, the diversion before the abyss of death allows the subject to partake in the magic of its own *méconnaissance* and thereby forestall the possibility of true self-recognition. In the case of Montaigne, essaying provokes a displacement of knowledge of which it is itself the cause.

My theoretical concern in exploring the dynamics of subjectivity in the essay 'De la diversion' is threefold: to investigate the relationship of the *topos* of diversion to self-portraiture; to explore how the figuration of subjectivity theorises desire and anticipates what are today considered psychoanalytic concerns; and to study how the preoccupation with death functions as the condition of narrative in its digressive movements or detours. Although the analysis presented here does not derive from the application of specific psychoanalytic models per se, my reading of 'De la diversion' attempts to demonstrate how in that chapter psychoanalysis occupies the place of literature by foregrounding the rhetorical processes and topological dynamics underlying the writing of the text. Montaigne's 'death sentences' in 'De la diversion' reveal the implications between literature and psychoanalysis by dramatising how the essay anticipates the preoccupations of psychoanalytic theory by speaking of itself in the language of literature. Through the fictions of desire that 'De la diversion' projects, one is able to make the essayist's drives come forth through a discourse that is contingent upon a series of identificatory representations from which the subject of enunciation is figured.

The essay 'De la diversion' is constructed around a series of displacements framed by repetitions of the diversion *topos*. For Montaigne, death is a source of anguish. The narrative constituting 'De la diversion' is, in great part, an account of how the human subject turns away from that anxiety. By playing on the root meaning of the word 'diversion' (derived from the Latin *divertere*, 'to turn one's attention away from'), the essay literally engages in the 'acting out' of diversion through the slippage of its meaning. Or to put it another way, the performative dimension of the essay identifies it with the processes of metonymy (as displacement) and repetition (as resistance to recognition) inasmuch as, through its rhetorical swerves, the diversions on 'diversion' enable the essay to defer the possibility of making death a self-contained presence.

Montaigne begins his essay by recounting how he was once charged with consoling a woman who was in distress because of her inability to come to terms with the grief resulting from the loss of her husband. In this narrative, the essayist assigns himself the role of physician who renounces the possibility of a cure, and instead opts for the ruse of diversion through the displacement of that malady into less anguished channels:

> Ny faire une charge de tout cet amas, le dispensant par occasion, comme Cicero; (B) mais, declinant tout mollement noz propos et les gauchissant peu à peu aus subjects plus voisins, et puis un peu plus esloingnez, selon qu'elle se prestoit plus à moy, je luy desrobay imperceptiblement cette pensée doulereuse, et la tins en bonne contenance et du tout r'apaisée autant que j'y fus. (p. 831)

> Nor did I attack her grief with the weight of all those arguments put together, dispensing them as required like Cicero: [B] but by gently deflecting our conversation and gradually leading it on to the nearest subject, and then on to slightly more remote ones depending on how she answered me, I imperceptibly stole her from her painful thoughts; and as long as I remained with her I kept her composed and totally calm. (p. 936)

The reference to the woman in pain at the beginning of the chapter will eventually have a meta-critical function within the context of the essay. To begin with, the text puts forth a topological displacement whereby rhetoric becomes a trope for psychological processes through the assimilation of *insinuatio* to *digressio*.[2] Accordingly the orator-physician cares for the interlocutor-patient by engaging in a diversionary practice ('J'usay de la diversion ... ', p. 831) ('I made use of a diversion', p. 936) that releases tension through the inducement of a forgetfulness that is the product of digression. What is most striking in this context is the reference to rhetoric, conceived here in anti-Ciceronian terms, as an antidote to the uncontrollable force of passion. From an intersubjective standpoint, the essayist is represented as an omnipotent being whose therapeutic strategy is derived from a form of rhetorical deception. The expression 'je luy desrobay imperceptiblement cette pensée doulereuse' ('I imperceptibly stole her from her painful thoughts') reveals the diversionary tactics necessary for the survival of a subject who must be left unrepresented as a lack in the manifest narrative of the dialogue. The so-called affective attunement established between the essayist and the widow in pain is paradoxically sustained by the tension between separation and connection.

The projection of the active forgetting of pain onto the woman ultimately becomes a figure for survival and self-definition. To be sure, language is conceived as a form of action (*actio*) capable of regulating affect through its persuasive force. Without the outside other, there is indeed nothing to help the helpless subject tolerate the pain associated with internal tension. Through the subterfuge of the orator-physician the female figure, once viewed in Juvenal's *Satires* (VI, 272–74) as the site of simulated affect ('car la plus part de leurs deuils sont artificiels et ceremonieux', p. 830) ('mostly their mourning is affected and ritualistic', p. 935), now becomes the *locus* where the rhetorician effects a simulation of change through the power of the *logos*. The subjectivity of the woman in pain is demarcated as the object of rhetorical mastery whereby the representation of the essayist's desire ostensibly motivates the desire of the other. To achieve the release of tension the subject has to take a detour, one that is motivated by the duplicitous discourse of another.

In this initial narrative Montaigne's text demonstrates how the will-to-say something transforms itself into the will-to-say nothing through the magical movement of a floating signifier; desire is figured as a detour, an imposed delay in the playing out of painful feelings. The diversion *topos* as it is used here thus demonstrates how the displacement of affect defers re-cognition and perpetuates non-knowledge as the defining feature of a motivated repression. If the text foregrounds the importance of 'rhetoric' as a bridge to the mind, it is in order to show us how life deceives us through the magic of language.

In drawing upon a military example taken from Philippe de Commines' *Mémoires* (II, iii), Montaigne's text narrates in a subsequent part of the essay an allegory of diversion whereby the displacement of affect (the rage of the citizens before the possibility of surrender) short-circuits the possibility of rebellion:

(B) Ce fut un ingenieux destour, dequoy le Sieur de Himbercourt sauva et soy et d'autres, en la ville du Liege, où le Duc de Bourgoigne, qui la tenoit assiegée, l'avoit fait entrer pour executer les convenances de leur reddition accordée. Ce peuple ... print à se mutiner contre ces accords passez ... Luy, sentant le vent de la premiere ondée de ces gens qui venoyent se ruer en son logis, làcha soudain vers eux deux des habitans de la ville ... chargez de plus douces et nouvelles offres ... Ces deux arresterent la premiere tempeste, ramenant cette tourbe ... Somme que, par telle dispensation d'amusemens, divertissant leur furie et la dissipant en vaines consultations, il l'endormit en fin et gaigna le jour, qui estoit son principal affaire. (pp. 831–32)

It was an ingenious diversion by which the Sieur de Himbercourt saved himself and others in the town of Liège which the Duke of Burgundy who was besieging it, had obliged him to enter so as to draw up agreed terms of surrender ... The citizens ... began to rebel against what had previously been agreed ... He at once dispatched two of the inhabitants ... bearing new and milder conditions ... These two men calmed the storm ... In short, by managing to waste their time that way he diverted into frenzy, dissipated it in vain deliberations and eventually lulled it to sleep. (pp. 936–37)

In its reinscription of the diversion *topos*, this episode literalises the previous reference to the woman in pain by demonstrating how language functions as a diversionary tactic to dissipate the irrational forces of desire. Quite clearly, the structure of this historical example reflects in some sense the structure of the human mind – its natural drive to diversion – by situating a subject within a narrative that functions as the site of a ruse. The subject's survival, endangered by the possibility of revolt, is guaranteed through a subterfuge realised within a history that allegorically represents the displacement of a threatening energy and thus quells instability. The motivation of the citizens into vain deliberations, a form of empty discursive meandering, represents an attempt to undo their imaginary relation to the symbolic. The general's ability to manipulate and displace, to turn one thing into another (the passion of rebellion into discursive emptiness) realises an ingenious negation of reality derived from a simulation of mastery.

If Montaigne's text draws on these examples of displacement, it is to demonstrate how diversion is proposed as an ideal for survival. This idea is amplified in a subsequent passage drawn from Ovid's *Metamorphoses* (X, 666–67) in which Atalanta is diverted by Hippomenes' apples. In that story Atalanta tried to rid herself of potential suitors by only accepting those who could run a race as fast at she could and punishing those who failed with the loss of their lives. Montaigne's rewriting of Ovid's narrative in this context appears to emphasise how the 'goddess who protects all amorous passion [had] come to his [Hippomenes'] aid' (p. 937) through the gift of the apples that were thrown in Atalanta's path and thus slowed her down. By its reference to diversion as a strategy to protect passion, the story of Hippomenes' survival is linked to the maintenance of his desire (and love) as a means of passing from the dangers of death to the pleasures of life. The goddess's gift of the apples functions as the cure which prolongs the narrative and recaptures the potentially doomed energy of passion in a life that is subject to plot.

Ironically, each repetition of the diversion *topos* decentres the narrative, creating new objects of observation that transform the essay into a series of detours that dramatise the psychology of displacement. 'Quand les medecins ne peuvent purger le catarre, ils le divertissent et le desvoyent à une autre partie moins dangereuse. Je m'apperçoy que c'est aussi la plus ordinaire recepte aux maladies de l'âme … (B) On luy faict peu choquer les maux de droit fil; on ne luy en faict n'y soustenir ny rabatre l'ateinte, on la luy faict decliner et gauchir' (pp. 832–33) ('When our doctors cannot purge a catarrh they divert it towards another part of us where it can do less harm. I have noticed that to be also the most usual prescription for illnesses of our soul … Doctors can rarely get the soul to mount a direct attack on her illness: they make her neither withstand the attack nor beat it off, parrying it rather and diverting it', pp. 937–38). The veering off that is figured here installs a lack or absence that ensures the estrangement of a malaise; thus diversion can be seen as a means of exiling pain and discomfort and masking its origin through an act of avoidance.

As the essay proceeds through its many digressions concerning diversions both public and private, it puts forth an ego ideal exemplified by the figure of Socrates who is described as capable of avoiding diversion and is thus able to confront death head on. This *exemplum* carries a symbolic value in its representation of Socrates as a presence made perfect. What is striking in this narrative fragment is that death is directly named ('le mourir'). In that process it constitutes itself as an act of reference, as a starting point of a narrative transference whereby the writing subject (Montaigne) acts out his own story which is always already articulated in the shadow of an exemplary other (Socrates). 'Il apartient à un seul Socrates d'accointer la mort d'un visage ordinaire, s'en aprivoiser et s'en jouer. Il ne cherche point de consolation hors de la chose; le mourir luy semble accident naturel et indifferent; il fiche là justement sa veüe, et s'y resout, sans regarder ailleurs' (p. 833) ('It behoves none but Socrates to greet death with a normal countenance, training himself for it and sporting with it. He seeks no consolation not inherent to the deed: dying seems to him a natural and neutral event; he justly fixes his gaze upon it and, without looking elsewhere, is resolved to accept it', p. 938). By facing death and by focusing his gaze directly upon it, Socrates finds no need for diversion (entertainment or temporal deferral) and its concomitant state of deviance (detour or spatial displacement). Socrates' psychic omnipotence, as manifested by his resolution, is represented as the counterpart to the anxiety produced by the fear of death inasmuch as the lack of tension between inside and outside in that exemplary figure enables an absolute relationship of the self to itself. Montaigne's text seems to suggest that Socrates enjoys an immediate proximity to the 'real'. Mastery as it is depicted here is an expression of omnipotence and resolution; the object of the gaze (death) receives the energy the subject directs toward it by an unmitigated willingness to accept it for what it is, 'sans regarder ailleurs' (p. 833). Unlike those fearful others who use language as a form of consolation to alleviate fear, Socrates retains the *logos* within the self and thereby affirms his mastery in silence.

In the context of this essay, humankind is described as being anti-Socratic in its drive to avoid the infelicitous anguish provoked by the thought of death. 'A ceux qui passent une profondeur effroyable, on ordonne de clorre ou destourner leurs yeux' (p. 833) ('Those who have to cross over some terrifyingly deep abyss are told to close their eyes or to avert them', p. 938). To be sure, death keeps us off balance for it constitutes an empty abyss, a centre that induces anguish and which we therefore seek to avoid. The human subject, characterised as naturally drawn to diversion, inevitably becomes a subject without a centre (a 'vuide') whose desire is incapable of reaching a fixed point. If 'our thoughts are always elsewhere' (p. 939), it is because the subject is made to derealise the specificity of the object of loss (death) and opt instead for the condition of loss produced through the repetition of displacement.

Montaigne's text depicts the ways in which the differing symptoms of death anxiety are embedded in literary and cultural representations. The collective impact of these representations demonstrates how the various categories of diversion anticipate the Lacanian revision of psychoanalytic theory by rejecting the concept of a self-contained subject and proposing instead one that forever exceeds itself. From that perspective, the essay narrates an example of religious piety and transforms it into a case of psychological weakness. Given what it is, that is to say its substantive lack of being, the human subject is bound to decentre the centrality of death by focusing on that which is external to it:

> Ces pauvres gens qu'on void sur un eschafaut ... les yeux et les mains tendues au ciel, la voix à des prieres hautes, avec une esmotion aspre et continuelle ... On les doibt louer de religion, mais non proprement de constance. Ils fuyent la luicte; ils destournent de la mort leur consideration .... (p. 833)

> Those poor wretches to be seen on our scaffolds ... while their arms and their eyes are lifted up to Heaven and their voice raised in loud prayer full of fierce and sustained emotion ... We must praise them for their faith but not strictly for their constancy. They flee the struggle, they divert their thoughts from it. (p. 938)

By diverting their thoughts, 'those poor wretches' not only demonstrate a lack of courage, but a logic of desire in which the perception of lack is assuaged by the magical thinking realised through the language of prayer. '(B) Nous pensons tousjours ailleurs; l'esperance d'une meilleure vie nous arreste et appuye, ou l'esperance de la valeur de nos enfans, ou la gloire future de nostre nom, ou la fuite des maux de ceste vie, ou la vengeance qui menasse ceux qui nous causent la mort' (p. 834) ('Our thoughts are always elsewhere. The hope of a better life arrests us and comforts us; or else it is the valour of our sons or the future glory of our family-name, or an escape from the evils of this life or from the vengeance menacing those who are causing our death', p. 939). In this context, the essay characterises hope, in a somewhat sacrilegious way, as a means of substituting new objects of desire for the dissatisfaction associated with the unnamed thing (death).

In the course of the essay, ontological concerns open up to epistemological preoccupations. The language of philosophy creates confusion between sign and substance and diverts us from the possibility of ever isolating the meaning of the thing in itself. '(C) Voire les arguments de la philosophie vont à tous coups costoiant et gauchissant la matiere, et à peine essuiant sa crouste' (p. 834) ('(C) In fact the arguments of philosophy are consistently skirting the matter and dodging it, scarcely grazing the outer surface with its fingertips', p. 940). In constructing its own language the rhetoric of philosophy can never simply refer to itself; philosophy is therefore a source of diversion inasmuch as it moves elsewhere in the wake of its own pronouncements.

Further in 'De la diversion', the familiar Montaignian *topos* concerning the arbitrary relationship between words and things appears as the essay once again undergoes another detour. Montaigne's text relates how we can be distracted by small things that sometimes say more by simply saying less. By showing how words can deflect the referential meaning of things while at the same time carrying within themselves the possibility of affective response, the essay demonstrates how euphemisms for death are transmitted through signifiers evoking memories of things past. Language is shown to incarnate the ghostliness of a spectre capable of generating a response that stimulates grief more from the sound of words than from their content:

> Le son mesmes des noms, qui nous tintoüine aux oreilles: Mon pauvre maistre! ou, Mon grand amy! Hélas! mon cher pere! ou, Ma bonne fille! quand ces redites me pinsent et que j'y regarde de pres, je trouve que c'est une plainte grammairiene et voyelle. Le mot et le ton me blessent. Comme les exclamations des prescheurs esmouvent leur auditoire souvant plus que ne font leurs raisons et comme nous frappe la voix piteuse d'une beste qu'on tue pour nostre service …. (p. 837)

> Take the forms of address which stay ringing in our ears – 'My poor Master': or 'My dear friend'; or 'Dear Papa' or 'My darling daughter': if I examine them closely when their repetition grips me, I discover that the grief lies in grammar and phonetics! What affects me are the words and the intonation (just as it is not the preacher's arguments which most often move a congregation but his interjections – like the pitiful cry of a beast being slaughtered for our use). (pp. 942–43)

If the human subject can be swept away by the sounds of language, it is because it is able to absorb affect representations through aurality. Yet this incorporation bases itself upon a partial disavowal of the object of grief. Through a series of linguistic turns, the subject in pain displaces the object of its loss; it focuses its attention less on the 'what' of the loss than on the 'who' that can now only cathet onto that other through the sound of words.

In yet other examples Montaigne's text narrates the ways in which the human subject attempts to overcome death through a displacement which requires a form of repression engendering an othering of the self. 'Celuy qui meurt en la meslée, les armes à la main, il n'estudie pas lors la mort, il ne la sent ny ne la considere: l'ardeur du combat l'emporte' (p. 833) ('A soldier who dies in the melee, his weapons in hand, is not contemplating death: he neither thinks of it nor dwells on it; he is carried away by the heat of battle', p. 939). Set in these terms, diversion is represented as something heroic. The energy derived from the power of battle requires the repression of the narcissism associated with fear. In essence, the denial of the possibility of loss functions as a mechanism defending the self from the reality of loss itself.

As the essay progresses, it demonstrates how the substitution of one passion for another enables the human subject to escape itself by allowing simulation to replace reality. 'J'ay veu aussi, pour cet effect de divertir les opinions et conjectures du peuple et desvoyer les parleurs, des femmes couvrir leurs vrayes affections par des affections contrefaictes. Mais j'en ay veu telle qui, en se contrefaisant, s'est laissée prendre à bon escient, et a quitté la vraye et originelle affection pour la feinte ...' (p. 836) ('I have known women too who have hidden their true affections under pretended ones, in order to divert people's opinions and conjectures and to mislead the gossips. But one I knew got well and truly caught: by feigning a passion, she quitted her original one for the feigned one', p. 942). The woman's 'acting out' results in the forgetting of the self that becomes the founding moment of exile and desire. This diversion of affect enables 'seeming' to become 'being' paradoxically at the very moment that the woman in question accedes to a newly born subjecthood founded on a kind of alienation. If Being attains a sense of self in this context, it is motivated by the staging of a desire derived from the image through which the self is constructed.

Throughout the essay, diversion becomes the master trope that enables desire to be realised. Accordingly, Montaigne evokes the loss of his friend La Boétie as the motivation to seek refuge from the pain of his grief in distraction:

> Je fus autrefois touché d'un puissant desplaisir ... je m'y fusse perdu à l'avanture si je m'en fusse simplement fié à mes forces. Ayant besoing d'une vehemente diversion pour m'en distraire, je me fis, par art, amoureux, et par estude ... L'amour me soulagea et retira du mal qui m'estoit causé par l'amitié. (p. 835)

> Once upon a time I was touched by a grief ... I might well have died from it if I had merely trusted to my own strength. I needed a mind-departing distraction to divert it; so by art and effort I made myself fall in love ... Love comforted me and took me away from the illness brought on by that loving-friendship. (p. 941)

As I have attempted to demonstrate in another context, the engendering of Montaigne's writing is a compensatory gesture for the loss of La Boétie; the feeling of absence and the anxiety of separation are dealt with through the essayist's endeavour to substitute his dialogic relationship with the text for the lost friend.[3] To be sure, the disappearance of the friend's gaze has resulted in the loss of the essayist's self image and the subsequent use of language as mediator of that lack: 'He alone enjoyed my true image, and carried it away. That is why I myself decipher myself so painstakingly'.[4] Here the dissolution of the sacred bond of friendship forces the essayist to assimilate the nothingness of death; it describes his self-alienation as a phenomenon that manifests itself in the dismembered fragments of his textual *corpus*.

Lack of being or the perceived sense of emptiness is thus the organising condition of the writer's subjectivity in 'De la diversion'. Victim of an ontological void resulting from an encounter with death, the writing subject, in order to survive, must compensate for this lack through a series of references which enable self-definition to be situated elsewhere. Accordingly, the staging of desire in this essay is derived from the various narrative fragments through which the self is constructed; the text always acts as a supplement for the man who, as Richard Regosin suggests, 'can never simply be'.[5] The multiple references to displacement and deferral as a means of survival throughout the essay enables Montaigne to live desire from someplace else; storytelling becomes the mechanism through which the essayist's subject-position is obliquely articulated. Subjectivity is the result of a kaleidoscope of images (i.e. the widow in pain, the leader threatened by rebellion) that retrospectively build the foundation for the subject of enunciation, and act as a substitute supplying the content that the subject itself lacks. Just as Montaigne explains how he was able to realise a young prince's hidden desire by turning his attention away from vengeance to ambition ('Je le destournay à l'ambition', p. 835), so too the essayist's desire can be fulfilled through a sublimatory displacement that liberates unconscious drives through narrative supplementation.

Although Montaigne does not endlessly draw attention to his own 'obsession' with death, the form of the essay, nevertheless, represents it in the substitutions and recombinations through which the unconscious makes itself known. To be sure, to name directly the object of fear functions as a kind of death sentence because of the congealing of its meaning. However, to 'essay' it through indirection is to make the subject of enunciation come forth by reflecting the desire for deferral that defines its subjectivity. If to write is to survive, then to live is to be caught in the signifying web of the language constituting the writing of the essay.

In this chapter, the writing subject thus declares himself better able to deal with death by viewing it nonchalantly. 'Je voyois nonchalamment la mort, quand je la voyois universellement, comme fin de la vie; je la gourmande en bloc; par le menu, elle me pille' (p. 837) ('When I looked upon death as the end of my life, universally, then I looked upon it with indifference. Wholesale, I could master it: retail, it savaged me', p. 943). Yet ironically the essayist seeks refuge in the very details that his own desire wishes to transcend. Painful thoughts, he proclaims, can be liquidated through a fascinating tendency for diversion in anxiety, producing details which, in principle, should be consigned to erasure. The memory of 'la robe de Caesar' (p. 937) ('Caesar's toga', p. 942) is more powerful than the reality of his death. '(B) Peu de chose nous divertit et destourne, car peu de chose nous tient. Nous ne regardons gueres les subjects en gros et seuls; ce sont des circonstances ou des images menues et superficieles qui nous frapent, et des vaines escorces qui rejalissent des subjects' (p. 836) ('(B) We can be distracted and diverted by small things, since small things are capable of holding us. We hardly ever look at great objects in isolation: it is the trivial circumstances, the surface images, which strike us', p. 942). As a corrective to the displeasure associated with powerful passions, Montaigne's text suggests the possibility of converting energy to lesser intensities as a means to dissipate unruly drives and regulate desire. 'Si vostre affection en l'amour est trop puissante, dissipez la ... car je l'ay souvant essayé avec utilité: rompez la à divers desirs, desquels il y en ayt un regent et un maistre, si vous voulez; mais, depeur qu'il ne vous gourmande et tyrannise, affoiblissez le, sejournez le, en le divisant et divertissant' (p. 835) ('If when in love your passion is too powerful, dissipate it ... I have often usefully made this essay. Break it down into a variety of desires, one of which may rule you as master if you like, but enfeeble it and delay it by subdividing it and diverting it, lest it dominate and tyrannize over you', p. 941). The dissipation of affect prevents true re-cognition from being realised; it therefore facilitates a mollification of that which threatens the subject.

Within the logic of the essay, the trope for change, metonymy, dislocates pain by forcing it elsewhere; it represents the movement by which an idea (diversion) serves as the nodal point of different associative chains:

Une aigre imagination me tient; je trouve plus court, que de la dompter, la changer; je luy en substitue, si je ne puis une contraire, aumoins un'autre. Tousjours la variation soulage, dissout et dissipe. Si je ne puis la combatre, je luy eschape, et en la fuyant je fourvoye, je ruse: muant de lieu … je me sauve dans la presse d'autres amusemens et pensées, où elle perd ma trace et m'esgare. (pp. 835–36)

Some painful idea gets hold of me; I find it quicker to change it than to subdue it. If I cannot substitute an opposite one for it, I can at least find a different one. Change always solaces it, dissolves it and dispels it. If I cannot fight it, I flee it; and by my flight I made a diversion … by changing place … I escape from it into the crowd of other pastimes and cogitations in which it loses all track of me and cannot find me. (p. 941)

Montaigne's attempted transcendence of pain is nothing less than a forgetting of its origins through a form of trickery (he proclaims 'je ruse') that provokes the dissolution of the subject.[6] The act of displacement introduces a disorganising sense of flux whereby the loss of a painful idea originates in a process ('la variation' or variability) through which it loses its own origin by becoming subject to change. Here diversion ('la variation') simulates a partial killing of the subject of narration, but the repression that results from the ruse of rhetoric keeps it embodied in its many returns through references to associative subjects.

If Socrates was able to resolve himself to the reality of death, Montaigne can only confront it through the diversionary process of writing. For Montaigne, writing therefore becomes a form of entertainment that acknowledges both a closeness with and a distance from death. In this way, Montaigne anticipates Freud's *Beyond the Pleasure Principle* (1920), written over three centuries later.[7] That text foregrounds the trope of the spool in the child's game of *fort-da* (here-there) ; it represents the fiction describing how the child attempts to overcome separation anxiety produced by the absence of the mother. In that game, the child throws a reel out of the crib and pulls it back to the alternating cries of *fort* and *da*. When the child makes the toy disappear in the game, it may be viewed symbolically as an attempted mastery of an unpleasurable situation from which the child may not escape. Like the child in Freud's study, the essayist, in the writing of the text, 'works out' unpleasurable experiences by active engagement with his anxiety rather than a passive acceptance of it. For Montaigne, displacement (diversion) is a simulation of mastery. Desire is figured in the digression of the essay, an imposed delay (deferral) in the playing out of painful feelings concerning death. The drama of salvation narrated in the text (the many stories about 'diversion') repeats itself in the engendering of the text itself (the digressive form that the discourse on diversion takes). In a way the essayist functions in the same manner as the classical orator who, claims the narrating subject, when acting out his case 'will allow himself to be taken in by the emotion he is portraying' (p. 944). In the example of 'De la diversion', the text presents itself as an imaginary space of escape where the symptomatically-marked ego attempts to replace itself with something else. By becoming other through the act of simulation (the relief produced by the essayist's vain writing), the Montaignian subject becomes in Lacan's terms 'the playing out of his thought'.[8]

Montaigne's obsession with death thus emerges over the course of the essay as the motivating force behind the compulsion to repeat. Quite clearly, the repetition that is actualised at the level of writing – the reinscription of the diversion *topos* – derives from an unconscious desire to liquidate uncomfortable thoughts which leads to a simulation of mastery. Ironically, this impulse to master that which is painful carries within it the radical unbinding that characterises the rhetorical detours that point to the narrative subject's impulse to approach his subject (death) and yet somehow avoid it. Changing places results when similar yet differentiated narratives are repeated as the result of what Freud described as the work of 'some demoniac force'. The mastery that the Montaignian essay works out is linked to the desire for an end (the liquidation of the death anxiety) that paradoxically leads us back to new beginnings (the impossibility of ever truly mastering it).

In the end, the narrative interpretation of 'De la diversion' is the result of a semiotic trajectory that emerges from the metonymic effect produced by the writing of the essay. By its endless references to the idea of diversion, Montaigne's text manifests the symptomology of the failed repression of its grammatical subject in the displacements that constitute the text of the essay. In this chapter, the self is not given in advance, but only emerges from the various fragments that the essay transcribes.

Perhaps the underlying lesson of 'De la diversion' is that loss can be transformed into a creative productivity that is paradoxically based on the vanity of life. 'Il n'en faut point pour agiter nostre ame: une resverie sans corps et sans suject la regente et l'agite' (p. 839) ('To excite our souls we need not causes; they can be controlled and excited by some raving disembodied fancy based on nothing', p. 945). The discourse on diversion is born from the fictions that supplement the ontological nothingness of the writing subject by compensating its absence through endless repetition. If the 'disembodied fancies' constituting the body of the essay become 'real', it is through a rhetorical effect that accepts them as such. Writing thus becomes a form of self-deception or trickery (*ruse*) whose diversionary tactics offer proof of the essayist's desire for self-deception. The metonymic displacement of grief keeps it alive and retroactively installs it as a series of living fictions refracted through the prism of language. Before the emptiness of the essay, the constitutive trope of diversion marks the subject's accession to language that, in the end, only produces a simulation of mastery derived from the emptiness of words. 'C'est priser sa vie justement ce qu'elle est, de l'abandonner pour un songe' (p. 839) ('Abandoning your life for a dream is to value it for exactly what is worth', p. 945).

# Notes

1 Michel de Montaigne, *Les 'Essais' de Montaigne: Édition conforme au texte de l'exemplaire de Bordeaux*, ed. Pierre Villey and V.-L. Saulnier, Paris, Presses Universitaires de France, 1965, volume 2; and Michel de Montaigne, *The Complete Essays*, translated by M.A. Screech, Harmondsworth, Penguin, 1991. Page references in my text refer to these editions.

2 See Jean-Paul Sermain, '*Insinuatio, circumstantia, visio et actio*: L'itinéraire rhétorique du chapitre III, 4: "De la Diversion"', *Bulletin de la Société des Amis de Montaigne* vol. 7, 1985, p. 127.

3 See 'Montaigne's Family Romance', in *The Rhetoric of Sexuality and the Literature of the French Renaissance*, Cambridge, Cambridge University Press, 1991, pp. 73–92; and 'Montaigne and Psychoanalysis', in *Approaches to Teaching Montaigne's 'Essays'*, ed. by Patrick Henry, New York, Modern Languages Association of America, 1993, pp. 110–16.

4 Montaigne made this addition to the 1588 edition of the *Essais*, in the chapter 'De la vanité' (3.9). Here I use the translation of Donald M. Frame in *The Complete Essays of Montaigne*, Stanford, Stanford University Press, 1976, p. 752, n. 14.

5 Richard Regosin, 'Sources and Resources: The "Pretexts" of Originality in Montaigne's *Essais*', *Sub-stance*, vol. 21, 1978, p. 114.

6 Randle Cotgrave in *A Dictionarie of the French and English Tongues* [London, 1611], Columbia, University of South Carolina Press, 1950, defines the verb 'ruser' as: 'to beguile, to deceive, to shift, to use tricks, to deale cunningly, to proceed by sleights'.

7 See Sigmund Freud, *Beyond the Pleasure Principle*, New York, W.W. Norton, 1961.

8 Jacques Lacan, *Ecrits. A Selection*, New York, W.W. Norton, 1977, p. 166.

# Select Bibliography

The following bibliography is intended as a list of select further reading, relating both to critical methodologies and French Renaissance literature. For more detailed bibliographies, readers are advised to consult the notes to the Introduction and to the individual contributions.

Apter, E. and Pietz, W. (eds), *Fetishism as Cultural Discourse*, Ithaca, Cornell University Press, 1993.

Bakhtin, M., *Rabelais and his World*, trans. Hélène Iswolsky, Cambridge, (Mass.), MIT Press, 1968; Bloomington, Indiana Press, 1984.

Barthes, R., *Oeuvres complètes*, 3 vols, Paris, Seuil, 1993–95.

Beaujour, M., *Le jeu de Rabelais*, Paris, L'Herne, 1970.

——, *Miroirs d'encre: Rhétorique de l'autoportrait*, Paris, Seuil, 1980.

Berriot-Salvadore, E., *Les femmes dans la société française de la Renaissance*, Geneva, Droz, 1990.

Bideaux, M., *L'"Heptaméron' de Marguerite de Navarre: De l'enquête au débat*, Mont-de-Marsan, Editions Interuniversitaires, 1992.

Bowie, M., *Freud, Proust and Lacan: Theory as Fiction*, Cambridge, Cambridge University Press, 1987.

——, *Lacan*, London, Fontana Press, and Cambridge, (Mass.), Harvard University Press, 1991.

Brody, J., *Nouvelles lectures de Montaigne*, Paris, Champion, 1994.

Burke, P., *Varieties of Cultural History*, Cambridge, Polity Press, 1997.

Carron, J.-C., (ed.) *Rabelais: Critical Assessments*, Baltimore and London, Johns Hopkins University Press, 1995.

Castor, G., *Pléiade Poetics: A Study in Sixteenth-Century Thought and Terminology*, Cambridge, Cambridge University Press, 1964.

Cave, T., (ed.) *Ronsard the Poet*, London, Methuen, 1973.

——, *The Cornucopian Text: Problems of Writing in the French Renaissance*, Oxford, Clarendon Press, 1979.

——, *Pré-histoires: Textes troublés au seuil de la modernité*, Geneva, Droz, 1999.

Cazauran, N., *L'"Heptaméron' de Marguerite de Navarre*, Paris, Société d'Edition d'Enseignement Supérieur, 1976; second ed., 1991.

Clements, R.J., *Critical Theory and Practice of the Pléiade*, Cambridge, (Mass.),

Harvard University Press, 1942.

Compagnon, A., *La seconde main ou le travail de la citation*, Paris, Seuil, 1979.

Culler, J., *Structuralist Poetics: Structuralism, Linguistics and the Study of Literature*, London, Routledge and Kegan Paul, 1975.

——, *The Pursuit of Signs: Semiotics, Literature, Deconstruction*, London, Routledge, 1981.

——, *On Deconstruction: Theory and Criticism after Structuralism*, Ithaca, Cornell University Press, 1982.

Curtius, E.-R., *European Literature and the Latin Middle Ages*, trans. W.R. Trask (Bollingen Series XXXVI), Princeton, Princeton University Press, 1973.

Davis, N. Z., *Society and Culture in Early Modern France*, Stanford, Stanford University Press, 1965; repr. 1975.

——, *The Return of Martin Guerre*, Cambridge, (Mass.), Harvard University Press, 1983; Harmondsworth, Penguin, 1985.

——, *Fiction in the Archives: Pardon Tales and Their Tellers in Sixteenth-Century France*, Stanford, Stanford University Press, 1987.

Defaux, G., *Pantagruel et les sophistes: Contribution à l'histoire de l'humanisme chrétien au XVIe siècle*, La Haye, M. Nijhoff, 1973.

——, *Marot, Rabelais, Montaigne: L'écriture comme présence*, Paris and Geneva, Champion-Slatkine, 1987.

Fallon, J., *Voice and Vision in Ronsard's 'Les Sonnets pour Hélène'*, New York, Peter Lang, 1993.

Felman, S. (ed.), *Literature and Psychoanalysis: The Question of Reading: Otherwise*, Baltimore, Johns Hopkins University Press, 1982.

——, *Jacques Lacan and the Adventure of Insight: Psychoanalysis in Contemporary Culture*, Cambridge, (Mass.), Harvard University Press, 1987.

Ferguson, M., Quilligan, M. and Vickers, N. (eds), *Rewriting the Renaissance: The Discourses of Sexual Difference in Early Modern Europe*, Chicago and London, University of Chicago Press, 1986.

Foucault, M., *Les mots et les choses: Une archéologie des sciences humaines*, Paris, Gallimard, 1966.

Freccero, C., 'Economy, Woman and Renaissance Discourse', in *Refiguring Women: Perspectives on Gender and the Italian Renaissance*, ed. Marilyn Migiel and Juliana Schiesari, Ithaca and London, Cornell University Press, 1991, pp. 192–208.

——, 'Gender Ideologies, Women Writers and the Problem of Patronage in Early Modern Italy and France: Issues and Frameworks', in Jonathan Hart, ed., *Reading the Renaissance: Culture, Poetics and Drama*, New York and London, Garland Publishing, 1996.

Frelick, N., *Délie as Other: Towards a Poetics of Desire in Scève's 'Délie'*, Lexington, French Forum, 1994.

Freud, S., *The Standard Edition of the Complete Psychological Works of Sigmund Freud*, 24 vols, trans. and ed. James Strachey, London, Hogarth Press, 1953–66.

Fumerton, P., *Cultural Aesthetics: Renaissance Literature and the Practice of Social Ornament*, Chicago, University of Chicago, 1991.

Genette, G., *Mimologiques: Voyage en Cratylie*, Paris, Seuil, 1976.

——, *Palimpsestes: La littérature au second degré*, Paris, Seuil, 1982.

Giudici, E., *Louise Labé: Essai*, Paris, Nizet, 1981.

Goyet, F., '*Imitatio* ou intertextualité? (Riffaterre revisited)', *Poétique*, vol. 71, 1987, pp. 313–20.

Gray, F., *Rabelais et l'écriture*, Paris, Nizet, 1974.

——, *La balance de Montaigne: Exagium/essai*, Paris, Nizet, 1982.

——, *Rabelais et le comique du discontinu*, Paris, Champion, 1994.

Greenblatt, S., *Renaissance Self-Fashioning, From More to Shakespeare*, Chicago, University of Chicago Press, 1980.

——, *Shakespearean Negotiations: The Circulation of Social Energy in Renaissance England*, Oxford, Clarendon Press, 1988.

——, *Marvelous Possessions: The Wonder of the New World*, Oxford, Clarendon Press, 1991.

Greene, T.M., *The Light in Troy: Imitation and Discovery in Renaissance Poetry*, New Haven and London, Yale University Press, 1982.

——, *The Vulnerable Text: Essays on Renaissance Literature*, New York, Columbia University Press, 1986.

Hendricks, M. and Parker, P. (eds), *Women, 'Race', and Writing in the Early Modern Period*, London and New York, Routledge, 1994.

Henry, P., *Montaigne in Dialogue: Censorship and Creative Writing, Architecture and Friendship, the Self and the Other*, Stanford French and Italian Studies, 57, Saratoga, ANMA Libri, 1987.

—— (ed.), *Approaches to Teaching Montaigne's 'Essays'*, New York, Modern Language Association, 1993.

Irigaray, L., 'Ce sexe qui n'en est pas un', in *Ce Sexe qui n'en est pas un*, Paris, Minuit, 1977.

——, *Speculum de l'autre femme*, Paris, Minuit, 1974.

Iser, W., *The Implied Reader: Patterns of Communication in Prose Fiction from Bunyan to Beckett*, Baltimore, Johns Hopkins University Press, 1974.

——, *The Act of Reading: A Theory of Aesthetic Response*, Baltimore, Johns Hopkins University Press, 1978.

Jakobson, R., *Essais de linguistique générale*, traduits et préfacés par Nicolas Ruwet, Paris, Editions de Minuit, 1963.

Jeanneret, M., *Des mets et des mots: Banquets et propos de table à la Renaissance*, Paris, Corti, 1987.

——, *Le défi des signes: Rabelais et la crise de l'interprétation à la Renaissance*, Orléans, Editions Paradigme, 1994.

Jones, A.R., 'Assimilation With a Difference: Renaissance Women Poets and Literary Influence', *Yale French Studies*, vol. 62, 1981, pp. 135–153.

——, 'Nets and Bridles: Early Modern Conduct Books and Sixteenth-Century Women's Lyric', in *The Ideology of Conduct*, ed. Nancy Armstrong and Leonard Tennenhouse, New York, Methuen, 1987, pp. 39–72.

——, *The Currency of Eros: Women's Love Lyric in Europe, 1540–1620*, Bloomington, Indiana University Press, 1990.

Jordan, C., *Renaissance Feminism: Literary Texts and Political Models*. Ithaca, New York, Cornell University Press, 1990.

Kelly, J., *Women, History and Theory: The Essays of Joan Kelly*, Chicago, University of Chicago Press, 1984.

Kelso, R., *Doctrine for the Lady of the Renaissance*, Urbana and Chicago, University of Illinois Press, 1956; reprint 1978.

Kritzman, L., *Destruction/Découverte: Le fonctionnement de la rhétorique dans les 'Essais' de Montaigne*, French Forum Monographs, 21, Lexington, Kentucky, 1980.

—— (ed.), *Le signe et le texte: Etudes sur l'écriture au XVIe siècle en France*, Lexington, French Forum Publishers, 1990.

——, *The Rhetoric of Sexuality and the Literature of the French Renaissance*, Cambridge, Cambridge University Press, 1991.

Labé, L., *Oeuvres complètes*, ed. François Rigolot, Paris, Garnier/Flammarion, 1986.

Lacan, J., *Ecrits*, Paris, Seuil, 1966.

——, *Le Séminaire*, multivolume work, Paris, Seuil, 1973-.

Lanham, R., *A Handlist of Rhetorical Terms*, second ed., Berkeley, University of California Press, 1991.

Larson, A. R. and Winn, C. H. (eds), *Renaissance Women Writers: French Texts/ American Contexts*, Detroit, Wayne State University Press, 1994.

Lyons, J.D. and Nichols, S.G. (eds), *Mimesis: From Mirror to Method, Augustine to Descartes*, Hanover, NH, and London, The University Press of New England, 1982.

Lyons, J.D. and McKinley, M.B. (eds), *Critical Tales: New Studies of the 'Heptaméron' and Early Modern Culture*, Philadelphia, University of Pennsylvania Press, 1993.

Maclean, I., *The Renaissance Notion of Woman: A Study in the Fortunes of Scholasticism and Medical Science in European Intellectual Life*, Cambridge, Cambridge University Press, 1980.

Marguerite de Navarre, *L'Heptaméron*, ed. M. François, Paris, Garnier, 1991.

Mathieu-Castellani, G., *Montaigne: L'écriture de l'essai*, Paris, Presses Universitaires de France, 1988.

——, *La conversation conteuse: Les 'Nouvelles' de Marguerite de Navarre*, Paris, Presses Universitaires de France, 1992.

Ménager, D., *Rabelais en toutes lettres*, Paris, Bordas, 1989.

Miller, N. (ed.), *The Poetics of Gender*, New York, Columbia University Press, 1986.

Moss, A., *Printed Commonplace-Books and the Structuring of Renaissance Thought*, Oxford, Clarendon Press, 1996.

O'Brien, J. (ed.), *(Ré)Interprétations: Etudes sur le seizième siècle, Michigan Romance Studies*, vol. 15, 1995.

Parker, P., *Literary Fat Ladies: Rhetoric, Gender, Property*, London, Methuen, 1987.

Parker, P. and Quint, D. (eds), *Literary Theory/Renaissance Texts*, Baltimore and London, Johns Hopkins University Press, 1986.

Pot, O., *Inspiration et mélancolie: L'épistémologie poétique dans les 'Amours' de Ronsard*, Geneva, Droz, 1990.

Quainton, M., *Ronsard's Ordered Chaos: Visions of Flux and Stability in the Poetry of Pierre de Ronsard*, Manchester, Manchester University Press, 1980.

Rabelais, F., *Oeuvres complètes*, ed. Mireille Huchon, Paris, Gallimard, 1994.

Regosin, R., *Montaigne's Unruly Brood*, Berkeley, University of California Press, 1996.

Rigolot, F., *Le texte de la Renaissance, des rhétoriqueurs à Montaigne*, Geneva, Droz, 1982.

——, *Les métamorphoses de Montaigne*, Paris, Presses Universitaires de France, 1988.

Ronsard, P. de, *Oeuvres complètes*, 20 vols, ed. P. Laumonier; revised and completed by I. Silver and R. Lebègue, Paris, Hachette; then Droz, then Didier, 1914–75.

Rose, M.-B. (ed.), *Women in the Middle Ages and the Renaissance: Literary and Historical Perspectives*, Syracuse, NY, Syracuse University Press, 1986.

Russell, D. A. and Winterbottom, M. (eds), *Ancient Literary Criticism: The Principal Texts in New Translations*, Oxford, Oxford University Press, 1972.

Screech, M., *Rabelais*, London, Duckworth, 1979.

Sonnino, L., *A Handbook to Sixteenth-Century Rhetoric*, London, Routledge and Kegan Paul, 1968.

Tetel, M., *Marguerite de Navarre's 'Heptaméron': Themes, Language and Structure*, Duke University Press, 1973.

Tompkins, J.P. (ed.), *Reader-Response Criticism: From Formalism to Post-Structuralism*, Baltimore and London, Johns Hopkins University Press, 1980.

Vickers, N. J., 'Diana Described: Scattered Woman and Scattered Rhyme', in *Writing and Sexual Difference*, ed. Elizabeth Abel, Chicago, University of Chicago Press, 1982, pp. 95–109.

——, 'This Heraldry in Lucrece's Face', *Poetics Today*, vol. 6, 1985, pp. 171–184.

Villey, P. and Saulnier, V.-L. (eds), *Les 'Essais' de Montaigne*, Paris, Presses Universitaires de France, 1965.

Weber, H., *La création poétique au XVIe siècle en France*, 2 vols, Paris, Nizet, 1956.

Whitford, M., *Luce Irigaray: Philosophy in the Feminine*, London, Routledge, 1991.

Worton, M. and Still, J. (eds), *Intertextuality: Theories and Practices*, Manchester, Manchester University Press, 1990.

Zima, P.V., *La déconstruction: Une critique*, Paris, Presses Universitaires de France, 1994.

# Index